The Portable Lawyer for Mental Health Professionals

An A–Z Guide
to
Protecting Your Clients,
Your Practice, and Yourself

Barton E. Bernstein, J.D., LMSW
and
Thomas L. Hartsell, Jr., J.D.

JOHN WILEY & SONS, INC.

New York • Chichester • Weinheim • Brisbane • Singapore • Toronto

Authors' Note: Sample forms should be used only after review by a local lawyer. Jurisdictions differ in their technical requirements, and every mental health professional should use forms specifically drafted for each individual practice, organization, or agency.

This book is printed on acid-free paper. ∞

Copyright © 1998 by John Wiley & Sons, Inc. All rights reserved.

Published simultaneously in Canada.

This publication is designed to provide accurate and authoritative information in regard to the subject matter covered. It is sold with the understanding that the publisher is not engaged in rendering professional services. If professional advice or other expert assistance is required, the services of a competent professional person should be sought. Sample forms should be reviewed by a lawyer in each jurisdiction.

Library of Congress Cataloging-in-Publication Data:

Bernstein, Barton E.
    The portable lawyer for mental health professionals : an a–z guide
to protecting your clients, your practice, and yourself / Barton E.
Bernstein and Thomas L. Hartsell, Jr.
        p.   cm.
    Includes index.
    ISBN 0-471-24869-X (pbk. : alk. paper)
    1. Mental health personnel—Legal status, laws, etc.—United
States—Popular works.   2. Mental health laws—United States—
Popular works.   I. Hartsell, Thomas L., Jr.   II. Title.
KF3828.Z9847   1998
344.73′044—dc21   98-10048

Printed in the United States of America.

10 9 8 7 6 5 4 3 2 1

My children, Alon and Talya.

My aunt, Anita Springer Bloch, who took me in when I was discharged from the Navy, and who patiently nurtured me and my career during my entire life.

My sisters, who always thought I could exceed my native ability.

And in loving memory of my father, Samuel Bernstein, and my mother, Suetelle Springer Bernstein Antine, who passed away in October 1997, before this book was published. I feel they know.

B.B.

My earliest mentors, my parents, Tom and Julie Hartsell, who, by admonishment and example, taught me the value of education and knowledge and instilled in me the independence and discipline to seek them both.

My professional mentor, Bart Bernstein, who helped teach me the practice of law, the joy of being an educator, and so much more that I can never hope to repay him. Along the way, he inspired me and challenged me to become a better lawyer and educator and, in the process, became a true and dear friend.

My wife, Barbara, who endured with patience the long hours I spent working on this book, running a law practice, teaching, and lecturing, at a time in her life when she would have benefited much more from my undivided attention.

My sons, Ryan and Jason, who have been both a delight and a constant source of consternation. Hey, maybe they will read this book. . . . Nah.

T.L.H.

Preface

Lawyers don't know what therapists really do, so how can they know when (if) they do it wrong.

    —Anonymous; first heard by the authors about 30 years ago.

In 1963, Bart Bernstein was just completing his term as president of a Toastmasters club when he was invited by the program director of a local mental health (nonmedical) organization to talk about mental health malpractice. No lawyer admits unfamiliarity with a legal subject, nor turns down an invitation to speak; further, a theme of Toastmasters is that, with a little research, a good speaker can present any topic with enthusiasm and interest. The scheduled talk was about two months away, so the invitation was accepted and inquiry commenced. But there was one nagging question: How could any person be liable to another if all that person did was talk or listen? This had never been discussed in law school.

With research of numerous cases from psychiatry, psychology, and allied mental health professions, the analysis began and the information flowed in—from early English cases to United States precedent. Suddenly, what had begun as a theoretical problem became a reality. Mental health professionals had actually been sued for negligence and malpractice over the years, and few current practitioners were aware of their vulnerability as clinical therapists who treated clients.

The talk piqued an interest in the interrelationship of law and mental health and led to further checking with local educational institutions that offered courses in the mental health professions. Soon, the obvious became more obvious. No local course was available to inform potential mental health providers that they were vulnerable in their treatment of clients/patients. Recent graduates might engage in conduct that could lead to liability, not because of intentional wrongdoing, but because of ignorance of the laws that apply to mental health providers.

A course on law and mental health was offered by Bernstein to a local graduate school, then to another, then to a medical school. Now, more than thirty years later, most mental health professionals, as part of their training, receive information concerning the interrelationship of law, therapy, ethics, liability, and malpractice.

Some 30 years ago, few licenses were granted to or required of a mental health professional. One earned a degree from an accredited institution of higher learning, hung up a diploma, and began practice. Now, most states require a graduate degree plus a license to practice independently. But the license is not permanent; it is "loaned" to the licensee, who may act only within the authority granted by the license. If a license violation occurs because of an ethical infraction, as defined by the licensing law; or continuing education credits are not sought and maintained; or a renewal is late; or a check does not clear the bank, the license can be revoked or suspended, thus ending or interrupting a professional career. The power of the licensing board is awesome and seriously applied.

The need for continuing education has increased. Mental health professionals face harsh consequences if they act negligently or unethically with clients and/or the institutions with which they are associated. They may not be allowed to renew their malpractice insurance policies; or they may fail to qualify as managed care providers because of a blemish on their record. In short, accountability requires in-depth knowledge of the law that applies to mental health in all its ramifications.

The Portable Lawyer is primarily directed to mental health professionals of all disciplines who can benefit from a quick and ready reference to legal and ethical issues. The book is organized to cover nine general topics. When practitioners/providers of mental health services recognize a question or situation that has possible legal overtones, they can consult the contents listing and be guided toward rules and principles that apply to the specific problem at hand, without extensive research. Armed with fundamental knowledge and examples of relevant documents, the practitioners can make informed decisions, including consulting with a lawyer for further clarification and advice.

The Portable Lawyer is secondarily directed to consumers of mental health services who feel something has gone wrong with the services available or already being provided. Because of the mystique surrounding mental health (from consumers' point of view), the recipients of mental health treatment often do not know where to go to discover whether the actions of a therapist or provider are appropriate. This book offers a compendium of what can go wrong. A consumer can then decide whether the treatment received was appropriate or actionable. In most instances, we would hope that the therapy will be found competent, caring, and helpful.

Recent movies—*Deconstructing Harry, First Wives' Club, Prince of Tides, Tin Cup*—have primary plots or cameo situations that depict mental health professionals in questionable postures, which consumers of mental health services—and the general public—might assume to be proper conduct. *The Portable Lawyer* will indicate that generally acceptable movie scenarios are or might be depicting illegal or unethical conduct. The public should be educated in this regard. The authors still await a movie in which the hero or heroine is an honorable, ethical, and competent mental health service provider who somehow saves the day just before the credits scroll on the screen.

Acknowledgments

In the process of writing this book, the authors had many friends, acquaintances, and colleagues who provided inspiration, nurturing, and mentoring—all necessary for any work worthy of publication.

We want to thank John Wiley & Sons, Inc. for creating the idea, and Kelly A. Franklin, Executive Editor and Associate Publisher, for her enthusiasm, help with the organization, and ability to conceptualize an overview, so essential to a book of this type. We also thank Dorothy Lin, Assistant Editor, who helped to reorganize the chapters and was able to digest legal concepts and help us translate legalese into English.

Encouragement came from many special friends, some of whom we want to mention by name. James W. Callicutt, PhD, Associate Dean, Graduate School of Social Work, University of Texas, Arlington, was Bart's mentor, initial source of inspiration, and first contact in the interactive field of law and mental health. He helped organize the first course in Law and Social Work and has facilitated the interaction ever since. Myron ("Mike") F. Weiner, MD, Vice Chairman for Clinical Services, Department of Psychiatry, Southwestern Medical School, and a friend for over thirty years, bridged the gap between psychiatry and law, encouraging participation in the residents' program at the Medical School and service on the adjunct faculty. Drs. Paul C. Mohl, John W. Cain, and J. Douglas Crowder have continued this tradition.

Our personal thanks go to Judy Meagher, MEd, who brainstormed the creative and promotional ideas and served as devil's advocate during the creative process; David Shriro, a close friend and confidant for almost forty years, for constantly encouraging (some might call it nagging) an addiction to writing; and to Anthony Paul Picchioni, PhD, for emphasizing the need for continuing education in the area of ethics and malpractice.

BARTON BERNSTEIN
THOMAS L. HARTSELL

Dallas, Texas

Sample Forms

CLIENT FORMS

CONSENT FORMS

WAIVER FORMS

MISCELLANEOUS FORMS

Contents

SECTION FOUR
FEES

SECTION FIVE
FORENSIC ISSUES

SECTION SIX
PRACTICE MODELS

SECTION ONE

CLINICAL RECORDS
Protected or Not

1

Clinical Notes

Melody had been a client of Ms. Ford, MSSW and a licensed clinical social worker, for about five years, on and off. Melody called Ms. Ford during times of crisis but ignored her in between. There had been a sixteen-month lull between visits, and Ms. Ford assumed Melody was doing all right. Melody had called once, indicating that she was in love and had found the ideal man. Ms. Ford dutifully recorded the call in Melody's file. Within a few years after Melody had married and had a child, her marriage began falling apart. A contested divorce followed, in which custody or conservatorship was the issue. Both Melody and her husband petitioned the court to be designated as the primary parent of the child—the parent with whom the child would live, and who would receive child support. The other spouse would be allowed visitation only at certain specified times. As part of the custody battle, a process server shows up at Ms. Ford's door with a subpoena, seeking all the clinical records Ms. Ford has maintained in Melody's file.

Does Ms. Ford have to turn over the original records to the process server? If there is a deposition, does Ms. Ford have to appear and bring all Melody's clinical records to the deposition? If there is a court hearing and Ms. Ford receives a subpoena, duces tecum (she is to come in person and bring all Melody's records), does she have to comply with the subpoena and testify, revealing every aspect of the records and commenting on each response given during cross-examination?

The ultimate question is: Are the records of a mental health professional protected from the curious or interloping eyes of the information-seeking public *or* an investigative reporter *or* the attorney for the opposition in a contested suit? When therapists pick up a pen or sit at a computer, do they have to keep in mind that whatever they write down for their own purposes can and might become part of the public domain? Have we discovered a true intellectual conflict when clinical notes created to assist in the therapeutic process become involved in the legal process in a manner that was never intended?

Are the records of a mental health professional protected?

Does every therapist need to keep notes with the "withering cross fire of cross-examination" in mind?

Clinical Records/Clinical Notes Must Be Maintained

Gone are the days when therapists could keep clinical records in their heads. When a threat of malpractice arises, or when a complaint is filed with the licensing board, the clinical notes are often the first line of defense. The board or the attorney for the plaintiff requests all clinical notes as the initial procedure in the investigation.

Whether we like it or not, clinical notes—including computer files—cannot be fully protected from the intrusive eyes of the legal system.

Preserve clinical notes for five to seven years for adults, and longer for minors.

Every therapist must keep and maintain clinical notes, in some cases preserving them for five to seven years for adults, or five to seven years past majority for clients who are minors.

A change of therapists is another reason for keeping complete, current clinical notes. Vacation, death, or other circumstances may require having a relief or new therapist take over a client. The clinical file is the only professional indication of treatment to date.

Clients have to also be told the limits of therapist–client confidentiality.

Customs of the profession indicate what records must be maintained. The operative issue is: What notes would a reasonable and prudent therapist keep under the same or similar circumstances? In addition, the ethical canons of many jurisdictions, usually stated in guidelines published by the various licensing boards, require that certain records be maintained on each client.

For example, in various states, the code of ethics and professional standards of practice might include these themes:

- **"Therapist shall base all services on an assessment, evaluation, or diagnosis of the client."** This standard would suggest that therapists must maintain notes that contain clinical information and the rationale for the assessment, evaluation, and diagnosis of the client. It also implies that the treatment plan should be supported by the same factors.

- **"Therapist shall evaluate a client's progress on a continuing basis."** The notes on each client must be maintained and updated throughout the treatment process. All changes in the assessment, evaluation, prognosis, and diagnosis, as well as the treatment plan, are updated continuously, as long as the client is in treatment.

- **"For each client, therapist *shall* keep records of the dates of services, types of services, and billing information."** Routine, accurate billing records and third-party payment forms provide the means of fulfilling this requirement.

- **"Therapist shall not disclose any confidential information [but will take] reasonable action to inform medical or law enforcement personnel if the professional determines that there is a probability of imminent physical injury by the client to the client or others, or there is a probability of immediate mental or emotional injury to the client."** Although the exact confidentiality requirements vary greatly from jurisdiction to jurisdiction, confidentiality canons should always raise a red flag. In general, confidentiality is to be protected. But when the specter of homicide or suicide appears, the state statute must be consulted. In some jurisdictions, there is a duty to warn the identifiable, apparent intended victim; in others, the therapist must alert the police or a medical facility. In some instances, the therapist is required to call a client's family to prevent a possible suicide; in other states, such a call might be a breach of confidentiality and could have secondary consequences. Research the requirements of your state carefully when confidentiality is at issue.

For the "duty to warn," check the state statute.

Can Clinical Records and Notes Be Protected?

Statutes granting the therapist–client privilege vary, so make sure to consult the statutes in your state. In general, the confidentiality of mental health information is guaranteed. But, in some cases, a different maxim is operative: "What the big print giveth, the small print taketh away." That is, the guarantee of privilege is made hollow by exceptions to the statute. For example, generally there is *no mental health privilege* when a parent–child relationship is involved and custody is an issue; or when a crime has been committed; or when the mental health of a party is an issue in litigation; or when there is child or elder abuse; or when a suit is filed against a therapist.

There is no mental health privilege in parent–child custody situations.

When professionals discuss the confidentiality of mental health records, they have to inform clients of the limits on confidentiality, as mandated by the state. For the therapist's protection, the limits on confidentiality should be clearly spelled out in the original intake and consent form signed by the client before therapy begins. (See Chapter 2 for a sample form.)

Privilege rests with the client, not the therapist.

Practitioners must also keep in mind that the privilege (i.e., the desire to protect the record) belongs to the client. If the client tells the therapist to make the record public, then the therapist must do so. (The client's request should be written, signed, and dated. In some states, it may have to be notarized.) If a therapist feels, as a matter of professional judgment, that the file should not be made public, he or she may file a motion with the appropriate court to restrict publication of the file. This motion will lead to a hearing and a judicial determination. The therapist does not possess the right to refuse to disclose the file if the client and court determine it should be made public. The burden of proof is on the therapist. The court must be shown that revealing the file to the client would be harmful to the client, and that the best interest of the client would be served by keeping the file confidential, even from the client.

Two remedies are available when the therapist seeks to preserve the confidentiality of a file when a subpoena is served: (1) a **Motion to Quash,** and (2) a **Motion for a Protective Order.** Generally, a Motion to Quash points out a technical problem that renders a subpoena invalid. A Motion for a Protective Order acknowledges the validity of the subpoena but argues against the scope of the subpoena. A therapist who wishes to introduce either of these legal remedies would be well advised to seek representation and engage an attorney. When the court rules on the motions, the therapist must, of course, abide by the ruling.

The Bottom Line

• Clinical records must be maintained on every client.

• Clients have to be informed what is confidential and privileged and what is not confidential and privileged. Ms. Ford has an ethical and legal obligation to inform her clients what is and is not confidential and privileged.

- Subpoenas cannot be ignored. The therapist has to take affirmative action to protect a file.

- Computer records are subject to subpoena.

- If a discipline issues a state license, the licensing board usually publishes guidelines that set out the minimum standards necessary for clinical records and notes.

- A therapist can maintain only one set of records. Private records, or personal notations, are usually subject to subpoena. Court testimony indicating that the therapist had two sets of records, one for the client and the other for the therapist, can be embarrassing.

Computer records are subject to subpoena.

Legal Lightbulb

- A privilege must be granted by statute or there is no privilege.
- Don't promise clients that everything they tell you will be kept confidential.
- It takes a lawyer to protect a file.
- In the intake and consent form, set out *in writing* the exceptions to confidentiality.
- It only takes an evening to:
    ⇒ Read the state statute concerning privilege and confidentiality.
    ⇒ Read the state board requirements regarding clinical records, and the duty to warn when a client is a danger to self and/or others.
    ⇒ Read the state standards for record keeping, if published.
    ⇒ Attend a seminar on the subject of confidentiality and take copious notes. If a therapist attends a lecture, reads a book, or takes a class concerning therapy and law, the words of the lecturer are educational and *not* the practice of law. That is, a student or seminar participant can't sue the professor if the participant follows the professor's advice given in a lecture and the advice turns out to be incorrect. Hiring a lawyer is a different matter. If a lawyer is hired, the lawyer is professionally responsible for the advice given. There is a difference, for professional liability purposes, between the practice of law and the educational experience.

- Questions regarding homicide, suicide, and other "duty to warn" situations are in a constant state of legislative and judicial flux. When a problem arises, call your lawyer and your malpractice insurance carrier. A court decision or a new statute can change the rules between the time of publication and the time of the incident.

- If a record, in the interest of the therapist and the client, is to be protected, both, as a team, should consult a lawyer, who can then take the necessary legal steps to protect the file, the therapist, and the client.

Clinical notes can never be fully protected, even when they may contain information detrimental to the client. Efforts can be made to protect confidentiality. The privilege that safeguards records must be exercised when necessary. Both clients and therapists must know the limits imposed under the law.

2

Consent Forms

A client's lawyer calls and says he wants a copy of all your records—including all your personal notes—regarding the client. He says it is OK to send them directly to him; after all, he is the client's lawyer.

~

An investigator from the district attorney's office briskly walks into your office and insists on seeing you immediately. Your startled receptionist interrupts you in a therapy session, and you come out to see what the fuss is all about. The investigator gives you his card and demands the opportunity to review the original files of one of your clients, who has been charged with sexual assault of a minor child.

~

A husband and wife come to you for couples therapy as well as for individual counseling sessions. Eventually, the wife discontinues therapy and files for divorce. The husband asks you for a copy of both his and his wife's records. What do you do?

Disclosure to Third Parties and Clients

Have you maintained separate records for each client (the husband and the wife), or are the records commingled? Can they be easily separated?

Under what circumstance should a therapist produce records upon receipt of a request for information or records pertaining to a client?

The general rule is: Never release records or information regarding a client without the informed consent of the client. There are circumstances when a therapist has a duty to warn or make a report, and serious consequences will be imposed on a therapist who fails to do so. Securing a client's consent to the release of documents or information

Never release records or information regarding a client without prior client consent, and try to obtain permission in writing.

Securing client's consent to release documents or information is not an option; it's usually a necessity.

under duty-to-warn circumstances is not an option. There also may be occasions when a therapist will have to provide records or information regarding a client in response to a subpoena or a court order. Even under these circumstances, it is best to attempt to secure the client's consent via a consent form.

When should you use a consent form? Each and every time a request for information or records is received from a person or entity other than the client. A therapist's arsenal of protective weapons should include ready-to-use client consent forms. The consent form should include:

- Client's name.

- Address, telephone number(s), and social security number of client.

- A direction to the therapist to produce clinical or billing records to a specifically identified person or entity.

- A description of the records to be produced, or a reference to "any and all records."

- Any restrictions on the time period during which the authorization will be in effect.

Always give the client a copy of any form he or she signs. Once you secure the client's signature on a written consent form, the specified records or information can be disclosed with impunity as long as the disclosure is consistent with the scope of the written consent. You may use the sample form on page 11 as a model when preparing a consent form.

The sample consent form would offer protection in the scenarios outlined at the start of the chapter. For example, if a lawyer telephones and says, "Send me my client's records," you should politely respond, "My policy is that if and when I receive a consent for release of records from a client, I will comply with the request."

If an investigator from the district attorney's office starts to throw some weight around, you should state, "In connection with criminal investigations, it is my policy that, upon receipt of a court order or a signed consent for release of records from a client, I will comply with the request."

If one spouse in marital therapy requests both partners' records, you may say something like, "I will be happy to supply you with copies of *your* records but, until such time as I get a signed consent from your spouse to release those other records to you, I cannot comply with your request."

Sample Form

CONSENT TO DISCLOSURE OF CLIENT RECORDS/INFORMATION
TO A GENERAL THIRD PARTY

I, the undersigned, hereby consent to and authorize Dr. Anthony Kindheart to release or disclose to my attorney, Thomas L. Hartsell, Jr., any and all records, documents, notes and information Dr. Kindheart may have in his possession or subject to his control pertaining to my treatment with Dr. Kindheart for the period of time from January 1, 1996, through the date this consent is signed by me. I acknowledge and understand that I am waiving my right to confidentiality with respect to the records and information released and disclosed pursuant to this consent and hereby release Dr. Kindheart and his staff from any and all liability arising from release and disclosure of the information and records requested to my attorney, Thomas L. Hartsell, Jr.

SIGNED this _____ day of _____ , 20__ .

WITNESSED BY:

_____
Anthony Kindheart, LPC

_____
Client

_____
Address

_____
City and State

_____
Telephone Number

_____
Social Security Number

_____
Date of Birth

Photocopy the driver's license, business card, and photo ID of any person seeking information about your client.

Do not blindly trust any person regarding disclosure of records—not even lawyers or law enforcement personnel. Be wary and be vigilant in protecting your client's right to confidentiality. Beware of a pushy attorney, an aggressive investigator, or an ingratiating caller who seeks information. Such contacts often come from the individuals who are least entitled to the information. If someone enters your office seeking client records, ask for and photocopy the person's driver's license, business card, and photo ID (if there is one). Most government personnel have permanent identification cards.

Disclosure among Therapists

In many instances, consent forms not only offer a valuable means of protection against disclosure to third parties, but also, when a change of therapist occurs, they provide the new therapist with a way to review the prior therapeutic history and an indication of the success of earlier methods of treatment. In a therapist-to-therapist disclosure, the client should complete a consent form that will allow the release of records or information to the new therapist. To make sure there is proper identification of the client and the relevant records, this form should include the address and social security number of the client. The form should also specify the precise information that the client is agreeing to have disclosed.

Sample Form

CONSENT TO THERAPIST-TO-THERAPIST DISCLOSURE
OF CLIENT RECORDS/INFORMATION

TO: James Longley, LPC

      2407 Forest Lane, Suite 624
      Dallas, Texas 75208

CLIENT: Henry Joseph Harrison
           Birthdate: 6/14/52
           Social Security #453-67-8932

   I, the undersigned, hereby consent to, direct and authorize James Longley, LPC, to release or disclose to Dr. Anthony Kindheart, 6880 N. Central Exp., Suite 402, Dallas, Texas 75206; (214) 452-7698, confidential records or information pertaining to my treatment with James Longley, LPC, for the period of time from January 1, 1996, through the date this consent is signed by me. The information or records to be released or disclosed should include:

_____ Initial Evaluation/History

_____ Psychiatric/Psychological Reports

_____ Medical Information

_____ Therapy Notes

_____ Billing Records

_____ Transfer/Termination Summary

_____ Tests Taken and Testing Scores

_____ Other

_____ Any and all records/information

(continued)

Sample Form
(continued)

    This consent is subject to revocation at any time, except to the extent that action has been taken in reliance thereon; this consent, unless sooner revoked, will expire on _____ .

    I acknowledge and understand that I am waiving my right to confidentiality with respect to the records and information released pursuant to this consent and hereby release James Longley and his staff from any and all liability arising from release and disclosure of the information and records to Dr. Kindheart.

SIGNED this _____ day of _____ , 20__ .

_____   WITNESSED BY:

Client

_____

Address

_____   _____

City and State   Anthony Kindheart, LPC

_____   _____

Telephone Number   James Longley, LPC

Legal Lightbulb

- Information contained in a client's records should not be shared without a written consent form, signed by the client.

- The more aggressive the person asking for information, the more reluctant the therapist should be to divulge information.

- In certain situations (e.g., child abuse), information may be required by statute to be reported. State statutes set the limits of disclosure and the guidelines.

- A supply of limited and general consent forms should be a part of the therapist's office inventory. They should be available to be signed by clients whenever appropriate.

- Spouses and lawyers do not, by virtue of their legal or marital relationship, have a right to review their spouses' and client's files.

- Certain blank test forms cannot be released because of a contractual and proprietary relationship between the therapist and the owners or creators of those tests.

- If the sample forms in this book are to be used as models, they should be reviewed by a local attorney to see whether they conform to state requirements or meet specific modifications.

- All forms have to be periodically reviewed and updated to insure that they are current and conform to the most recent legal and state licensing board requirements.

3

Correcting Errors

A client, Bob, presented himself for counseling regarding communication in marital difficulties. Bob had had five sessions with the therapist when he called to tell her that his wife had filed for divorce, and had accused him—in a written pleading filed with the court—of being physically abusive. His wife was seeking custody of the couple's children and permission to move to another state. Bob also informed the therapist that, according to his attorney, his wife and her lawyer might subpoena his therapy records. Bob wanted to sign a consent for release of a copy of his file to his attorney. The therapist complied with Bob's request and released his record to his attorney.

*Upon review of the file, the attorney for the husband was startled to find the following note in Bob's records: ". . . discussed his physical abuse **of Karen**." (Karen was Bob's wife.) The attorney immediately called Bob, who advised him that what he and the therapist had actually discussed was Karen's recent behavior. She had spit on him and hit him on the back with a stick. Bob and his attorney called the therapist and demanded an explanation and the removal of that specific word or line from the notes. The therapist recalled the conversation and realized she had meant to write down "his physical abuse **by Karen**." This error in the clinical record could be devastating to Bob if quoted verbatim as part of the trial testimony.*

Under these facts, what should the therapist do, and what is she permitted to do? Would the situation change if the wife's attorney had been able to secure a copy of the therapist's notes first?

A therapist should get into the habit of reviewing notes and records.

Therapists are human, and mistakes are inevitably made with respect to mental health records. But a careful approach to transcribing records, and reviewing them soon after they are transcribed, can help prevent embarrassing problems from surfacing months or even years in the future. Therapists should get into the habit of reviewing notes and records soon after they are written, when recollections are fresh and strong. But even the best procedures and the most diligent concern for the accuracy of records will not prevent errors from occurring occasionally.

Most states do not have statutes or regulations regarding corrections to health care records, but several do. The rules prescribed by these states establish sound safeguards and guidelines to be followed by a mental health practitioner who wishes to correct a client's record. In Arkansas, pursuant to "Rules & Regulations for Hospitals & Related Institutions in Arkansas," Section 601 G (1988), errors in medical records must be corrected by drawing a single line through the incorrect entry, dating it, initialing it, and labeling it as an error. Pursuant to Massachusetts Regulations Code, Title 105, Section 150.013 (B) (1990), Massachusetts health care facilities are prohibited from erasing mistakes, using ink eradicators, or removing pages from the record.

How to Make Corrections

Common sense would dictate that only the person who originally made the error should correct it. At stake when an error is made is the credibility of the record and of the person who made the entry. In litigation, attorneys must establish the credibility, or lack thereof, of witnesses and admissible evidence introduced at trial. When examining a therapist about a client's file, in a deposition or at trial, a prudent attorney will ask whether any corrections, alterations, additions, or deletions were made to the records after they were originally transcribed. A therapist who has made an undisclosed change to a record is under oath and is faced with two choices: commit perjury or admit to changing the record. A therapist who has "whited out" or erased information and then written over it will have a more difficult time explaining his or her actions than a therapist who has written a single line through the error, initialed it, dated it, and marked it "Error." Much more suspicion will be raised in the minds of a judge, jury, and opposing counsel when an entry is completely removed and no one but the therapist knows what was originally recorded. Indecipherable notations are always suspect. (In the Nixon tapes, far more attention has been paid to the eighteen missing minutes than to the hours of accurate audiotape.)

Only the person who originally made the error should correct the record.

If you need more space than the record allows to correct an entry, attach an addendum on a separate sheet of paper, and reference the addendum at the point in the record where the mistake occurred.

Correct an error by drawing a single line through it, labeling it "Error," inserting the correction above it, and dating and initialing the correction.

Bob's therapist should correct her record by striking through the word "of," marking it "Error," inserting the word "by," and then dating and initialing the correction. The same procedure should be followed regardless of when the error is discovered—even if the records have already been produced in a lawsuit, with copies delivered to all concerned. In such a case, make the correction, date and initial it, then send the correction to all parties.

In case you are tempted to make undisclosed changes to a mental health record, remember that such conduct could lead to revocation of a professional license for unethical conduct, and criminal prosecution for perjury or evidence tampering.

The Bottom Line

- Never surreptitiously change a client's record.

- If an error is made, correct it by drawing a single line through it, labeling it "Error," inserting the correction above it, and dating and initialing the correction.

- License revocation and criminal prosecution await those who make undisclosed changes to mental health records.

- Jurors and judges are as willing to forgive an admitted error as they are a repentant sinner, but they have little sympathy for a therapist who erases or "whites out" to hide an unpleasant fact.

- If there is a state regulation concerning the procedure to correct an error, the therapist must become familiar with that procedure.

- When an error is discovered, review the error, the reason for the error, and the reason for correcting the error. Be prepared, should the case come to trial and testimony be required, to explain the error.

- Computer records present a unique problem because a hard drive or disk can be easily deleted and corrected. Be very careful when correcting computer copies, especially if hard copies have been printed. If a therapist testifies that a recent printout is correct, and then a different, older hard copy is located, the consequences are dire—charges of perjury, loss of credibility, and ethics concerns.

- When correcting a computer record, do not delete but insert, in parentheses, the date of correction and the initials of the person modifying the record. The computer record should then contain both the original and corrected versions.

- Consult state statutes when correcting computer records.

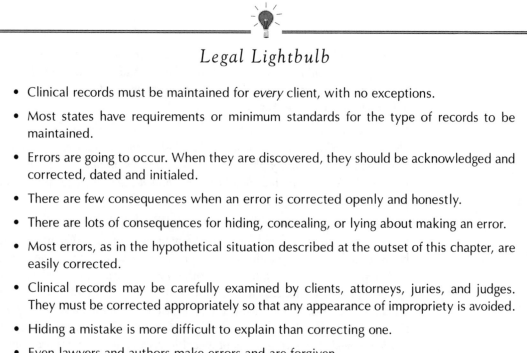

Legal Lightbulb

- Clinical records must be maintained for *every* client, with no exceptions.

- Most states have requirements or minimum standards for the type of records to be maintained.

- Errors are going to occur. When they are discovered, they should be acknowledged and corrected, dated and initialed.

- There are few consequences when an error is corrected openly and honestly.

- There are lots of consequences for hiding, concealing, or lying about making an error.

- Most errors, as in the hypothetical situation described at the outset of this chapter, are easily corrected.

- Clinical records may be carefully examined by clients, attorneys, juries, and judges. They must be corrected appropriately so that any appearance of impropriety is avoided.

- Hiding a mistake is more difficult to explain than correcting one.

- Even lawyers and authors make errors and are forgiven.

4

Discharge or Termination

A depressed client, Joshua, failed to appear for a scheduled appointment with a therapist and did not call to reschedule. Joshua had been in counseling approximately six months and told family members he was functioning well and didn't need to continue therapy.

In reality, Joshua was seriously depressed, and the therapist had concerns about his stability and well-being. When Joshua failed to appear, the therapist tried to reach him by phone—at all of Joshua's numbers—but was unsuccessful. Afterward, the therapist, who had a busy practice, put Joshua out of her mind.

One month later, the therapist received a call from Joshua's sister, who notified the therapist that her brother had committed suicide. When the sister began to ask probing questions, the therapist refused to discuss the matter with her, citing confidentiality concerns. The sister was appointed executor of her brother's estate and used this legal authority to secure copies of the therapist's records. Upon review, the sister accused the therapist of malpractice for failing to advise her brother of the therapist's concerns and of the brother's need for continuing mental health services when he stopped coming to therapy.

~

Amy was terminating therapy. Both the therapist and Amy were pleased with the results. They both realized the goals of therapy had been achieved. Amy was very satisfied and had become capable of coping with the problems of life. The time had come for Amy and her therapist to shake hands and go their separate ways.

What should the therapist do?

What methods are used to appropriately terminate, when either the client or the therapist does not feel continued therapy would be helpful, or when the goals of therapy have been accomplished?

What is the appropriate method to terminate when the client has essentially voluntarily terminated the therapy, but the therapist feels that therapy should have continued? A continued "no show" sends a message. The therapist should be especially concerned when clients who are obligated (perhaps by court order) to make an appointment fail to call to set up a date and time.

There will come a point in every therapeutic relationship when termination should occur. This can be the result of the client's achieving all therapeutic goals, or can occur when the client stops making progress and a referral to another provider is indicated. At that time, it is important to document the termination, and the reason for it, in appropriate detail. At any point prior to termination, a client's file should reflect the need for continued therapy. As soon as the need ceases to exist, termination of the therapeutic relationship with that client should take place. The file should also reflect that a client is benefiting from the mental health services provided. If, after an appropriate length of time, it becomes apparent that the client is not benefiting from therapy, termination and referral should occur.

How Should Termination Occur?

It is best to schedule an exit session or termination interview with the client so the therapist can be sure that the client fully understands what is taking place, the reasons behind it, and any recommendations the therapist has for the client. A termination letter should be prepared, reviewed with the client, and signed by the client. The client should be given a copy of the signed termination letter when the session ends. The termination letter should indicate that the therapist will:

A termination letter should be prepared, then reviewed with and signed by the client.

- Be happy to consult with any subsequent therapist.
- Make the file available to other professional individuals in response to a written request from the client, and signing of a consent form.
- Be available personally, if possible, should the client feel, in the future, that further therapy is needed.
- Provide a tickler follow-up file if desired by the client. The therapist would then check, at specified times, how the client is doing. The client would furnish an acceptable phone number(s) or address(es) for

Obtain a phone number and alternate address where the client can be contacted.

future contact and give written permission to the therapist to contact the client at the number or location.

If an exit or termination interview session is not possible, a phone conference should be attempted, and a copy of the termination letter should be sent to the client at the mailing address authorized by the client. If neither an office visit nor a phone conference is possible, two copies of the termination letter should be sent to the client: one by certified mail, with return receipt requested, and another by first-class mail. This same procedure should be followed when a client skips an appointment and then stops all contact with the therapist, especially if the therapist believes the client is in need of additional mental health care. Don't just dismiss a client who drops out of sight and refuses to return phone calls. Write to the client, explain the need for continuing mental health services, and recommend at least three competent referral sources.

Don't dismiss a client who drops out of sight and refuses to return phone calls.

Termination Letter Checklist

The termination letter should include the following:

- Client's name.
- Date therapy began.
- Termination date.
- Primary (and any secondary) diagnosis.
- Reason for termination.
- Summary of treatment, including need for additional services.
- Referral sources, including addresses and phone numbers (try to list at least three).
- A statement that the client understands what termination of treatment means and accepts the responsibility to seek further treatment if needed or appropriate.
- Signature lines for both the therapist and the client, and a date line for each signature.
- Enclose a self-addressed, stamped envelope, and indicate "Enclosure" at the bottom of the termination letter.

Sample Form

CLIENT TERMINATION LETTER

ANTHONY KINDHEART, LPC
6894 Forest Park Drive
Suite 268
Dallas, Texas 75206
July 17, 20__

Mr. Kevin Jones
1425 Centenary
Dallas, Texas 75210

Re: Termination of Treatment

Dear Mr. Kevin Jones:

It has become necessary, for the reasons stated below, to terminate our professional and therapeutic relationship. I will maintain your records for the period required by law and will make copies of your records available to you upon written request. You may be charged a reasonable fee for the cost of duplicating the records.

Our work together began on July 1, 1996, and ended on this date. During this time, we worked on improving your occupational and social functioning and alleviating your depression by addressing factors that may have caused, contributed to, or aggravated your depression.

In the exercise of my professional judgment, I have concluded that you have not made satisfactory progress in improving your social and occupational functioning and with your depression. I believe you are in need of additional mental health services for treatment of your depression and possible chemical dependency. These services can be best provided to you by one of the following:

Richard Lewins, MD, (214) 489-3624, 1900 Main Street, Suite 120, Dallas, TX 75201

Sylvia Jones, LCDC, (972) 270-9142, 689 LBJ Freeway, Suite 410, Dallas, TX 75214

Harold Jones, PhD, (214) 814-3621, 48764 Mockingbird, Suite 206, Dallas, TX 75206

(continued)

Sample Form
(continued)

I recommend you contact one of these providers, or another provider of your choosing, as quickly as possible to schedule an appointment. With your written consent, I will consult with any professional of your choosing and will forward the file or a summary of your treatment to my successor.

Your primary discharge diagnosis is: 296.32 Major Depression, recurrent.

This termination is not due to any personal reasons but solely due to my desire for you to achieve the highest possible level of mental health wellness and social and occupational functioning. I believe referring you to one of the providers listed above presents the best possibility for this to occur. I wish you success and want you to know that I will make myself available for consultation with anyone you choose to work with, in order to make this transition as easy as possible.

Sincerely,

_____
Anthony Kindheart, LPC

I acknowledge receipt and review and accept and understand the terms of this termination letter, dated the 17th day of July, 20__ .

_____   _____
Kevin Jones   Date

                                       _____
                                       Social Security Number

Closing a File

It is imperative for the therapist to document the completion of a client's file with a termination letter or form similar to the one suggested here. A therapist has an ethical obligation to terminate a client who is not benefiting from the relationship, and to make an appropriate referral when the client can be better served by another provider. The surest way to prove compliance with these ethical obligations is to maintain a written record in the client's file. Don't put yourself in the same situation as the therapist described at the beginning of the chapter. Be proactive; document your file.

Make notations, in the client file, of all attempts to contact the client.

A client's record is not complete until it has a written record of termination.

Legal Lightbulb

- The therapeutic relationship with a client should continue only so long as it is benefiting the client.

- A client's file should always reflect the need for additional mental health services. When that need ceases, it is time to terminate.

- Develop and use a termination form or letter.

- Try to schedule a face-to-face termination session, and have the client sign the form or letter in your presence. If an exit interview isn't possible, try to make phone contact with the client. Either way, mail the form or letter to the client's authorized mailing address. It's a good idea to make two copies of the letter. Send one by certified mail, with return receipt requested, and the other by regular mail. Regular mail is delivered; certified mail can be refused.

- If termination is necessary and the client needs additional mental health care, provide the client with at least three competent referral sources. (Remember, a tort action can be brought against you for negligent referral. Any person, agency, or organization on your referral list must be capable of treating the client, on terms the client can accept financially and clinically. See Chapter 26, "Acts of Omission," for more specifics.)

- Documentation is critical. It is your best defense.

A similar letter is necessary for voluntary termination, when both the therapist and the client agree that the therapy has accomplished its goals. Most important would be these provisions:

- The therapist is available for future sessions if the client desires.
- The therapist will make the client's file available to any future therapist, if the client consents, in writing, to its release.
- If the client leaves the area, referrals can be made to a therapist in the new location.

5

Electronic Records

A worried therapist called his lawyers. He had brought his personal computer to a major repair facility and returned two weeks later to pick up the instrument. However, it could not be found! After a long and diligent search, the shop offered to replace it with an upgraded computer—a new product with double the market value of the lost PC. The only problem was that the original computer's hard drive had not been erased (nor a backup file created), and some person now had possession of numerous client files, all of which were privileged, confidential, and private. Fortunately, there had been no repercussions. Whoever had the computer was probably only interested in the hardware and was ignorant of the significance of the stored data. The therapist responsible for the security of the file had been lucky—there had been no reported breaches of confidentiality. On the other hand, the therapist lost all the data and notes that had been saved on the hard drive.

In the current electronic age, therapists are using desktop computers to create, store, and design client files, and are transmitting documents via fax and e-mail. In addition, new client records are constantly being created, generated, and maintained on computers, and the need for hard copies stored in voluminous, space-eating files is diminishing.

Because maintaining floor space for files costs money, many mental health professionals prefer the convenience of a disk to the bulk of a thick paper file. When a client file is needed, the press of a few buttons retrieves the file onto the screen or printer in a matter of seconds. The main concern, when a therapist chooses to convert to computerized record keeping and storage of client files, is whether the computer system will preserve both the confidentiality and the integrity of the client's health care information.

The computer system used by the therapist should preserve the confidentiality and integrity of the client's health care information.

Maintaining Correct Files and Confidentiality

With a printed paper file, it is easy to secure client information. The office and the file cabinets can be locked, and only designated persons can have access to the file on a "need to know" basis. Paper files can also be counted on to survive the time period for which the therapist is required, by law and good practice, to maintain and preserve case records. However, with computers, the rules and procedures of storage have changed. Indeed, there is little similarity between a computer disk and a printed, paper-intensive file secured in a cardboard file folder.

Gone are the days when a hard copy of each client file was maintained in a neat manila folder, which could be pulled out when needed. Now, in addition to hard copies, there are floppy disks, hard drives, and, possibly, central storage systems. Maintaining security, confidentiality, privacy, and privilege has become a nightmare.

"Computerizing patient records could improve coordination of care, decrease duplication of tests, simplify outcomes research and, ultimately, allow more comprehensive treatment," health care experts say. But they caution that, without adequate security controls, computerization could give unscrupulous individuals access to sensitive information in medical records. ("Electronic Records Require Safeguards," *Healthweek*, October 21, 1996, Vol. 1, No. 21, p. 1.)

Access to computer files can be safeguarded with codes, but absolute security cannot be guaranteed.

A mental health professional's obligation to maintain the confidentiality of a client's file is not altered by a change in the method by which the record is created or stored. It does not matter whether the file is created by hand, computer, audio tape, or video tape. Computerization of client information, however, does increase the risk of unauthorized disclosure to hackers—individuals who, for the sheer pleasure of displaying their technical expertise, randomly invade, disclose, or rearrange files. Access to computer files can be safeguarded with codes, but absolute security can usually not be guaranteed.

System security measures, such as user passwords or computer locks, should be considered. To satisfactorily comply with a therapist's legal and ethical obligation to preserve the confidentiality of a client's record, reasonable effort must be made and reasonable safeguards must be implemented.

Call for Backup

Every mental health provider, regardless of discipline, should back up each file regularly, perhaps daily, onto a floppy disk, a tape, or some other backup system. Clients have a right to copies of their files, and they will take a dim view of a therapist or provider who has, by negligence or inadvertence, allowed a file to be lost, destroyed, or negligently placed into the public domain.

As a precaution, when a computer needs repair, copy information to the backup system, and erase the files from the hard drive. If the computer is lost or stolen, only the computer is lost, not client information, substance, or material. Remember, the client has not given informed consent for a computer repairer to review his or her file.

Computer files can easily be deleted, lost, erased, corrupted, or overwritten. The typical system—whether as a result of inadvertent or accidental operator error, or such unforeseen events as electrical storms, major power surges, or power shortages—can lose data very quickly. Frequent backup is a necessity.

The therapist should give thought to the durability of a computerized record—the medium on which the information is stored. A disk or tape will have to survive for at least the minimum period of time the therapist is required to maintain records. (See Chapter 7, "Maintaining Records"). In addition, technology is rapidly advancing and changing. If a therapist upgrades his or her computer system, it is important for the new and the old systems to be compatible. If they are not, old equipment may have to be preserved and maintained so the therapist can comply with the requirements for the minimum record-keeping period.

How should the therapist keep computerized records?

Remember to regularly back up each client file onto a disk, tape, or other storage system.

When a computer needs repair, copy information to the backup system, and erase the files from the hard drive.

Some Hints for Keeping Computerized Records

- Make sure the hard drive and any backup disks are locked and secure at all times. They should be protected against fire, flood, curious cleaning people, and inquisitive clients who have the habit of draping themselves over the therapist's desk and peering at the computer screen.

- A password protects access to the computer system; secure passwords from detection.

- If a celebrity is in treatment at any time, devise a fictitious name and keep all records under the assumed name. Have the "key" to the name in a protected place. (Investigative reporters and private detectives have been known to gain entry surreptitiously and copy files. A diligent hacker can access most instruments.)

- Back up the computer to a disk, tape, or other backup system regularly, and give the backup system the same respect as the hard drive.

- Copy the records to a disk, tape, or other backup system, and then delete the hard drive, whenever the computer is taken in for repair or whenever a repairer must examine it.

- When you purchase a computer, ask the computer salesperson to show you how to protect stored information and to explain the durability of the medium (i.e., disk or tape) used to back up and store information.

Regular or temporary support staff who have access to computer files should sign a confidentiality form.

- Have *every person* who will have access to files read and initial a published protocol that indicates the importance and relevance of safeguarding the files. This is especially important for temporary and other support staff who may not be aware of or trained in important principles concerning the sanctity, privacy, or confidentiality of clients' records or names.

- Adequately train yourself and the support staff about the computer system employed. Know how to use it properly.

A client who has a right to view his or her file would have a right to a copy of the disk.

- Consider the files of all clients to be valuable property which, if lost or stolen, produces dramatic consequences.

- Position computer monitors so that only the operator can see the screen.

- Use virus protection software.

- Take the potential problem of computer theft or crash seriously enough to establish reasonable safeguards.

The New Communications Media

Technology has created new methods of communication and has the capacity to put into the public domain information that is thought to be private and personal. Many of the current communication methods were not available even a few years ago. They make communication and publication easier, but confidentiality and privacy are more difficult to maintain.

New transmission media include the Internet, fax machines, cordless telephones, cellular telephone communications networks, computer communications, "private network" communications, "semipublic network" (password-protected or encrypted) communications, unencrypted Internet e-mail, and other creative methods of communication.

All are in use, and many are presumed by clients to be private and confidential—and perhaps privileged as well. But all these methods are relatively new in the global, long-term view of legal history and case precedents, and legal determinations have not yet been solidified into dependable rules of law. To some extent, the rules of computer technology and the responsibility of therapists to create, maintain, and guard records are in the process of evolution. To date, there are few case precedents, and most lawyers will give advice with a caveat: "This is my best guess regarding the legal consequences as of this day. Tomorrow it may change."

Modern communication methods permeate all phases of mental health practice, from the keeping and maintaining of clinical records to the written and oral transmission of information over the wires and air waves of mass communication. Speed and accuracy are mandated, but so too are confidentiality and, where appropriate, privilege. Each method of communication has its own developing body of law. The mental health professional who has "gone modern" should stay abreast of the developing law in his or her jurisdiction before going public with information that might place a client, and later the provider, in jeopardy.

Alongside the benefits of technology, there are some disadvantages to consider. Copy machines offer an opportunity for roving eyes to glance at documents that were intended to be private. Fax transmissions can go to the wrong place because of a simple error of pressing the wrong digit. Telephone answering machines can generate messages to unidentified listeners, or information may be offered before the absolute identity of the original caller is determined. Cellular phones carry conversations over the air waves, and anyone with the proper equipment can listen in while a call is being made. Voice pagers can blurt out information in closed sessions. The caller assumes confidentiality and will have no idea that the voice message has entered the public domain.

Advances in technology help communication; however, use caution when dealing with faxes, pagers, voice mail, and e-mail.

Voice mail messages are often unprotected if the access code is in writing and placed near the machine. Computer terminals are often in plain view, so a person can peer around the counter or workstation and see the mental health history of a client on the screen.

In these circumstances, common sense must prevail. No rules are always "fail safe" in all situations. However, certain standard methods of protection can be practiced in most office settings, and individual therapists will create others to satisfy their own needs and purposes.

Some Suggested Safeguards

- Prevent the copy machine from becoming a social gathering place. Make sure that discarded copies are shredded and not left to be viewed by anyone who might go through the trash.

- Turn down the volume on your telephone answering machine, or turn it off, when third parties are in the room.

- When answering a message left on your answering machine, verify the identity of the person who made the call, and make sure you are alone in the room.

- On a cellular phone, assume "Big Brother" is listening in on your call. One can't be too careful. Careers have been ruined by talking too freely to a wrong, and unseen, person. "Big Brother" can be a gossipy neighbor, an investigative reporter, a government agency, or a political rival.

- Don't use a loud voice pager in public. Turn the volume down or off.

- Insure the integrity of your voice mail code. Only the mental health professional and others who have a real "need to know" should have it available.

- Consider getting the client's written consent prior to sending any fax or e-mail transmissions. Advise the client of the potential risk of disclosure. In some cases, ask the recipient to wait by the machine while the fax is being sent. Ask for confirmation of receipt.

- Consider encryption technology for e-mail transmissions.

- Contact the intended recipient prior to transmission, to advise that a transmission is imminent.

- Double-check all fax transmissions, and keep the printout (staple it to the transmission) so there is always evidence of the recipient's number.

- When using the fax, have a "fail safe" system to see that all numbers are accurately pressed. Include a confidentiality page in each transmission.

Advancing technology will continue to create new difficulties and areas of exposure—in terms of liability and professional ethics—for the mental health practitioner. The client assumes everything shared with the

The therapist is responsible for maintaining the confidentiality of a client's file, regardless of the method by which the record is created or stored.

Legal Lightbulb

- A computer file is the same as a hard file, when confidentiality, privacy, privilege, maintenance, and security are to be considered.

- Legally, files are files, regardless of the method of preservation.

- Computers must be secure from roving eyes.

- Presumably, a client who has a right to view his or her file would have a right to a copy of the disk on which it is stored.

- A lawyer who states "This is the law concerning computer files" is overstating the facts. The law is in a developing stage and will be as long as computers are being constantly created, updated, and upgraded within a few years after their creation. Imminent obsolescence seems to keep the law and the anxiety level of lawyers on a constant high plane. If a lawyer renders an opinion, ask him or her to reduce it to writing.

- The transmission of sensitive information using modern technology creates a legal nightmare. There is no fail-safe advice. Just be careful.

- Most breaches of confidentiality are covered by malpractice policies. A therapist who is worried should increase his or her coverage.

- Be careful of what you discard as trash.

- Create a therapist–employee (regular or temporary) contract. Employees have no reason to copy files onto a personal disk, and no client files should ever be removed from the office.

professional is confidential and will be kept confidential. The best way for the therapist to maintain that level of confidentiality is to continue to be cautious.

When in doubt, call your lawyer, the malpractice hot line, your professional organization, or the licensing board. New laws will be published on a regular basis. Read the latest bulletins on law and therapy and on the need for confidentiality preservation, and maintenance of electronic and computer files. Knowing the content of the most current bulletin will help you in the future and may even save your practice.

6

Intake and Consent Forms

Dr. Shapiro was notified by her licensing board that a complaint had been filed against her by a client whom she had reported to the state authorities for suspected child abuse—pursuant to Dr. Shapiro's legal duty to make the report. In the complaint to the licensing board, the client stated that he had sought mental health treatment from the therapist for problems when dealing with his children, and the therapist had never advised him that suspected child abuse was an exception to his right to confidentiality.

~

Dr. Chen was practicing under supervision, with the approval of his licensing board. He received notice of a complaint filed against him with his licensing board for allegedly failing to advise a client that he was practicing under supervision. The client stated that the supervision was never disclosed to her, and that she never would have consented to treatment with the therapist had she known about the supervision. She wanted the therapist to refund the $1,800.00 she had paid from her own pocket for counseling and therapy over a fifteen-month period. She was complaining only about the failure of the therapist to disclose to her that he was under supervision, not about the quality of the therapy.

How does a therapist defend against these and other allegations from unhappy clients?

Many state licensing statutes require a mental health professional to discuss several important matters with a client before, or at the onset of, the very first counseling session with the client. To proceed with treatment, the therapist must have the *informed consent* of the client. *Uninformed consent is no consent at all.* Remember that licensing statutes have evolved primarily from a concern to protect the consumer. Public policy demands a protected and well-educated consumer. Fortunately or unfortunately, the therapist has the task of educating the consumer/client.

To help accomplish that end, a mental health practitioner is required to discuss, at the outset:

- The licensing of the therapist.
- Supervision and restrictions.
- Information regarding the services to be provided.
- Purposes, goals, and techniques of treatment.
- Confidentiality and its exceptions.
- Fees and payment.
- Consent for treatment.

The best evidence to present to the licensing board when a complaint is filed is an intake and consent form signed by the client.

Without a written record that these matters were discussed with the client, the therapist's word must stand against that of a client who complains to a licensing board. The best and easiest evidence to present to the licensing board when a complaint is filed is an intake and consent form signed by the client on the date of the very first therapist–client session.

There is no basis for argument when a written record indicates coverage of all the matters that need to be addressed. Prepare a consent form, go over it with the client, have the client sign it in your presence, and send the client home with a copy of the consent. If the client returns for a second session, he or she will find it even harder to support a complaint or to allege failure to cover the requisite matters.

Every intake and consent form should be carefully crafted for each therapist's individual practice and clientele.

This chapter gives you a checklist of issues to be addressed in an intake and consent form. The list should not be considered exhaustive. Every intake and consent form should be carefully crafted for each therapist's individual practice and clientele.

Throughout this book, model forms are presented to cover specific problems. When constructing your own forms from the models, include all circumstances that have a possibility of happening, and eliminate areas that are so remote or statistically improbable for your practice that they do not need inclusion.

In general, all clients will sign almost anything placed in front of them.

Anyone entering a hospital within the past few years signs an admission form consisting of pages and pages of small print. Anyone watching the procedure observes that arriving patients will sign almost anything placed in front of them. Few question the admission form, which has been carefully crafted by the hospital lawyer *to protect the hospital, the attending physician, and the staff.* Mental health professionals might not need such detailed protection, but in our litigious society, the printed and signed form is important.

What to Include in Your Intake and Consent Form

1. A description of yourself and your credentials: Include information regarding your licensing status; restrictions, if any; and, if you are practicing under supervision, the name and address of your supervisor. State your relationship to any referring entity, such as: "Independent Contractor/Provider for ABC Managed Care." Mention your employer if you work for a group or agency. If you are in private practice, advise the client of your independent status.

2. A description of the services you provide: Tell the client what you do during a typical session, and what types of services you provide (e.g., "psychological services including but not limited to play therapy and psychological testing"). The idea is to make sure the client is an educated consumer. The client should acknowledge, in writing, what the therapist does and does not provide, the competence of the therapist, and the limits of that competence.

The client should never begin and continue in therapy with unrealistic expectations.

3. Procedures for appointments: Tell the new client how far ahead you schedule appointments and how much notice you expect for a cancellation. Provide the client with specific information on scheduling and canceling appointments, including the times and the numbers to call. State whether there is a charge for canceled or missed appointments.

4. Length and number of sessions: Advise the client when a finite number of sessions is approved initially by an insurance carrier or managed care company. Start planning—and encourage the client to do so as well—the steps that will be needed if additional sessions are required. If there are no session limitations, advise the client that you cannot predict how many sessions may be required to appropriately address his or her problems or concerns. At least discuss the managed care or insurance limitations, and what might be the plan if third-party payments are not available.

5. Relationship between the therapist and client: Dual relationship problems can be effectively avoided if the therapist has a frank discussion with the client regarding the nature of the therapeutic relationship between therapists and clients. Explain to the client what a therapeutic relationship means, and the limitations concerning nontherapeutic personal contact. Advise the client that, for your work to have the best chance of success for him or her, the therapeutic relationship is the only relationship the two of you can have. Advise the client that it is inappropriate for you to exchange or bestow gifts, spend time with each other socially, or attend family functions, graduations, marriages, or religious ceremonies.

It is not appropriate for a client to try to engage you in conversation at your home or anywhere outside your office.

It is not appropriate for a client to try to engage you in conversation, in person or by phone, at your home or anywhere outside your office. Urge the client not to call you outside the office unless it is to discuss a future appointment or a genuine emergency.

A client can cross the line into a dual relationship with impunity, but the therapist can't. Many therapists have been unwittingly drawn across the line by a client. Deal with the issue when establishing the initial relationship, and advise the client that, if the line is crossed, you will have to terminate the therapeutic relationship and refer the client to another therapist. Blurred relationships or fuzzy contacts are to be avoided. When a therapeutic relationship begins to blur, handle the problem at once. Don't wait until the therapeutic contact becomes a crisis.

Therapists cannot cross the line into a dual relationship.

Let the client know how far ahead he or she must cancel an appointment, to avoid incurring a charge.

6. Fees/payment: Give the client accurate information about all special charges and about your fees for services you provide to clients. State when payment is due. For a managed care referral, calculate and communicate the amount of co-pays the client is responsible for.

A matter not often addressed by mental health professionals is the time and expense that may be incurred in response to a subpoena to produce records or give testimony. Most often, a therapist will not be a *litigation expert witness*—someone who meets the client for the first time after a lawsuit has been filed, and is retained to give testimony on behalf of the client. Usually, the therapist has provided mental health services to a client before any lawsuit is filed or even contemplated. For example, one therapist began treating a woman for depression, and, six months later, was subpoenaed by the client's husband, who was filing for divorce and seeking custody of the couple's children.

Provide clauses for the time and expense that may be incurred in responding to a subpoena.

Unfortunately, there is usually no court protection for therapists who may wish to petition for reimbursement for time and expenses incurred in responding to a subpoena. A therapist, like an eyewitness to an accident, can be subpoenaed to testify in court about what he or she has observed. To give yourself an option to present an invoice for your time and trouble, include in the intake and consent form, clauses that make the client responsible to pay a fee for your time and expense spent in responding to a subpoena, regardless of who issued the subpoena.

Is it fair for the client to have to pay for the therapist's time if her husband and his attorney issued the subpoena? Perhaps not, but is it fair for the therapist to incur financial loss—in the form of canceled appointments and missed opportunities—and inconvenience, because the client and her husband are seeking a divorce? It is fairer to place this unexpected loss on the client/litigant, who has more control over and more involvement in the events that gave rise to the litigation.

7. Confidentiality and the duty to warn: Clients come into your office with the expectation that everything told to you will be kept strictly confidential and will not be disclosed to any third parties. They may believe that you will take their secrets to the grave and will never give them up or testify about them, no matter what the price. In reality, however, absolute therapeutic confidentiality is a myth. There are so many exceptions to confidentiality that, upon consideration of all of them, a person might reasonably conclude that confidentiality no longer exists.

A mental health professional has the duty to explain confidentiality to a prospective client and to reveal the exceptions. Cover this matter thoroughly, and list as many exceptions as you can think of; use the clause "including but not limited to." If you open a practice in a jurisdiction where it is unclear whether you have the right or duty to contact an intended victim, have all your new clients authorize your right to contact any person in a position to prevent harm to the client or a third party. Consent is the number one exception to confidentiality. Ask the client to provide you with addresses and phone numbers of specific persons you can contact if you reasonably suspect the client or a third party is in danger.

A therapist is obligated to explain the limits and exceptions of confidentiality to the client.

Consent is the number one exception to confidentiality.

8. Addresses/phone numbers for communication with client: Be sure to have the client provide you with an address where mail can and may be sent, if you need to contact the client and one or more phone numbers (work/daytime, evening, weekend) where you can contact the client if necessary. Remember, disclosing client identity can constitute a breach of confidentiality, and area codes, phone numbers, and addresses change over time. Check the validity of your client information file at regular intervals.

9. Risks of therapy/counseling: Tell your new clients that therapy involves risks. Therapy sessions can be very painful at times. Clients may learn things about themselves that they don't like. Pain often precedes growth, and clients should be made aware that they may experience pain, sorrow, depression, and anxiety along the way.

10. After-hours emergencies: Clients should be given a phone number to call in the event of a true emergency. If your practice provides twenty-four-hour access to a therapist, provide clients with the phone numbers to call during and after normal office hours. If twenty-four-hour service is not available, list on your intake form the phone numbers for hotlines or prevention organizations that should be contacted in the event of an emergency, and for local hospital emergency rooms.

11. Therapist's death/incapacity: Confidentiality survives death—the therapist's as well as the client's. Very few mental health practitioners consider what to do about client records, or how clients should be contacted, if the therapist should die or become incapacitated. Some states impose a duty on therapists to plan for these contingencies, but not all have specific statutory provisions or ethical canons that set out procedures to follow in the event of the death or incapacity of the therapist or the death of a client. One approach would be for therapists to state in their wills that all of their records and files are to go to the appropriate licensing board in the event of the therapist's death. The therapist's concern is breach of confidentiality. It is not appropriate for a therapist's spouse, or any third party not consented to by the clients, to review files or appointment calendars, when the therapist dies or becomes incapacitated.

There is an exception for court-appointed executors, administrators, guardians, or receivers, but it takes time to secure a court appointment. In the meantime, how should current and/or needy or desperate clients be protected? In your intake and consent form, provide for the client to consent to having another mental health professional of your choosing take possession of the client's file and contact the client, in the event you become incapacitated or die.

12. Consent to treat: A client must consent to having you provide mental health services to that client. When the client is a child, make sure you have a signed intake and consent form from a person who has the legal authority to consent for that child. (See Chapter 17.) The consent authorizes you to provide services, and it states the client's or a third-party payer's obligation to pay. It establishes a contract between

Remember, disclosing client identity can constitute a breach of confidentiality.

Therapists should appoint the licensing board as the executor for all their files and records.

Make sure you have a signed intake and consent form from a person with the legal authority to consent for a child.

you and the client, and it gives you all the rights and duties to provide professional mental health services for compensation.

However, one problem can still plague the therapist. What happens when the appropriate call is made; authorization is given; therapy is offered, accepted, and concluded; and then, after internal review, the insurance carrier or managed care company declines the claim as being unauthorized or inappropriate because of some technicality? In one case, the parties were divorced and the carrier was not notified. The divorce had terminated the client's coverage. Everyone acted in good faith and yet the claim was denied.

Provide specifically in the consent form that ultimate responsibility for the bill is with the client/patient, and if the claim is later denied for any reason, the client/patient is fully responsible for paying the bill within a reasonable period of time—for example, thirty days after the date the claim is denied. (In one case, the claim was denied after payment had been made, and the insurance company demanded reimbursement from the therapist a year later!)

The responsibility for payment is ultimately with the client.

13. Waiver of right to child's records/information: If you deal with children, especially adolescents, it may be advisable to secure a waiver of a parent's right to information about a child, in the event that you determine it is in the best interest of the child to withhold information from the parent. Generally, parents have the right to access the mental health records and files of their children. But a teenager may be reluctant to be candid with a therapist if a parent will have access to the information shared in a counseling session. The waiver may prove helpful later on, in dealing with difficult parent–child issues raised by the child. For the child to achieve success in therapy, trust and a right to assured privacy are critical.

It is advisable to secure a waiver of a parent's right to information about a child—if it is in the best interest of the child.

14. Signature lines: After you have developed your intake and consent form with your lawyer and reviewed it with your client, don't forget to have the client sign it. You should also sign it and make a copy of the signed form for the client to take home. At that point, you should have a client who is a well-educated consumer, and adequate proof of having satisfied your professional responsibilities in educating, informing, and advising the client.

Consider forms carefully, and engage the help of lawyers or other professionals who are familiar with the mental health statutes of your state.

It may be necessary to develop more than one information and consent form to satisfy different areas of your practice. A therapist who solicits forensic work may wish to tailor a form for criminal, custody, and other

Sample Form

CLIENT INFORMATION AND CONSENT

Therapist

The undersigned therapist is a licensed professional and chemical dependency counselor and a licensed marriage and family therapist engaged in private practice providing mental health care services to clients directly and as an independent contractor/provider for various managed care entities. In addition, as shareholder and employee, the undersigned therapist provides all mental health services through Life Experiences, Inc. d/b/a New Life Counseling Center.

Mental Health Services

While it may not be easy to seek help from a mental health professional, it is hoped that you will be better able to understand your situation and feelings and move toward resolving your difficulties. The therapist, using his [or her] knowledge of human development and behavior, will make observations about situations as well as suggestions for new ways to approach them. It will be important for you to explore your own feelings and thoughts and to try new approaches in order for change to occur. You may bring other family members to a therapy session if you feel it would be helpful or if this is recommended by your therapist.

Appointments

Appointments are made by calling (972) 432-2636 Monday through Friday between the hours of 9:00 A.M. and 5:00 P.M. Please call to cancel or reschedule at least 24 hours in advance, or you will be charged for the missed appointment. Third-party payments will not usually cover or reimburse for missed appointments.

Number of Visits

The number of sessions needed depends on many factors and will be discussed by the therapist.

Length of Visits

Therapy sessions are 45 minutes in length but may take longer for psychological testing.

Relationship

Your relationship with the therapist is a professional and therapeutic relationship. In order to preserve this relationship, it is imperative that the therapist not have any other type of relationship with you. Personal and/or business relationships undermine the effectiveness of

Sample Form
(continued)

the therapeutic relationship. The therapist cares about helping you but is not in a position to be your friend or to have a social or personal relationship with you.

Gifts, bartering and trading services are not appropriate and should not be shared between you and the therapist.

Cancellations

Cancellations must be received at least 24 hours before your scheduled appointment; otherwise YOU will be charged the customary fee for that missed appointment. You are responsible for calling to cancel or reschedule your appointment.

Payment for Services

The charge for your initial session is _____ and the charge for any subsequent sessions is _____ . The undersigned therapist does not normally accept assignment of insurance benefits but may be required to do so in connection with certain managed care contracts. **The undersigned therapist will look to you for full payment of your account, and you will be responsible for payment of all charges.** Different co-payments are required by various group coverage plans. Your co-payment is based on the Mental Health Policy selected by your employer or purchased by you. In addition, the co-pay may be different for the first visit than for subsequent visits. You are responsible for and shall pay your co-pay portion of the undersigned therapist's charges for services at the time the services are provided. It is recommended that you determine your co-payment before your first visit by calling your benefits office or insurance company.

Although it is the goal of the undersigned therapist to protect the confidentiality of your records, there may be times when disclosure of your records or testimony will be compelled by law. Confidentiality and exceptions to confidentiality are discussed below. In the event disclosure of your records or testimony is required by law, you will be responsible for and shall pay the costs involved in producing the records and the therapist's normal hourly rate for the time involved in preparing for and giving testimony. Such payments are to be made at the time or prior to the time the services are rendered by the therapist.

Confidentiality

Discussions between a therapist and a client are confidential. No information will be released without the client's written consent unless mandated by law. Possible exceptions to confidentiality include but are not limited to the following situations: child abuse; abuse of the elderly or disabled; abuse of patients in mental health facilities; sexual exploitation;

(continued)

Sample Form
(continued)

AIDS/HIV infection and possible transmission; criminal prosecutions; child custody cases; suits in which the mental health of a party is in issue; situations where the therapist has a duty to disclose, or where, in the therapist's judgment, it is necessary to warn or disclose; fee disputes between the therapist and the client; a negligence suit brought by the client against the therapist; or the filing of a complaint with the licensing board. If you have any questions regarding confidentiality, you should bring them to the attention of the therapist when you and the therapist discuss this matter further. By signing this information and consent form, you are giving your consent to the undersigned therapist to share confidential information with all persons mandated by law and with the agency that referred you and the managed care company and/or insurance carrier responsible for providing your mental health care services and payment for those services, and you are also releasing and holding harmless the undersigned therapist from any departure from your right of confidentiality that may result.

Duty to Warn

In the event that the undersigned therapist reasonably believes that I am a danger, physically or emotionally, to myself or another person, I specifically consent for the therapist to warn the person in danger and to contact the following persons, in addition to medical and law enforcement personnel:

NAME   **TELEPHONE NUMBER**

_____

_____

_____

I consent for the undersigned therapist to communicate with me by mail and by phone at the following addresses and phone numbers, and I will IMMEDIATELY advise the therapist in the event of any change:

ADDRESS   **TELEPHONE NUMBER**

_____

_____

_____

Risks of Therapy

Therapy is the Greek word for change. You may learn things about yourself that you don't like. Often, growth cannot occur until you experience and confront issues that induce you

Sample Form
(continued)

to feel sadness, sorrow, anxiety, or pain. The success of our work together depends on the quality of the efforts on both our parts, and the realization that you are responsible for lifestyle choices/changes that may result from therapy. Specifically, one risk of marital therapy is the possibility of exercising the divorce option.

After-Hours Emergencies

A mental health professional or your therapist is on call when your therapist's office is closed, and can be reached for emergencies on a twenty-four-hour, seven-days-per-week basis, by calling (214) 845-8761. Emergencies are urgent issues requiring immediate action.

Therapist's Incapacity or Death

I acknowledge that, in the event the undersigned therapist becomes incapacitated or dies, it will become necessary for another therapist to take possession of my file and records. By signing this information and consent form, I give my consent to allowing another licensed mental health professional selected by the undersigned therapist to take possession of my file and records and provide me with copies upon request, or to deliver them to a therapist of my choice.

Consent to Treatment

I, voluntarily, agree to receive Mental Health assessment, care, treatment, or services, and authorize the undersigned therapist to provide such care, treatment, or services as are considered necessary and advisable.

I understand and agree that I will participate in the planning of my care, treatment, or services, and that I may stop such care, treatment, or services that I receive through the undersigned therapist at any time.

By signing this Client Information and Consent form, I, the undersigned client, acknowledge that I have both read and understood all the terms and information contained herein. Ample opportunity has been offered to me to ask questions and seek clarification of anything unclear to me.

_____   _____
Client/Parent   Date
_____
Social Security Number and Address

as witnessed by:

_____   _____
Anthony Kindheart, MA, LPC,   Date
LCDC & LMFT, Therapist

Sample Form

PARENTAL WAIVER OF RIGHT TO CHILD'S RECORDS

I hereby waive my right as parent/guardian to obtain information from and copies of any records from <u>Anthony Kindheart</u> and <u>New Life Counseling Center</u> pertaining to the evaluation and treatment of the following child: _____ , age _____ . I understand that <u>Anthony Kindheart</u> and <u>New Life Counseling Center</u> may refuse to provide me, or any third party acting upon my request or authorization, with information and records pertaining to this child's mental health evaluation and treatment, if disclosure in the opinion of the child's therapist would negatively impact the child or the child's evaluation and treatment. I hereby release <u>Anthony Kindheart</u> and <u>New Life Counseling Center</u> from any and all liability for good-faith refusal to disclose the child's information or records.

_____   _____
Parent/Guardian   Date

_____   _____
Parent/Guardian   Date

as witnessed by:

_____   _____
Anthony Kindheart, MA, LPC,   Date
LCDC & LMFT, Therapist

specific types of cases. Clients in these cases must understand that the therapist may come to a conclusion, or be forced to give an opinion, that is adverse to the client or the client's position in a lawsuit. Do not use forms blindly; consider them carefully, and engage the help of lawyers and other professionals to make sure they suit your practice and give you maximum protection.

The Bottom Line

- Documentation is a therapist's best defense against a complaint lodged by a client.

- The most important document in a client's file is a detailed information and consent form that has been carefully drafted and then reviewed by a lawyer.

- Without a signed, comprehensive information and consent form, it is the therapist's word against the client's in the event a fact dispute occurs, or a complaint is filed against the therapist, or any other dispute arises.

- Generally, in disputes before a licensing board or in malpractice litigation, differences in testimony are resolved against the professional. Therefore, written instruments give the professional valuable support.

- As the reviewer of your consent form, select a lawyer who is familiar with state statutes concerning mental health, state licensing laws, and the cases that interpret them. Mental health law may not be a recognized specialty, but familiarity with professional information is necessary to draft a coordinated contract that protects the professional.

- A contract is usually construed against the entity that has drafted it and presented it to the other party for signature. In our consumer-oriented society, a precise document is critical.

- The checklist is not complete. Each therapist must complete it with specifics that apply to his or her individual practice.

Legal Lightbulb

- A written contract is an enforceable legal agreement.

- Because we live in a consumer-oriented society, the intake form will be construed against the professional if there is a dispute.

- There is nothing wrong with practicing defensive mental health therapy.

- Clients will generally sign any forms presented to them during an intake session.

- Before creating the information and consent form, contemplate areas of vulnerability, and, if possible, contractually guard against them.

- Sex, boundary violations, dual relationships, and conscious breaches of confidentiality are the subjects of numerous claims. Therapists must protect against them—in writing (and in personal conduct).

- In the event a client or therapist dies, post-death provisions should be included in the contract.

- Obligations to the client and the client's file survive the death of both the client and the therapist.

- Children's rights should be protected in the information and consent form. Some states have different rules if the child is sixteen or seventeen years of age, is married, is living apart from his/her parents, or is emancipated (the "disabilities" of minority have been removed).

7

Maintaining Records

After practicing privately for fifteen years in the same office, Richard, a therapist, was forced to relocate to a new office when the building owner decided to sell the entire building to a developer. Richard began searching for new office space and, because of financial restrictions, was forced to rent a smaller office. As moving day approached and the packing began, Richard decided to discard the retained client records from the first eight years he was in practice. He had limited space in his new office and wanted to discard old files. State law required therapists to maintain client records for seven years. So Richard discarded files that were older than seven years, and files for which the last contact had occurred at least eight years before.

Two months after he was happily situated in his new office space, he was visited by an investigator from the district attorney's office. A former client had mentioned to her current counselor that she once had a sexual relationship with Richard while in therapy. The current counselor was legally bound to report the sexual exploitation to the district attorney and to Richard's licensing board.

Richard was charged with a criminal offense (sex with a client is a criminal offense in a number of states), and faced a licensing board hearing for revocation of his license. The accuser did not realize that a sexual relationship was inappropriate until a few months before, when she was so advised by her present counselor. The statute of limitations for prosecuting sexual offenses in Richard's state is ten years. Richard could not even recall whether his accuser had entered his office. There was no written documentation of any therapy, and no recollection. The alleged victim claimed she had paid in cash because she was married at the time and did not want her husband to know she was seeing a therapist.

Without a file, Richard's defense became even more difficult.

How Long Should Client Records Be Maintained?

Records should be maintained for a minimum of ten years, or ten years after majority if the client is a minor.

Statutes of limitations govern the time period when a client can bring a complaint to a licensing board, or initiate a malpractice lawsuit.

The discovery rule provides that the statute of limitations does not begin until the person knows or should have known there were grounds for a claim of negligence or misconduct.

The legal requirements set out by statutes, regulations, and licensing boards vary from state to state and within each mental health discipline and licensing body. These legal requirements are published and available to every practitioner. The average maintenance period appears to be seven years; the shortest term is five years, and the longest is ten years. In light of Richard's problem, common sense would dictate a minimum maintenance period of ten years, or ten years after majority if the client is a minor.

The most conservative and safest advice for mental health professionals is: Never destroy client records; maintain them even after death, at least until the deceased therapist's estate is fully probated. One can never know when a claim based on charges of professional negligence or misconduct will rear its ugly head. If the means are available to maintain and store client files permanently, keep them; if not, be sure to maintain them for at least ten years.

In all jurisdictions, statutes of limitations define the time allowed for a client to bring a complaint to a licensing board or initiate a malpractice lawsuit for alleged negligent acts of omission or commission by a therapist. The limitation periods vary from state to state, board to board, and discipline to discipline. Limitation periods may be longer than the minimum record-keeping period, as seen in Richard's situation. Often, a *discovery rule* comes into play and further confounds the problem with respect to record keeping. The discovery rule provides that the statute of limitations does not begin to run until a reasonable person knows or should have known that he or she had a claim for professional negligence or misconduct against a therapist. If a client represses a memory and does not recover the memory until ten years later, an argument based on a discovery rule could be raised to defeat a statute of limitations defense. The suit might be allowed even though it was not brought within the ten-year limitation period.

As a result of these overlapping statutes and principles of law, it is abundantly clear that the only truly safe position a therapist can take is to preserve records for as long a period as possible. **A therapist's first, and often best, line of defense against allegations of misconduct is a**

well-documented client file. Without documentation, even the most re-sourceful attorney will have a difficult time mounting a spirited and competent defense. In our consumer-oriented society, when conflicting evidence is admitted in court or before a licensing board, the word of the consumer is often given greater weight than that of the professional.

A therapist's first and best line of defense against allegations of misconduct is a well-documented client file.

In the event that the client is a minor at the time the mental health service is provided, all states require records to be maintained for a period of time after the minor reaches the age of majority. (In some states, majority is achieved by marrying or having the disabilities of minority removed before the normal age of majority is reached—a procedure sometimes called "emancipation.") The general rule is that after a child reaches the age of majority, his or her records must be preserved for the same number of years that a therapist is required to maintain adult records. For example, if the state requirement is seven years, then a child's records must be maintained until the child reaches twenty-five years of age (18 + 7).

A therapist should know what his or her jurisdiction requires, but whatever the minimum legal requirement, it is suggested that records be kept for as long as possible, and certainly well beyond the minimum required time period. If space constraints become a factor, save at least basic information: intake forms, dates of treatment, diagnoses, termination forms, and perhaps, case summaries.

How Should Clients' Records Be Discarded?

When the decision is made to eliminate files in whole or in part, destruction of records must be accomplished in a manner that protects confidentiality. Have the records shredded or burned or, for preservation of the environment, opt for shredding and recycling. Be sure there is no possibility for any third party to determine client information from the discarded and destroyed files. In one situation, a semiretired therapist, practicing part-time in a small community, emptied old files, "as is," into an outdoor dumpster. Later, local children playing in the dumpster found some very interesting reading material about people they knew, and soon the information was spread all over town. Former clients who had consulted with the therapist some twenty years earlier were very unhappy, and that was only the beginning of the story.

When discarding a file, make sure the method of eliminating the record preserves client confidentiality.

Take the time and expense to shred or burn all files selected for destruction. Oversee the process yourself, to guarantee that the job is completely private and that prying eyes are not reviewing the contents before the files are consigned to oblivion.

Securing Files against Third Parties

Files should be secured at all times to prevent access or review by third parties. Only the therapist and office personnel who have a legitimate need to access information should be allowed contact with a client's file. Any access by office personnel should be limited to only the information needed. A staff person performing a billing function would not normally need to review the therapist's session notes in order to properly and accurately bill for services provided. Access should be permitted only under the supervision of the therapist. It is the therapist's legal duty and responsibility to safeguard the confidentiality of clients' records, and the therapist will be held accountable for breaches by office personnel or third parties.

The therapist will be held accountable for breaches by office personnel or third parties.

Regardless of the recording medium used—printed paper, computer disks or tapes, microfilm, or video or audio tapes—records should be kept under lock and key. Individual cabinets and the rooms in which they are stored should be secured. A therapist will not be held liable if a burglar breaks into a locked room and pries open a locked cabinet to gain access to clients' files. But a therapist will be held liable if the files are not secured, and a husband waiting for his wife to emerge from her therapy session slides down the hall, opens an unsecured door and a file cabinet drawer, and reads notes in his wife's file about an undisclosed affair. The same liability would apply if the husband is a computer hacker and easily cracks the therapist's security code.

A therapist is held liable if files are not secured by a lock, security code, or computer password.

It is important for every therapist to establish office procedures and policies regarding maintenance and security of, and access to client files. These procedures and policies should be clearly presented in an office manual and signed by each person working in the office or practice. Even a therapist practicing alone, without any support staff, should ponder these matters from time to time, to ensure that every possible means of protecting and securing clients' records has been employed.

If there is ever a question about a particular person's access to a client's file, the therapist should seek written consent from the client.

Clients' Right to Access Files

Do clients have the absolute right to access their own records? Generally, the answer is Yes, but many jurisdictions have statutes that allow a mental health professional to withhold records or information from a client if the therapist, in the exercise of professional judgment, reasonably believes the disclosure would be harmful to the client. If a therapist practices in a jurisdiction where there is no statutory authority to withhold information or records from a client, and the therapist believes they should be withheld, he or she should petition an appropriate court for a protective order to keep the records from the client. The petition will be reviewed, a hearing will be set, and a ruling will be made by the court.

Many jurisdictions have statutes that allow mental health professionals to withhold records and information from a client.

Although keeping multiple files is tedious, notes on *each person* in a family—perhaps a husband, wife, and child—or in any group treated with a family systems approach should be filed separately. Commingled or integrated files are a nightmare to separate, and each family member has the right to view only his or her personal file, not that of a spouse, a sibling, a parent, or any other adult family member. Erasing is impossible, and "whiting out" or "blacking out" (with a felt pen) is evidence of tampering. Each client should have a personal file, which the therapist can produce without breaching the confidentiality of any other family member.

Each individual should have a separate file, even if both spouses, or the entire family, are involved in the treatment process.

Parents of a child generally have the right to access their child's mental health records, but a few jurisdictions allow the therapist, pursuant to statute, to withhold records from a parent. In the absence of statutory authority, a therapist who is concerned about a parent's access to a child's records should seek a protective order from a court of competent jurisdiction to keep records from the parent. As discussed earlier, it would be good practice for the therapist to ask the parent to waive his or her right to access the records prior to beginning therapy with the child.

In a perfect world, only the client and therapist would ever have access to a client's records. But the world is far from perfect, and many eyes are legally entitled to gain access to a client's mental health information. It's the therapist's duty to limit, as much as possible, the number of contacts third parties have with a client's file. Although the confidentiality of mental health information is set down as a rule of law in many jurisdictions, the exceptions to the rule emasculate the perceived right to privacy. In most cases, the therapist has scant legal grounds for keeping a file absolutely private from everyone.

Legal Lightbulb

- Maintain files for *at least* the minimum time period required in your jurisdiction. (States do not coordinate with each other, nor do various national and state professional organizations.)

- Best practice is to *never discard* client files because it is impossible to know when a claim or complaint will be made by a former client.

- Remember that claims can be brought after a therapist is no longer required to maintain records, or after a therapist retires, leaves the jurisdiction, changes agencies, or loses control of a file.

- If you must eliminate old client files, consider maintaining a partial file with basic information such as intake forms, dates of treatment, diagnosis, and termination forms. At least have some documentation of who your clients were and why they were there.

- If files are to be discarded, completely destroy them by shredding or burning them. Be present until the destruction is complete.

- It is difficult to defend against a complaint or malpractice suit in the absence of a well-documented and complete client file.

- Secure all file cabinets, as well as the room in which they are stored.

- Establish written policies and procedures regarding the maintenance and security of client files, and the limitations on access to them. Review the policies with each permanent or temporary staff person.

- Limit the number of people who have access to your office. Limit access to the information needed; do not open an entire file.

- If in doubt about a person's right to access information, obtain written consent from the client.

- If a client or parent wants access to a file and you wish to prohibit access but the law does not allow you to withhold the record, seek a protective order from an appropriate court.

- Remember, the therapist has the ultimate responsibility for his or her client files and should not rely on others (i.e., support staff) to maintain records.

8

Treatment Plans

Jane attended regular therapy sessions with Dr. Gold for four years. Her problem was depression. She was in an unhappy marriage and was unsure of her legal, therapeutic, and ethical options. Finally, Jane, with the input of Dr. Gold and her attorney, decided to divorce her husband and seek custody of her two minor children. At the trial, Dr. Gold testified as an expert for Jane, but the court ruled in favor of her husband. Despite the expert testimony and evidence in her favor, Jane was given only standard rights of visitation and had to pay child support. She was angry, devastated, and humiliated. Jane felt that if Dr. Gold's testimony had been more enthusiastic and spirited, she would have won the custody battle. As time passed, and as she talked to her friends, she became gradually more furious. What did Dr. Gold write in the clinical file that offered such (in her opinion) lukewarm testimony? Jane called Dr. Gold and asked for a complete copy of her clinical records—everything, from intake form to final assessment.

Does Jane have a right to see Dr. Gold's complete record?

In years past, the client file belonged to the therapist. Clients had a right to review a summary of the therapy but did not have a right to peruse the file itself. This protection has changed with the times.

The client file now belongs to the client. Copying expense is billable, but the client has the right to receive a *copy* of his or her file upon reasonable notice. The file includes the treatment plan, assessment, diagnosis, prognosis, and any notes entered in the file.

Clients' Rights Regarding the Treatment Plan

Clients **cannot** enter the therapist's office unannounced and expect to have their file copied immediately while they sit in the waiting room, nor

The client has a right to review a copy of his or her file, including the treatment plan, assessment, diagnosis, prognosis, and any other notes made during treatment.

can they suggest that the therapist should hand over the original file for review.

The client **can** call or write to request to see the file or to receive a copy of the file. The therapist must then make a copy (a reasonable fee can be charged for copying services) and allow the client to pick up the copy when ready. Or, the copy can be mailed or faxed according to the client's written instructions and authorization. The information in the client file, in theory, belongs to the client, and the client has a right to a copy.

On occasion, a file may contain information that the therapist, upon reflection, feels would be detrimental to the client—material that, if known to the client, might be injurious psychologically. For example, during therapy, a client constantly talked negatively about her mother. However, after therapy concluded, the client was reconciled with her mother, and then forgot the phrases that were dutifully recorded in her file. If the client's file were to be disclosed, old wounds would resurface and create new hostility. In another case, a therapist was granted permission to investigate her client's background by meeting with a school counselor, a former teacher, a relative, and a good friend. This information, although hearsay in legal terms, remained in the client file. If revealed, the investigative inquiries would be disturbing to the client.

The intake and consent form should state that if the file is requested, the therapist may, if clinically necessary in the therapist's opinion, withhold information in the file that is or might be, in the therapist's opinion, injurious to the client. Clients can also waive, in advance, the right to full disclosure of tests, notes, or an investigative summary. The waiver must be in writing.

In another scenario, a client had taken a psychological test. The test results might be available, but the test itself was not, for contractual reasons. Again, the importance of an intake form must be stressed. The intake form should contain a paragraph stating that, in the course of therapy, certain tests might be administered. These tests and their contents cannot be revealed to the client, and the client must agree in advance that no request for them will be made. Many are proprietary; they belong to the creator of the test, not the therapist.

The therapist who uses proprietary tests or copyrighted material has an obligation to protect the disclosure of the material.

Some therapists' ethical canons provide for maintaining test security. These canons state that therapists must make reasonable efforts to maintain the integrity and security of tests and other assessment techniques in a manner that is consistent with legal and contractual obligations and

Sample Form

CLIENT WAIVER OF FULL DISCLOSURE CLAUSE

" . . . I have been advised I have a right to copies of my entire file but acknowledge that some information may not be in my best interest to review. In the event my therapist, in the exercise of his/her professional judgment, determines that information in my file may be injurious to me, I waive my right to obtain such potentially injurious information and release my therapist from any and all claims, damages and causes of action that I suffer or could assert for his/her refusal to provide me with the information requested . . . . The therapist's discretion shall control."

permits compliance with the requirements of ethics codes. A therapist who uses proprietary tests or copyrighted material has an obligation to protect the disclosure of the material. If the client insists on disclosure, the therapist must seek legal protection. This is a double bind—there is an obligation to release client information to the client, and an obligation to protect a psychological test from disclosure, in accordance with the contractual relationship between the test owner and the therapist.

Therapists' Response to Demand to See Files

- Discuss the matter with the client. Ask whether the client will accept an oral summary of the file in a modified therapy session.

- If an oral summary is not acceptable, suggest that you furnish a written summary, rather than a complete file.

Legal Lightbulb

- In general, the client is entitled to a copy of his or her file upon payment of a reasonable copying cost ($0.25 to $1.00 per page).

- Certain test materials must be protected, and the client has no right to them.

- The intake and consent form should contain a paragraph that protects proprietary or contractually protected rights and information.

- When some clients demand their file, they are acting on an impulse. A free session might dissuade such a client from proceeding further.

- It is better to review the file with the client rather than just hand it over.

- Clients who are angry because they have lost contested litigation, at great expense to themselves, often seek some third party to blame, and an obvious and vulnerable person is the therapist. *Handle every demand for records as a potential lawsuit or complaint to the board. Proceed gingerly.*

- Do not withhold a file because of nonpayment of your bill.

- Remember the beginning point. Information in client files belongs to the client. The therapist is only the custodian of the original record.

- If the complete file is still demanded, and the file is thorough, appropriate, and ready for disclosure, make a complete copy and deliver it to the client in the manner requested by the client.

- Indicate to the client that certain tests, and perhaps other materials, are copyrighted, trademarked, or proprietary, and cannot be disclosed. Most clients will accept this as a correct statement. Alternatively, the therapist can expect an angry letter from the client or the client's lawyer (with a release-of-information form attached), demanding the complete file. The therapist would then be wise to seek a court order to protect the file. A judge, presented with the obligation to maintain test security, will usually issue a protective order guarding the right of the client to see the file while, at the same time, safeguarding the interests of the therapist. The judge will determine which part of the file is to be delivered to the client and which part is to remain in the therapist's sole control.

If a complete file is demanded, the therapist should seek a protective order to protect the file.

SECTION TWO

CONFIDENTIALITY

9

Couples, Family, and Group Therapy

Dr. Lowenstein, a licensed psychologist, conducted group sessions that included couples, single individuals, and teenagers. Before accepting each person into the group, he stressed the importance of confidentiality. What was said in the group session was not to leave the room. Each person had to affirm that he or she understood the principle of confidentiality. For added emphasis, Dr. Lowenstein insisted that each person sign a "guarantee of silence" form— an agreement that he or she would not, under any circumstances, share with any person outside the group, what was revealed in the group. In addition, at the beginning and end of each session, Dr. Lowenstein stressed confidentiality and trust. Participants, he explained, would be removed from the program if there was any possibility that the information was repeated.

Four weeks into a sixteen-week workshop series, a group member, Jill, discovered that another member, Maria, was a personal friend of Jill's employer. Jill had talked freely for three weeks about her employer (the cause of all her stress), and felt that if her boss found out what she had been saying, she would be in trouble or be fired. She became very intimidated and hesitant about sharing stress-causing incidents.

Can Jill be guaranteed absolute confidentiality? Or, if she became involved in a major discrimination suit or personal litigation, could all the group participants be subpoenaed? Could Dr. Lowenstein be compelled to reveal the names of the group members?

How can a mental health professional who conducts group sessions protect the members of the group from a harmful breach of confidentiality? Are there differences when the group is small (a couple), slightly larger (a family in family systems therapy), or very large (an assembly of strangers who gather because they have a common problem)?

Managed care has created pressure to cut costs while increasing services, and this phenomenon has led to handling an increased patient load via group sessions and group therapy. Is there anything the therapist can do

Group members are not under a professional ethical obligation to refrain from gossip.

to *guarantee* absolute privacy? Probably not, because, unlike the mental health professional, the group members are laypersons, and they are not obligated by professional ethics to refrain from gossip. However, if they sign a form in which they acknowledge the principle of confidentiality and agree to abide by it, they are then contractually responsible. NOTE: There are few, if any, cases against group members for breach of confidentiality.

To date, there is no litigation in which group members have been sued and substantial recoveries awarded because information received in the group was repeated to outsiders. The principal reason to create contractual responsibility is to create a deterrent, not establish punishment. Group members will undoubtedly limit what they repeat if they realize they are responsible financially, as well as morally, for what they say.

The best the therapist can do is make sure each prospective client in a group setting is aware of the confidentiality issue, as well as the limitations. The client must understand the risks involved in sharing facts and intimacies with strangers who might repeat what is heard, either inadvertently or as juicy gossip.

These limitations should be spelled out in the intake and consent form that is signed prior to the initial group session, and then signed by each individual who later enters the group. The original should be maintained by the therapist, and copies should be given to the clients.

Having signed an intake form of confidentiality, the client is contractually responsible for confidentiality.

When his or her signed statement acknowledging the limitations of confidentiality is in the therapist's file, a client, at a later date, would be hard pressed to claim ignorance concerning the need for confidentiality. Some states, in their ethical canons, require that clients be informed concerning the limits of confidentiality. It is always best to have this receipt of information in writing (i.e., that clients have been fully informed, in writing, that there are limits to confidentiality; that they have been told what those limits are; and that they accept the risk of those clear and specified limits).

Protective Measures for Confidentiality

Although confidentiality cannot be guaranteed, there are some methods to protect the therapist in the event a group member does not take the confidentiality concept seriously enough, including:

- In group sessions, have each individual sign a confidentiality statement.

- Insert a *hold harmless* clause indicating that, should a participant breach confidentiality, and should the facilitator be held responsible or sued, the participant will pay all damages incurred. This will serve as a deterrent to participants who feel that, as nonprofessionals, they are not liable for their own gossip. A legally drafted contract creates legally enforceable liability. Every adult knows this, or should know it (it might also deter an investigative reporter who joins in a group for information rather than therapy).

- The sign-in sheet must contain, in bold print, a confidentiality reminder.

- The policy of group therapy, enforced without exception, is that any-one who violates confidentiality will be dismissed from the group, for-feiting all payments made (and be liable for any damages they caused).

- Anyone in the group who hears of group gossip is obligated to report the infraction to the group leader, whether a therapist, a layperson, or a facilitator.

- Although there may be some "public policy" opinions against such language, the intake form should contain a clause that exonerates the therapist in the event a group member gossips inappropriately. Each person must sign an intake form prior to entering the group.

- Some obvious exceptions to confidentiality are: child abuse, elder abuse, a subpoena to testify under penalty of contempt of court, a par-ent–child relationship, litigation in which the mental health of the patient client is an issue, and some criminal prosecutions. The statu-tory exceptions to confidentiality vary from state to state and are sit-uational. Professional legal advice should be sought before assuming that any of the above circumstances justifies making therapeutic in-formation public.

- Many therapists have brochures that contain abbreviated vitae as well as descriptions of the treatment offered. If the brochure has a state-ment that describes the limits of confidentiality in group sessions, each participant can sign on the intake form that a copy of the brochure was received, read, and understood.

The sign-in sheet must contain, in bold print, a confidentiality reminder.

The exceptions to confidentiality by statute vary from state to state and are situational.

As group therapy, couples therapy, and family systems therapy become more common, an ever expanding number of individuals become privy to the innermost thoughts of their fellow clients. The therapist can make an effort to protect the shared information, but cannot guarantee absolute privacy. However, the therapist must take steps to protect group members as much as possible.

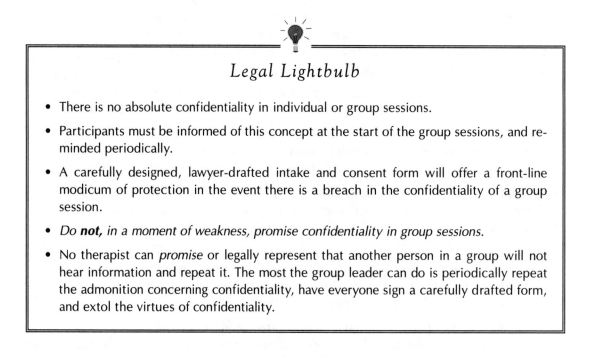

Legal Lightbulb

- There is no absolute confidentiality in individual or group sessions.
- Participants must be informed of this concept at the start of the group sessions, and reminded periodically.
- A carefully designed, lawyer-drafted intake and consent form will offer a front-line modicum of protection in the event there is a breach in the confidentiality of a group session.
- *Do **not**, in a moment of weakness, promise confidentiality in group sessions.*
- No therapist can *promise* or legally represent that another person in a group will not hear information and repeat it. The most the group leader can do is periodically repeat the admonition concerning confidentiality, have everyone sign a carefully drafted form, and extol the virtues of confidentiality.

Sample Form

GROUP CONFIDENTIALITY

As evidenced by my signature below, I agree to participate in group therapy with the undersigned therapist. I acknowledge that, with group therapy, there is risk of disclosure of confidential information by persons in the group to individuals outside of the group. I agree that I will not disclose information learned by me during the course of any group session and will protect each participant's right to confidentiality. I agree to hold the undersigned therapist harmless from any claims or liability resulting from my disclosure of confidential information to a third party outside of a group session. I further agree not to hold the undersigned therapist responsible, and release her/him from same, for/from any claims or liability that I could assert as a result of disclosure of my confidential information by coparticipants in my group therapy sessions.

I understand I may choose to discontinue group therapy at any time.

_____   _____
Client   Date

_____   _____
Therapist   Date

10

Insider Information

Susan was explaining her troubles to her therapist, Dr. Pick, during a regularly scheduled therapy session. She had just heard from a very reliable corporate source that her company, a large publicly traded corporation, was going broke. Only her accountant friend was privy to this secret information. Susan told Dr. Pick about it in a therapy session while discussing her work-related stress. Dr. Pick, unknown to Susan, had personal investments in Susan's company. Shortly thereafter, he sold all his stocks short, and garnered substantial profits when the stock plummeted.

~

Jack, a client, was explaining his troubles to Dr. O'Reilly. In the course of conversation, he mentioned that he had made a unique technological discovery which, when made public, would guarantee a stock rise. After hearing this news, Dr. O'Reilly bought a substantial stock position. When the discovery became public, the stock rose dramatically and Dr. O'Reilly's investment more than tripled.

A few weeks later, a representative of the Securities and Exchange Commission arrived with a subpoena for Dr. O'Reilly.

Are these instances of securities fraud? Prohibited insider trading? The wrongful use of confidential information?

These therapists didn't seek the data. The developments were revealed to them in a therapy session, and neither therapist told anyone the source of the information. In their orientation, not only is client information confidential, but so is the identity of the confidant. Can all information shared in a therapy session be guarded? When challenged, can it remain confidential?

The Paper Trail

A therapist has to keep in mind that there is a trail of paperwork in every transaction. There are notes of each session, billing information, reimbursement submissions, long-distance phone logs, and, if a buy or sell order is issued, records of the transaction. Few activities of life go on without some written objective evidence. And often, as in real estate, an exchange is publicly recorded in the Deed and Records Office at the county courthouse, and available for any curious citizen to discover.

Clients will share business information freely in most therapeutic situations, and some of these data might be potentially lucrative to an astute therapist. One must keep in mind: *The purpose of therapy is to help the client.* The client assumes that information shared with the therapist is confidential and private. There is a real probability that clients never, in their wildest imagination, consider that the therapist might use the information for personal gain.

The purpose of therapy is to help the client, not the therapist.

Making a One-Time Killing

Every so often, a client confides news that is potentially lucrative, developments that can make big bucks for the therapist. The event might involve real estate (a rezoning); the stock market (a new discovery); litigation (who is being sued, and the potential outcome); a rare painting coming to the market from a seller who is not knowledgeable about art or aware of the value of this particular work; or supposedly "worthless" land, bonds, stock, stamps, or currency that is actually valuable. Regardless of the particular circumstances, the therapist has insider knowledge not available in the public arena, and can be tempted to use this information to make money on the transaction.

Don't!

"*A California therapist pleaded guilty to insider trading* after using information obtained during a counseling session to make a *stock market killing.* . . . Final sentencing is scheduled for March, 1996. The case against his fellow investor is still pending." [Source: *Psychotherapy Finances*, 21:12 (December 1995).] Although this case has not been specifically followed to conclusion, the fact that it was reported is sufficient to raise a concern. The danger is obvious.

An income calculator would be helpful in computing the value of a professional license.

Don't take advantage of any information garnered in a therapy session. In the case cited above, the therapist made $177,235. You might make more, or less, but how much is your license worth? Possibly, over a lifetime, more than the sum above. An income calculator would be helpful in computing the value of a professional license.

Do not lead yourself into temptation.

The use of insider information is a clear breach of confidentiality.

Resist the temptation to make a business killing by using information gained in a therapy session. Information garnered confidentially will often have implications in areas other than therapy. The use of this information is prohibited and is a clear breach of confidentiality.

Even if a client suggests that the therapist should act on insider information or trade secrets for personal gain, the use of this information may be illegal or, possibly, unethical, and creates a dual relationship. After the therapist has netted large sums of money, the client may ask for a share of the profits, or else. . . . Legal and ethical nightmares can result.

Although there may be no obligation to report crimes a client may have committed, a therapist who offers advice concerning a crime can become an accomplice.

Although there may be no obligation to report most crimes a client may have committed (call a lawyer for particulars), a therapist who offers advice concerning a crime (stealing trade secrets, for example) can become an accomplice.

Insider information might include:

- When to buy or sell a stock.

- A zoning change that will affect the value of a property that is for sale.

- A commodity that will become scarce because of events not yet known to the public.

Ethical Requirements

General ethical requirements are contained in the codes of ethics of many jurisdictions. Although the wording may differ from state to state, or from one mental health discipline to another, the principles might be stated as follows:

- The therapist shall not engage in activities that seek to meet the professional's personal needs at the expense of a client.

- The therapist shall not promote the professional's personal or business activities to clients unless the professional informs the clients of his or her personal or business interest in the activity.

- The therapist shall not provide counseling to business associates.

- The therapist shall not have or engage in a dual relationship with a client.

- Boundary violations are to be avoided at all costs. Sometimes they are conceptually cloudy. When in doubt, DON'T.

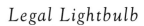

Legal Lightbulb

- Clients may indicate information that could be financially beneficial to the therapist. If used by the therapist, it is used at his or her peril.

- Remember this basic rule: The purpose of therapy is to help the client, not the therapist.

- The paper trail in therapy—as well as billing and third-party reporting procedures—makes information difficult to conceal, if challenged. Surrounding circumstances often indicate the sequence of clandestine personal and business transactions.

- In most major litigation, depositions may be taken of the parties or the witnesses. Each person is sworn, and the opposing attorney asks questions that must be answered under oath. A court reporter takes down the answers and later transcribes them. Depositions may also be recorded by audio or audiovisual equipment. When under oath, a lie (a false statement made under oath) is perjury and is a serious offense. Thus, once an event occurs, it is hard to conceal if it becomes involved in the civil or criminal justice system. Therapists cannot assume anonymity or ignorance, nor can they claim to have a faulty memory, the "oops" theory.

- Therapists are vulnerable. An appearance of impropriety in a transaction can be unethical, illegal, or, at the very least, embarrassing, especially if it becomes a media event.

- Not all publicity is career-enhancing.

- Be alert. Avoid the bad stuff. Usually, it will give you a gut feeling that cannot be ignored.

The purpose of conservative practice is not only to avoid a trial, but also to avoid even the appearance of an unethical or illegal act.

- The therapist shall not use relationships with clients to promote, for personal gain or profit, commercial enterprises or transactions of any kind.

The purpose of conservative practice is not only to avoid a trial, but also to avoid even the appearance of an unethical or illegal act.

11

Third-Party Payers

Dr. Anthony Kindheart, a licensed psychologist in private practice, agreed to accept assignment from his client's insurance benefits for payment of services. Dr. Kindheart's secretary completed the insurance claim form with assignment provisions furnished by the client, and forwarded it to the claims office of the insurance company. In response, the claims office requested backup data, including the psychological testing and session notes. The information in the psychological testing and session notes would be embarrassing to the client, and, if disclosed to his employer, could jeopardize his position with his company. In addition, his file contained proprietary tests that require permission for release. (Some testing tools cannot be shared because they belong to the test owner and/or may be copyrighted.)

Can Dr. Kindheart provide the claims examiner with the requested documents? What information can the claims office legitimately request in order to review the claim?

An insurance policy is a contract between an insurer and the insured, and may include specific provisions regarding information that must be supplied by the insured in support of a claim. By law, federal and state agencies regulate insurance company contracts with clients and often provide guidelines and regulations regarding claims information and the processing of claims. An insurance company will have the right to all information reasonably necessary to determine the validity of the claim and the extent of any benefits to which the claimant is entitled. Under most circumstances, this would not include therapy notes and psychological testing or raw data, but would include dates of treatment, test results, diagnosis, and prognosis. Problems result when the insurer challenges the claim and requests additional information beyond the submitted claim form.

Insurance companies are required to keep confidential the claims information received in support of a claim.

Insurance companies are required to keep confidential the information received in support of a claim. Federal and state laws prohibit disclosure of the information to the insured's employer, even if the employer provides the insurance as a benefit of employment. That does not mean information never "leaks" out; for example, representatives of the insurance company may play golf with a client's employer. Great concern must always be directed to records or information of a client that are shared with a third party, even an insurance company.

Requests for Additional Information

Client consent must be secured before information can be revealed to any third party, even an insurance company.

When additional information beyond the claim form is requested by an insurance company, the therapist is caught between the desire and need to be paid for services rendered, and the client's right to privacy and confidentiality. The therapist has a duty to protect the client's right to confidentiality, and even the disclosure of a client's name can constitute a breach of confidentiality. Client consent must be secured, in most cases, before information can be revealed to a third party. If the client asks that assignment of benefits be accepted in payment of services rendered, and the therapist agrees, one could safely argue that the client has consented to disclosure of the information requested on the insurer's claim form. Submitting the completed claim form would not be a breach of confidentiality.

But what happens when additional information, beyond the claim form, is requested? Has the client consented to submission of information beyond the claim form? A practitioner should secure the client's written consent before the release of any information or records requested in support of the submitted claim form. All clients should sign a consent form at the time the therapist accepts assignment of insurance benefits.

In some areas, public policy arguments have been raised by consumer protection advocates against "any and all" release forms. If any question exists in the therapist's mind about the release of a particularly sensitive document or piece of information, the client should be asked to sign a consent for release of that specific document or information. A good practice would be to attach a copy of the document or information itself as an exhibit to the signed release.

Caveats about Insurance Claims

What if there is *no* assignment of insurance benefits, but the therapist agrees to process an insurance claim form for a client as an accommodation?

Sample Form

CONSENT FOR RELEASE OF INFORMATION UPON INSURANCE ASSIGNMENT

I, the undersigned, on this date have requested that Anthony Kindheart, LPC, accept assignment of my insurance benefits for charges for mental health services rendered to me by Mr. Kindheart. Mr. Kindheart has agreed to accept assignment of my insurance benefits. I agree to sign any and all forms necessary for the submission of a claim for payment of benefits to Mr. Kindheart by my insurance company. I hereby consent and authorize Mr. Kindheart to provide my insurance company with any and all information requested by my insurance company in connection with its review and consideration of the claim for payment of benefits. I acknowledge and understand that I am waiving my right to confidentiality with respect to the records and information requested by my insurance company, and I hereby release Mr. Kindheart and his agents and employees from any and all liability arising from release of the information and records requested.

SIGNED this _____ day of _____ , 20___ .

_____
Client

WITNESSED BY:

_____
Address

_____
Anthony Kindheart, LPC

_____
City and State

_____
Telephone Number

_____
Social Security Number

_____
Date of Birth

Sample Form

CONSENT FOR RELEASE OF INFORMATION TO INSURANCE COMPANY

A request for records or information has been received by my therapist, Mr. Anthony Kindheart, LPC. I hereby consent and authorize Mr. Kindheart to provide XYZ Insurance Company with the document or information attached to this consent as Exhibit A, consisting of _____ pages.

I acknowledge and understand that I am waiving my right to confidentiality with respect to the records and information requested by my insurance company, and hereby release Mr. Kindheart and his staff from any and all liability arising from release of the information and records requested.

SIGNED this _____ day of _____, 20__ .

WITNESSED BY:

_____   _____
Anthony Kindheart, LPC   Client

                                 _____
                                 Address

                                 _____
                                 City and State

                                 _____
                                 Telephone Number

                                 _____
                                 Social Security Number

                                 _____
                                 Date of Birth

The same considerations come into play, and no information should be provided to the insurance company without the specific written consent of the client.

The easiest solution for the therapist is to avoid getting involved with billing insurance companies. Instead, take direct pay for services rendered, and provide the client with completed claim forms and information, which the client can choose to forward to an insurance company directly.

There are a few key points for the therapist to keep in mind when dealing with a request for information from an insurance company:

It is better for the therapist to take direct pay for services and not get involved with billing insurance companies.

- Disclosure of any information, including a client's name, can constitute a breach of confidentiality.

Legal Lightbulb

- Assume the confidentiality of every client and every client file.

- Be aware that clients assume absolute confidentiality as a beginning point.

- When there is to be a sharing of information, make sure the provider/therapist has the written consent of the client to give out any information.

- If the information requested may endanger or embarrass the client, discuss the request with the client and obtain written, informed consent to share the data. If, in the professional opinion of the therapist, the information should not be shared under any circumstances, discuss it with the client and, if needed, seek a protective order from a court.

- Keep the client informed. Remember, under certain circumstances, it is better to forgo payment for services than to allow confidential information to be disclosed.

- Insurance companies and third-party payers are staffed by ordinary humans, and there is no absolute guarantee that they will not share information that should remain private and confidential.

- The purpose of a lawyer-drafted or lawyer-reviewed Consent to Release Information form is to prevent a complaint of inappropriate release of information. Each jurisdiction has its own particularities.

- Secure the client's written consent to the release of any information to an insurance company.

- If possible, let the client deal directly with the insurance company; supply the client with completed claim forms and requested information to deliver to the insurance company.

Don't ever run the risk of forwarding a client's records or information without the client's written consent. If you choose to accept insurance assignment of benefits, be sure to have the client sign a consent for release of information at the very moment you make that agreement with the client. Getting the client to sign at a later date could prove to be difficult or even impossible, if the relationship with the client has deteriorated.

SECTION THREE

CONTRACTS

12

Capitation Agreements

A capitation agreement covers a specific population group and provides that a fixed fee per member will be paid to a provider for specified mental health services. The current trend in capitation agreements is toward lower fees. Competition among providers of behavioral health services continues to escalate, and purchasers are becoming more knowledgeable and sophisticated about available plans and services [Source: *Managed Care Strategies*, 3:2 (February 1995)]. This means that providers will be assuming a greater financial risk.

Under a capitation agreement, mental health care services are provided during a set period of time to a group of potential clients, and a flat fixed fee is charged for each client. If there are 1,000 clients in the population group and the contract rate is $3.50 per member per month, a provider must service the mental health needs of this group for one year for the sum of $42,000.

Because employers and insurance companies want to be able to predict with greater certainty their behavioral health care costs, capitation agreements are becoming increasingly attractive. With more provider groups competing for capitation contracts, the bid prices are dropping.

It is very unusual for a capitation contract to be considered by a single mental health provider or a small group of providers. However, as the trend continues, it may become increasingly common for employers to turn to smaller integrated groups that may be able to provide a higher quality of care at a cheaper rate.

Under a capitation agreement, mental health care services are provided during a set period of time to a group of potential clients, and a flat fixed fee is charged for each client.

How Will the Trend toward Capitation Affect the Average Practitioner?

As the capitation rates that employers are willing to pay to a managed care company fall, so will the rates paid to the individual providers who contract with the managed care company. Everyone in the chain of behavioral health care delivery services will be impacted.

An inadequate bid will result in financial losses when demand for services exceeds projected rates.

Capitation involves tremendous risk. An inadequate bid will result in financial losses when demand for services exceeds projected rates. These types of contracts require a tremendous amount of sophistication and should not be approached without counsel from skillful and experienced legal advisers and industry consultants.

Before any consideration can be given to entering into a capitation agreement, a provider group must have a thorough knowledge of its own operating costs. Capitation agreements involve calculated risk assessment. Assumptions and projections will have to be made, and they should be based on solid and verified information and statistics.

Population Data

After operating costs are determined, it is important to identify the size and the nature of the population to be covered by the contract. The number of persons is easy to obtain, but, beyond a simple count, there should be a thorough investigation of the nature of the population: its history of mental health needs, number and nature of past claims, and utilization rates. The mental health provider should be patient and persistent, in order to maximize its own investigation and the accuracy of the data from the fiduciary who is representing the population group. A capitated provider wants to avoid having to provide mental health services without compensation because utilization has exceeded projected rates.

Examine carefully the records indicating the mental health needs of the population over a period of time.

Examine carefully the records indicating the mental health needs of the population over a period of time. Do you or your group of practitioners have the expertise, training, or experience to provide the kinds of services this identified group has needed in the past? If not, additional providers must be placed under contract.

Provider's Concerns

A provider group considering a capitation contract should have a nucleus of mental health practitioners who excel in brief solution-focused therapy and have good case management skills.

Generally, a summary plan description is prepared and made available for study by anyone interested in bidding on a capitation contract. Its provisions will define covered services or conditions, exclusions, medical necessity, and descriptions of employee contributions (i.e., copayments, deductibles, and maximums). Plan descriptions vary widely. Providers must examine each one closely and compare its requirements with their own practice standards.

Any managed care contract, whether it is capitated or simply a provider agreement, does not supersede the individual therapist's ethical and legal responsibility to a client. If a plan excludes mental health services that are normally provided by you, and you determine that a client needs those services, you could be forced to provide them for free. The contract should include a definition of medical necessity that every party understands and agrees to, and a statement regarding "who" makes the determination of necessity.

Any managed care contract does not supersede the individual therapist's ethical and legal responsibility to a client.

Here is a typical provision:

> "[Medically necessary] means services or supplies which are determined by
> _____ to be: (i) appropriate for the symptoms, diagnosis, or treatment of the medical condition; (ii) within acceptable mental health practice standards within the organized mental health community; (iii) not primarily for the convenience of the covered individual or any provider providing covered services to the covered individual: (iv) among only those services determined by _____ criteria and/or _____ as adequate and essential for the treatment of mental disorders or substance-abuse-related disorders, as defined by the standard nomenclature and the current version of the *Diagnostic and Statistical Manual of Mental Disorders* (DSM-IV; American Psychiatric Association, 1994), or any of its later amendments.

A key consideration of the mental health professional providing the mental health services should be: Who will determine when mental health services are medically necessary, and what criteria will be used to make the determination. Would the employer who is paying a fixed fee

The provider should consider who will determine when mental health services are "medically necessary" and what criteria will be used to make the determination.

per employee care if services are overutilized under a capitation agreement? Would the provider want an employee or agent of the employer making that determination? Would the employer care whether the criteria used to determine the obligation to provide services were weak? Careful consideration of these questions is critical. Overutilization could cause substantial financial losses under the contract, and place professional licenses in jeopardy if needed services are denied.

Underutilization—caused when a very stringent "medically necessary" provision is rigidly applied—could cause even more serious problems for the provider. A low and inadequate contract rate could present the provider with a dilemma: refuse to provide services, or lose money. Any denial of access to services could easily lead to a malpractice claim and a complaint lodged with a state licensing board.

The names or information that go into the blanks in the definition of "medically necessary" are critical to the financial success of the provider as well as to his or her professional future.

Study the list of covered services. Does it align well with the providers who will be servicing the population group? Do they have the ability and experience to profitably provide quality services? If not, what will it cost to bring the necessary providers on board?

Make sure the contract carves out and excepts risk for medical treatment interventions. It is not uncommon for mental health clients to experience medical needs while receiving mental health treatment (e.g., a therapy client might attempt suicide and be hospitalized). The cost of the medical services should not be borne by the provider who contracted to provide the mental health services.

Changes in Population, and Term of the Agreement

Two other areas of the contract should be carefully considered: (1) the eligibility of members of the population pool, and (2) the term of the agreement.

Two other areas of the contract should be carefully considered: (1) the eligibility of members of the population pool, and (2) the term of the agreement. Is the population highly fluid, increasing and decreasing with the hiring and firing of employees? If so, will there be financial adjustments to the contract as new members are enrolled or terminated? If an employer lays off a substantial portion of its covered labor force, will the employer be entitled to a refund of part of the capitated amount paid?

If prosperity suddenly requires the addition of a substantial number of employees, will the provider be compensated for the addition to the population pool? If so, at what rate? Agreements negotiated in January may seem inadequate in November. And what about a traumatic work place death, homicide, or suicide, which necessitates emergency action and increased consultation and therapy?

Should you enter into a one-year capitated agreement to avoid the losses a longer term could generate if the bid rate proves to be too low? Or, is a longer term a sounder financial consideration because another provider may submit a lower bid after the one-year contract is up?

These are difficult questions, and they cannot be answered quickly or generally. Even with an abundance of information and caution, these considerations, like all aspects of capitated agreements, are difficult to

Legal Lightbulb

- Capitation involves tremendous risk. An inadequate bid will result in financial losses when demand for services exceeds projected rates.

- A therapist's ethical and legal responsibility to a client supersedes any provision of a capitated contract. Services that are not covered but are needed may have to be provided without additional charges.

- Retain control over, or at least maintain input into, the decision as to whether mental health services are "necessary."

- Be sure the contract carves out and excepts risk for medical treatment interventions.

- Negotiate for a sharing of profits (or losses) over (or under) certain amounts.

- Capitation is all about risk and the risk–reward ratio. Information is essential in assessing, weighing, and accepting the risk. At least know what risk is being assumed.

- Beware the fiduciary who refuses to provide specific requested information, and avoid bidding on the contract such a source offers.

- Never approach a managed care contract, **least of all a capitation agreement,** without the input of skillful and experienced legal advisers and industry consultants.

address. Appreciating, weighing, balancing, and, in the final analysis, *accepting* risk is what capitation agreements are all about.

A true balance of the risk to the employer and the provider might be arranged as a sharing in any profit or loss realized by the employer or the provider. Consideration might be given to establishing a profit (or loss) figure over (or under) which each party might share. Such an agreement would reduce the risk of financial loss for the provider and allow the employer to recover overpayment if the contract rate proved to be too high.

Capitation agreements are here to stay and apparently will be increasing in number, at least in the near future. The risk associated with these agreements, and the complicated nature of the provisions they contain make it imperative that competent advice be obtained from legal and industry sources and consultants.

13

"Gag Rules"

A group practice was formed to provide integrated behavioral health services by a psychiatrist, a psychologist, two social workers, a substance abuse counselor, and two licensed professional counselors. All were experienced mental health practitioners who wanted to pursue managed care contracts. One of the first managed care contracts they signed as a group, and individually, provided that in the event a referral was necessary, the treating therapist and the group would only refer the client back to the managed care company. Over a period of several months, one of the social workers, in conjunction with the psychiatrist, who prescribed and monitored medication, provided services to a young woman who was having serious difficulty both functioning on her job and getting along with family members and coworkers. The social worker, suspecting that the woman suffered from dissociative identity disorder, consulted with the other members of the group. None of them was experienced in treating persons with this disorder, and the group was unanimous in recommending termination and referral back to the managed care company. The client was instructed at a termination session to ask the managed care company for referral to a specialist who was experienced in working with multiple personality clients. The managed care company was advised of the perceived problem and needs of this client.

Unfortunately, the managed care company did not have under contract a provider who was experienced with this disorder. Instead, the client was referred to another social worker who had recently attended a dissociative disorder workshop. After two visits to the social worker, the young woman committed suicide. Her family hired an attorney, who asserted that the group, the social worker, the psychiatrist, and the managed care company had had a duty to make a referral to the best possible source for care of dissociative identity disorder. The managed care company, the group, the social worker, and the psychiatrist were all facing a suit for professional negligence.

Very few practitioners are able to sustain a private practice without entering into managed care provider agreements. "Private pay only" practices are vanishing in today's era of highly competitive behavioral health services. Therapists often join as many panels as possible without taking the time to review and carefully consider a proposed contract or a proposed managed care company. They adhere to a faulty philosophy that, because managed care is a necessity of successful practice, the more provider panels one can contract to join, the better. More is not always better, however, and the failure to review and understand a contract presented by a managed care company can lead to serious consequences for a provider.

A therapist cannot abrogate his or her professional and ethical responsibilities when they conflict with a contractual obligation in a provider agreement.

Managed care contracts are prepared by the attorneys for the managed care company. They have the company's interests and protection in mind, and provisions of the agreement may conflict with the interests of the therapist. A therapist cannot abrogate his or her professional and ethical responsibilities when they conflict with a contractual obligation in a provider agreement. It is imperative to review all contracts before executing them, and to consult a legal specialist who can advise on any terms or conditions that are unclear. The provider may finally elect to sign the contract as presented, but at least the terms of the agreement have been understood in all their ramifications.

Provisions That Deserve Careful Attention

Gag Clauses

Negotiate the elimination of a gag clause before you sign the agreement, or limit the clause to defamatory statements.

Gag clauses, commonly included in provider contracts, attempt to preclude the therapist from discussing, with third parties or clients, any disagreements with care standards, procedures, management, sharing rate, or referral information. Many states have moved to ban these types of clauses. If you practice in a jurisdiction where they are permitted, negotiate the elimination of that particular clause before you sign the agreement, or limit the clause to defamatory statements. An issue may arise on which you will have a moral or legal obligation to speak out.

The "Hold Harmless" Clause

Another common provision, the hold harmless clause, imposes a financial obligation on the therapist to reimburse the managed care company if the company becomes a defendant in a lawsuit or must pay damages for any negligent or fraudulent acts of the therapist. The following is a typical— but very broad and risk-laden—hold harmless provision:

> Provider shall indemnify and save harmless ABC, Inc. and its officers, agents, and employees from all suits, actions, losses, damages, claims, or liability of any character, type, or description, including, without limiting the generality of the foregoing, all expenses of litigation, court costs, and attorney fees for injury or death to any person or persons or property, arising out of, or occasioned by, the acts of Provider or Provider's agents or employees.

This clause means just what it says, and it goes to an extreme in providing protection for the managed care company. If the provider performs *any* act, justifiable or not, or is sued for *any* reason, (also justifiable or not) and the managed care entity is named in the suit as a party defendant, the provider pays all costs of defense and any judgment that is entered. It doesn't matter whether the provider was wrongfully accused and sued, or whether the suit is successfully defended by the provider and the managed care company. It simply says, "If we get sued, you pay."

As a practical matter, if the managed care entity is named in a suit, involving the provider, or receives a letter of complaint, or has to negotiate a settlement, the provider will ultimately be financially involved. The details will vary from case to case, but, in general, the responsibility for defense and damages shifts to the provider.

Unless endorsed on the malpractice policy of the provider, the provider's personal malpractice or professional liability policy will usually not cover expenses of the managed care entity's defense. The contractual "save harmless" agreement does not extend obligations of the malpractice carrier without endorsement.

It is virtually impossible to negotiate the elimination of a hold harmless clause in its entirety, but it is possible to negotiate a narrower and fairer provision and to make it mutual. If you must indemnify the managed care company for your mistakes, they should be obligated to indemnify you for its mistakes. Suits are now being filed for wrongful *denial of care*. These suits have a short history, but managed care entities are becoming sensitive to their vulnerability.

If the managed care company is named in a suit, the "hold harmless" clause shifts the responsibility for defense and damages to the provider.

Options

Cross out the clause entirely. Delete the paragraph by lining it out, and initial the change. It doesn't hurt to try.

- Make the clause reciprocal or mutual; place the managed care company under a similar indemnity agreement.

- Negotiate a narrower scope for the clause. Limit the indemnity obligations to a situation where the provider is found guilty of or liable for negligence or fraudulent conduct. Consider adding the following language:

  Provider shall indemnify and save harmless ABC, Inc. and its officers, agents, and employees from all suits, actions, losses, damages, claims, or liability of any character, type, or description, including, without limiting the generality of the foregoing, all expenses of litigation, court costs, and attorney fees for injury or death to any person or persons or property, arising out of, or occasioned by, the acts of Provider or Provider's agents or employees, **but only to the extent that Provider or Provider's agents or employees are found judicially liable for such losses.**

- Call the malpractice carrier and negotiate for coverage of a possible indemnity risk. For a premium, the carrier may be willing to extend its coverage.

- Ask the managed care company to extend its policy to cover you, as provider, and your group, and to unify protection in one policy. Offer to pay the additional premium if there is one.

Coverage and Payment

Learn the co-pays and deductibles, and study the demographics of the covered population, to determine whether you and your practice are a reasonable match.

When reviewing a contract, examine the specific benefits and exclusions of the plan for mental health services. Learn the co-pays and deductibles, and study the demographics of the covered population, to determine whether you and your practice are a reasonable match.

The most important consideration for therapists is usually the amount of compensation that will be paid for the services provided. Look for a fixed payment schedule, but don't stop there. Be sure the contract contains provisions for payment within a fixed and short period of time. Try to impose penalties and interest on the managed care company if payment is not made within the prescribed time period.

Find out whether the managed care company publishes a list of providers and, if so, what information you can include with your listing and what specialty listings are available. Be sure to review a proof of the listings before they are published.

Referral Restrictions

Referral agreements and restrictions should be carefully considered. Many contracts require referral back to the managed care company or only to another panel member. Some require the client to repeat the utilization review process for an alternate referral. A few contracts impose the assumption of financial responsibility on any referring therapist who makes a referral to a provider outside the plan. A therapist cannot contract away the ethical and legal duty to refer a client to the best possible source for care.

Negotiate for the right to make a referral to a provider outside the plan if you believe that such a referral is the best option for a client.

Negotiate for the right to make a referral to a provider outside the plan.

Confidentiality and Reviews

The contract should provide for confidentiality of client records. Any access by the managed care company or the employer should occur only with the consent of the client. Try to impose the most protection possible for the client. Learn who will be viewing client information and what their qualifications are. Narrow the scope of any provisions that compel access to information by the managed care company.

Know what types of reviews (i.e., prior, concurrent, retrospective) are required by the plan, and what rules are in place with respect to reviews. Ask about the appeal processes, and determine whether they are reasonable and fair. If they are too onerous or appear to be unfair, you should probably decline the provider agreement presented by that company. If the client has a problem with the managed care company, you, as the treating therapist, will be drawn into the legal fray.

Providing services through a bad managed care company is just inviting unwanted involvement in legal proceedings. Get as much information as possible about the company and its plan while contemplating the terms of a contract. Other providers and colleagues are a wonderful source of information and should be routinely consulted regarding company or contract issues.

Continuity of Care

Examine carefully what the plan contractually provides for continuity of care. Try to ascertain what happens when a client's insurance coverage—or care—is terminated. Your responsibility to a client is not as easily severed. You are taking on a client, not a managed care company, and your professional and ethical responsibilities to the client are independent of and supersede your managed care contractual obligations and duties. If the company won't pay for coverage and you feel the services are necessary, you may have to decide how to deliver those services to the client, or make a proper referral.

Some managed care contracts forbid the provider from charging the client for noncovered services, even if the client agrees to pay for them. If the client has a need for noncovered services, you may have a legal and ethical obligation to provide them or to refer the client to a private-pay therapist, if permissible under the managed care contract. Negotiate to have this clause stricken from the contract.

Legal Lightbulb

- Carefully review each provider agreement, and consult with a knowledgeable attorney before signing one.

- You are taking care of clients, not managed care companies. Your professional and ethical responsibilities to a client are independent of and supersede your managed care contractual obligations and duties.

- Carefully evaluate a company's offer to list you on its provider panel. Thoroughly inspect each term and provision of the provider contract.

- If the client is angry at and dissatisfied with the managed care company, you may be caught in a legal fray and named as a codefendant in any lawsuit filed.

- Consult peers regarding a company's reputation and contract issues.

- It is always worth the effort to negotiate important clauses.

Be sure that the term of the contract is consistent with your professional goals and needs. A long-term contract may appear to provide security and stability, but you may want the flexibility to get out of a contract quickly if it doesn't meet your expectations.

Not every provider contract is the same. Never assume that all provider agreements have the same standards. Contracts vary from company to company, and you must carefully review each provider agreement before signing. Consult with a lawyer and peers and, at the very least, put yourself in a position to make an intelligent risk assessment.

Rarely does a provider present a managed care contract to a managed care company. Uniformly, the contract is drafted by a managed care company's lawyers for the benefit and protection of the company (the lawyer's client), and delivered to the provider for acceptance. Some clauses can be negotiated and others eliminated. The potential mischief in gag and hold harmless clauses is enormous. A potential provider might finally agree to these clauses, but it is important to first view all their implications. Many managed care companies have some flexibility built into their contracts; with tact and persistence, some of these provisions might be amendable. Negotiation is always worth some effort. Once the contract is signed and operating, changes are almost impossible.

Check whether you have the flexibility to get out of a contract quickly if it doesn't meet your expectations.

SECTION FOUR

FEES

14

Sliding Fee Scales

A therapist received a call from her minister asking if she would see a member of the congregation whose husband had run off with another woman and taken all the couple's money. The minister informed the therapist that the congregant was extremely distraught, had four young children, no insurance, and limited financial resources. The therapist agreed to see the woman in therapy, and even reduced her normal hourly rate by 50 percent.

A managed care referral wished to continue in therapy after all authorized, covered benefits had been exhausted. But he was unable to pay the therapist's full fee in cash. The therapist agreed to see the client at a reduced rate.

A managed care referral, a widow with eight minor children and limited financial resources, struggled to pay her $20 co-pay for each session. The therapist, aware of the problem, waived the co-pay for future sessions.

These are examples of sliding or variable fees. To kindhearted therapists, they present serious risk of civil and criminal fraud and possible claims for breach of contract.

All states prohibit a health care provider from charging a higher fee to a client who has insurance coverage than to one without insurance, when insurance (or the lack of it) is the only differentiating criterion applied. Many statutes, such as Article 21.79 E of the Texas Insurance Code, criminalize the charging of different fees for the same service, where the higher price is based on the fact that an insurer will pay all or part of the fee.

The altruistic reasoning behind sliding fee scales is easy to grasp, but, in practice, flexible fee policies present a dangerous legal trap for the unwary mental health professional. Giving an uninsured client a break, and

Flexible fee policies present a dangerous legal trap for the unwary mental health professional.

charging a lower rate than would be billed to an insurance company could result in a criminal conviction. Fines and imprisonment are possible penalties, even for the best intentioned therapist.

Contract Restrictions

Insurance companies and managed care payers look very closely at the fee arrangements of their providers and will take a hard stand on such seemingly insignificant acts as waiving co-pays. If the therapist contracts with a managed care company for an hourly rate of $85 per hour, with a $10 co-pay, and then waives the co-pay, the rate is really $75 per hour. The therapist should be receiving only $65 per hour from the managed care company and $10 from the client. Several therapists who waived co-pays have been sued for refunds on fraud grounds. **Never waive a co-pay.**

Most therapists, when asked about their rate for services, will respond with an amount and a time period (e.g., "$75 per 50-minute session"). That is the information they circulate when asked by inquiring clients, insurance carriers, and managed care companies. Their rates might also be published in brochures and stated or implied when answering questions in public. When the therapist contracts to provide services at that rate with one client and subsequently charges another client a lower rate, misrepresentation of the fee can be argued and used to establish a basis for a civil or criminal fraud complaint.

If insurance or lack of insurance is the only differentiating criterion used by the therapist to determine who pays a higher or lower price, a criminal prosecution could result.

Suppose the $75 rate is disclosed to a managed care company and the therapist ultimately agrees to a provider contract for reimbursement by the managed care company at $60 per hour. Can the managed care company complain if the therapist sees a few private-pay clients at $65 or even $50 per hour? Yes. The managed care company could argue that if it had known that the therapist charged some clients less than $75 per session (the quoted rate), it would have negotiated to pay the provider an amount less than $65 per hour.

Some managed care companies have a negotiating strategy of compensating therapists at a fixed percentage of the therapists' quoted rate. Suppose a company typically contracts to pay a therapist 80 percent of the stated rate of $75, or $75 × 80% = $60. If the therapist then charges some clients $65 per session, the managed care company could assert "material misrepresentation" and sue to recover the excess fees paid. If lack of insurance was the only differentiating criterion used by the therapist to determine who paid $65 per session instead of $75, a criminal prosecution could also result.

Insurance Restrictions

These fee issues are being monitored nationwide by payers and governmental agencies, as reported by *Practice Strategies* (April 1997): "Therapists should, however, avoid routinely reducing fees or routinely waiving co-payments for clients while billing insurance for the full fee. Where the full fee is routinely reduced, it may appear *that the reduced fee is in actuality the full fee—and the therapist is charging a premium for services billed to insurance. In this case, **insurance and government fraud units may charge the private practitioner with misrepresenting the actual fee.**"*

Many provider agreements restrict the fees that can be charged to a client when benefits under the client's managed care plan have been exhausted or "when needed" services are not covered by the plan. It is imperative to read benefit summaries and provider contracts carefully before offering additional services to clients at reduced prices.

It is imperative to read benefit summaries and provider contracts carefully before offering additional services to clients at reduced prices.

Can a mental health practitioner have a sliding fee scale? Yes. If insurance or lack thereof is not the **only** factor considered in determining the rate, a therapist can have a sliding fee scale. Some state laws require a county hospital to look at the following factors in determining eligibility for free medical care:

- Number of persons in the applicant's household.
- Existence of insurance coverage.
- Transfer of real property within prior 24 months.
- Applicant's household income.
- Applicant's liquid assets.
- Work-related and child-care expenses.

Incorporating these and other factors into a sliding fee scale should prevent the therapist from violating a statute that prohibits charging a higher fee to persons with insurance coverage, when insurance is the only criterion. An intake form soliciting this information would have to be completed and signed by each client seeking a sliding fee scale, and maintained as part of the client's permanent record. Some therapists have a form on hand, similar to a bank loan application, which is offered to clients who seek sliding fees. The form is completed by the client prior to any reduction in the standard fee, and is submitted to the therapist at the time a sliding fee determination is requested.

Pros and Cons

If a therapist is going to have a sliding fee scale, it must be announced to each prospective client, insurer, or managed care company, and must be consistently applied.

If a therapist is going to have a sliding fee scale, it must be announced to each prospective client, insurer, or managed care company, and must be consistently applied. If the therapist has existing managed care contracts in which an hourly rate has been disclosed, but wishes to switch to a sliding fee scale, each managed care company must be informed of the change in the fee structure, schedule, and policy. One must be **very** careful about prior rate disclosures to, and contracts with, insurers and managed care companies.

Most managed care contracts contain an "audit" clause. The managed care entity has a right to audit the fees of the therapist to determine the actual fees charged and to ascertain whether the therapist is in compliance with the managed care contract.

Can a therapist have a fee policy whereby a reasonable fee is negotiated with each client? Yes, but this must be the therapist's stated fee policy and it must be universally applied. Most state licensing laws only require fees to be reasonable and consistent with law. It would be acceptable if a therapist chose not to establish a fixed session rate but had an announced policy of negotiating a reasonable fee with each client, insurer, or managed care company on a case-by-case basis. However, because such a policy would consume considerable time, and negotiating a fee would imply revealing personal financial status, many clients will opt not to come in. Looking for certainty on cost, the client will call the next name on his or her list of potential providers. People want to know what they will be charged before they take time out of their busy day to come to a therapist's office. Therapists are also concerned about time, a resource most would like to conserve and use efficiently.

A sliding fee scale can be implemented but the criteria must be documented, and this type of inquiry and documentation presents another layer of paperwork and complexity in the mental health practice. Any fee schedule except a stated fixed rate will result in great difficulties in billing. A variable fee schedule causes additional complexity and consumption of time and will make it an unattractive choice for even the most altruistic therapist.

To therapists who want to help out the less fortunate and don't want the headache of implementing a sliding fee scale, we suggest charging everyone the same rate but offering flexible payment plans when an insurer or managed care company is not providing payment. An increase in delinquent accounts may result, but the therapist will face much less risk for having a kindhearted attitude toward unpaid invoices than for reducing fees.

Questions continue to arise concerning sliding fee scales, reduced fees, waiving co-payments, the percentage of the full fee that is payable by insurance companies, the amount communicated to insurance companies as being the full fee, third-party payments, discounts, charitable or pro bono therapy offered to clients who cannot afford the full amount, and any number of arrangements that alter a fixed fee and create a flexible market price.

This is truly a case-by-case situation. Before establishing a sliding fee scale, reducing fees, devising methods of reducing fees for noninsured clients, or indulging in partial pro bono billing, it is advisable to call a specialist or lawyer for expert input. Insurance fraud is a very serious matter. In cases where insurance fraud has been proven, providers have faced jail time. Some providers, months or years after the treatment was completed, have received letters demanding reimbursement of all or part of the fee paid.

Careless billing practices can also be grounds for a complaint to the licensing board, and may result in investigation by a professional organization.

Debate continues in this volatile and often delicate area. Caution, careful planning, and a meticulous paper trail would be advisable. Remember, when dealing with managed care or third-party payments in any form, the payer has the right to audit the records of the provider. When audits are conducted by payers, they will be seeking to uncover fraudulent practices and recovery of payments made.

When dealing with managed care or third-party payments in any form, the payer has the right to audit the records of the provider.

Legal Lightbulb

- Altruism with respect to fee setting can subject an unwitting or naive therapist to claims of criminal and civil fraud and return of fees paid.

- Fraudulent fee practices can result in the suspension or revocation of a professional license.

- Avoid the appearance of charging lower fees simply because the client does not have insurance.

- If a variable fee structure is to be utilized, base the fee on a number of financial and personal factors, not solely on insurance coverage or the lack thereof.

- Whatever fee policy is adopted, apply it universally to each managed care organization, insurance company, and client.

- Review carefully each plan summary and provider contract. What fee restrictions are stated?

- Never waive a co-pay.

- If a sliding or variable fee scale is being considered, consult carefully with knowledgeable legal and industry advisers.

- A set fee, consistently applied but allowing for flexible or easy payment terms, may be the easiest policy to implement.

- Take insurance audits seriously.

15

Recovering Unpaid Fees

Jack and Susan saw Ms. Love, LMSW (Licensed Master Social Worker), for family therapy. At the end of each month, Ms. Love sent them a bill, which they promptly paid in accordance with the original agreement. After a few months, Susan indicated that a family financial problem had occurred and asked to have payment delayed a month or two while the couple put their resources in order. Not wanting to put added pressure on them, Ms. Love agreed. The couple continued in therapy for another six weeks, then separated and filed for divorce. Neither would pay Ms. Love for the last few sessions. Instead, each told her to seek payment from the other. The total unpaid bill was $530. Although they were satisfied with the treatment, both refused to pay. Three months after their last visit, Ms. Love had still not been paid.

~

Lynne was married to Bob, a long-term employee of a major company with excellent mental health insurance benefits. She felt depressed and sought long-term therapy with Dr. Wise, who was on the preferred provider panel for her husband's employer's insurance program. Dr. Wise called the insurance carrier, and the treatment was approved. For about two years, Dr. Wise treated Lynne. Finally, after excellent care from Dr. Wise, Lynne recovered and was discharged. During the two-year period, Dr. Wise submitted his monthly bills and was paid promptly.

An internal insurance company audit conducted six months after Lynne's discharge by the insurance company which paid Dr. Wise revealed that Lynne and Bob had been divorced about five months after Lynne's therapy began. Lynne had not revealed the divorce to Dr. Wise nor had she informed Bob's employer or the insurance company. The insurer had made payments for the benefit of a former wife who was not entitled to coverage. The auditor wrote a letter to Dr. Wise, indicating that Lynne was not covered after the date of the divorce, and demanded reimbursement. The amount involved was thousands of dollars. What are the options for both of these therapists?

Both the social worker and the psychologist had in their clients' files a carefully drafted, lawyer-reviewed intake and consent form, signed by the respective clients, which stated that the client was primarily responsible for the therapist's fees. Third-party reimbursement of any amount would be credited toward the bill, but the form clearly indicated a personal contractual obligation. Payment for the therapeutic services was the obligation of the client, if sums were not forthcoming from any third-party payer.

Ms. Love's Options

1. Forget the fee; write off the $530 as a loss.

2. Make numerous calls to the former clients, offering terms, a payout, a settlement for less than the amount due (half or three-fourths, for example), or let Jack and/or Susan suggest percentages.

3. Turn over the unpaid bill to a collection agency, which will charge 40 to 50 percent of the billable amount for collection services.

4. File a suit in small claims court and be her own advocate, as is permitted in most small claims courts.

5. Turn over the unpaid bill to a lawyer for collection. Most lawyers will consider a $500–$1,000 collection a favor, not a business venture.

6. Have a lawyer draft some collection letters for her to send, then pursue a small claims court action.

The best option? Ms. Love should drop the whole payment issue. True, the bill is owed. True, the client, jointly or severally (either or both of them) ought to pay the amount incurred as a legitimate debt. However, the payment is not worth pursuing.

An uncollected bill cannot be written off as a business loss, especially if taxes are computed on a cash basis.

Small bills involve aggravating phone calls, collection agencies' fees, and collection letters sent personally or through an agency or an attorney. Therapists earn a living by offering therapy, not collecting bills. Better to write off a "bad debt" than to pursue collection efforts that annoy everyone, including the therapist. The bad news: an uncollected bill cannot be written off as a business loss, especially if taxes are computed on a cash basis.

One other thought. Clients become disturbed when they are reminded of unpaid bills. In our litigious society, a disturbed client is apt to file a complaint with the licensing board or seek some sort of malpractice relief if collection is pursued. As an almost knee-jerk reaction, when a suit for collection is filed, the client consults with an attorney and then files a cross action or counterclaim for malpractice. The usual outcome: The therapist drops the collection claim, and the client drops the malpractice suit. The parties are back to where they were in the beginning, but only after time and money have been wasted, and tempers have flared.

There are business losses in every business. A relatively small unpaid bill is just another business risk, and should be written off. The goodwill of the client (and possible future referrals) is more important, when measured against the difficulties of collecting. There is no "nice" way to pursue collection efforts.

Dr. Wise's Options

In this scenario, everyone may have acted in good faith. Lynne may not have known that her divorce affected her eligibility, nor realized that her benefits would be terminated at the same time as the marriage. With hindsight, she understands the concept of coverage, but she was so happy with Dr. Wise she just continued working on her own problems. She was not paying, so she did not give much thought to payment.

Dr. Wise was unaware of the divorce or the fact that eligibility was terminated on the date of the divorce. For all sessions after that date, he was not entitled to reimbursement. He received authorization and payments in good faith, and he relied on the representations of the payer that coverage was appropriate and continuing.

The insurance company fulfilled its contract beyond the agreed-on limit (the divorce), and only asked for reimbursement when it was discovered that the facts had changed and the employee's wife was no longer entitled to coverage. Should the company "be a sport" and not pursue a just claim against Dr. Wise? What is the value of the contract, compared to the amount to be recovered?

*All contracts
provided by
insurance
companies and
drafted by
insurance
company lawyers
favor the
company.*

Dr. Wise is responsible for reimbursing the insurance company for all payments made to him after the date of the divorce (i.e., when Lynne lost her eligibility). In the contract Dr. Wise signed with the insurance carrier, all authorizations were contingent and temporary, and, in the event a client was later found to be ineligible, the company was entitled to reimbursement. All contracts provided by insurance companies and drafted by insurance company lawyers favor the company. In a clause read but not necessarily understood by Dr. Wise, he had a contractual obligation to refund the amounts paid to him after the divorce.

Dr. Wise also had a lawyer-drafted and lawyer-approved contract with Lynne, which makes her responsible for reimbursing him for the sum he had had to return to the insurance company. Although Dr. Wise was clearly entitled to be paid by Lynne, as soon as he pursued the matter she reminded him that she had divorced during the therapy, and, as a psychologist, he should have sensed the trauma she was going through and been aware of her increased stressors. She insinuated that his diagnosis was incomplete and the treatment plan was inaccurate, although the results were satisfactory and the present prognosis was excellent. Not wishing to be faced with a counterclaim or a complaint to the licensing board, Dr. Wise, sadder and wiser, closed Lynne's file.

Unpaid Bills and Reimbursement for Insurance Claims

- There is no "nice" way to collect an unpaid bill.
- Suing a client for failing to pay a bill can have adverse consequences for the therapist. They include:

  —The client might file a cross action or counterclaim.

  —The client might file a complaint with the therapist's licensing board.

  —The client might report the therapist to the Chamber of Commerce, the Better Business Bureau, or a local or national professional organization.

  —The dispute might come to the attention of the hospital where the therapist has privileges, the provider group where the therapist is on

*Handle every
unpaid bill as a
"problem," and
don't let your
accounts
receivable
accumulate.*

the panel, or professional colleagues who might be anxious about having in their midst a therapist who is vulnerable to media coverage.

- The justness of a claim for payment has little effect on the aggressiveness and creativity of an upset, angry, hostile, or borderline client.

- Therapeutic services are not like products. Therapy is an art form to some extent, and there is no singular way to offer therapy. An angry client can easily find fault, and an imaginative lawyer can effortlessly find a reason why any bill should *not* be paid.

Legal Lightbulb

- Read your malpractice policy carefully. Some policies state that the malpractice carrier will not defend against a malpractice suit filed as a defensive measure against a collection effort.

- Generally, lawsuits for the collection of fees are not cost-effective.

- Handle every unpaid bill as a "problem," and don't let your accounts receivable accumulate.

- Read managed care contracts carefully. Therapists are bound by the contract terms, which are usually drafted by the managed care company's lawyer for the benefit of his or her employer.

- Most clients pay, eventually. When they do not, accept the loss as a business risk.

- When a bill is unpaid, negotiate, mediate, compromise, or settle. Don't sue, unless you are so advised by a knowledgeable attorney who is willing to take the case to conclusion. In that event, compare the unpaid bill to the legal fees you will incur.

- In a dispute between a therapist and a consumer, the therapist is more vulnerable, especially if the case gains media attention.

- Before taking any legal action, talk to your therapist, your lawyer, your minister, and your colleagues.

SECTION FIVE

FORENSIC ISSUES

16

Abuse Allegations

*"A volunteer baby sitter at a Sunday school who was jailed without bail for two and a half years before being cleared of inflicting satanic ritual abuse on children is now suing **child therapists,** prosecutors and the church where he worked. . . . [He was] acquitted . . . of . . . sexually abusing nine children, . . . therapists . . . had prodded children into fabricating fantastic accounts of ritual abuse. . . . [The children] testified that he had killed a baby . . . slaughtered an elephant and a giraffe . . . [the plaintiff] alleges slander, libel, false imprisonment, professional negligence, civil rights violations and infliction of emotional distress [and] accuses the prosecutors of selecting therapists who they knew were inclined to find evidence of abuse. . . . " [Source: Mental Health Law Reporter (November 1994, Vol. 12, No. 11, p. 81).]*

Every state has a child abuse reporting statute that requires mental health professionals—and, in most jurisdictions, every citizen—to report suspected child abuse to legal authorities. These reporting statutes generally grant immunity, civil and criminal, to anyone who makes a "good faith" report of abuse or reports a reasonable suspicion that abuse has occurred.

A therapist who reports child abuse has a certain amount of protection under the law, although, if a suit were filed, the protection of the statute would have to be invoked. A fact issue could exist for a judge or jury: Was the report made in good faith and was it reasonable to suspect abuse had occurred?

Liability for False Allegation

In light of litigated cases filed against therapists, mental health providers are often concerned about being sued for a false allegation and may be reluctant to make a child abuse report. Many statutes make it a criminal

Many statutes make it a criminal act not to report child abuse.

act *not* to report child abuse, so declining to report should not be considered an option. In all jurisdictions, the potential risks and harm from reporting a case that may be invalid should be weighed against the potential risks from failing to report a case. A child may subsequently be abused, killed, or seriously injured. Making the report is definitely the lesser of two potentially bad options. Most judges charged with the responsibility of addressing custody or visitation issues admit that, when in doubt, they prefer to err on the side of the safety of the child. There should be only one rule of thumb for therapists: **The best interest of a *child* or the safety of a *child* is always paramount.**

All therapists know (or should know) that child abuse must be reported. The therapist should have some clinical reason or justification for reporting the abuse and be aware of the danger of encouraging children to speak up: the words and images of the therapist may become the words and images of the child.

Lawyers often hear of child abuse. The accusation may come from a spouse who is seeking custody of a child and who quotes the supposed words of the child to a lawyer. Upon investigation, the lawyer may discover that the words are those of the spouse, not the child. Or, the words of the child are taken out of context and are so exaggerated that they are meaningless.

The uncorroborated statements of a child whose parents are involved in custody litigation have to be reviewed and evaluated carefully.

A child, wishing to please a parent, especially an aggressive or controlling individual, may tell the parent what he or she wishes to hear. The child often has no inkling of the ramifications of the words or how the information will be used. In this situation, the therapist must tread carefully. The uncorroborated statements of a child whose parents are involved in custody litigation have to be reviewed and evaluated carefully. Don't dismiss them; just scrutinize them cautiously.

Any case involving abuse carries a clear warning: Child abuse is serious and must be reported. However, there are situations when the evidence must be weighed carefully to determine whether the allegations or evidence received truly come from the child reporting the abuse or from an overreacting therapist. Or, are the allegations the words that an angry or hostile parent put into the mind and mouth of the child? Has the parent, now an embittered divorcing spouse, made suggestions to a child that, after a period of time and constant repetition, the child now thinks are his or her own?

A clinical and defensible basis should be established for making the report, in the event that the "good faith" or "reasonableness" of the report is called into question.

Therapists receive some clinical training to determine abuse, but an allegation cannot exceed the individual mental health professional's level of competence. To do so would be an ethical violation. If a therapist suspects abuse, the statute in that jurisdiction will require reporting the suspicion to appropriate legal authorities. If a therapist does not have the expertise or experience to properly evaluate a suspected abuse case, a referral should be made to a therapist who possesses the requisite learning, training, education, and experience to evaluate the situation. This may be accomplished after the initial report is made.

A clinical and defensible basis should be established for making the report, in the event that the "good faith" or "reasonableness" of the report is called into question.

Children's Truthfulness

Can a child make everything up? Can a child allege child abuse, convince a psychiatrist that such abuse occurred, observe his or her parents being arrested, and then recant and sue the mental health professional who reported the alleged abuse?

"A jury . . . awarded more than $272,000 to a couple and their teenage daughter, who had joined in a suit charging a psychiatrist with failure to properly evaluate the girl's accusations of parental sex abuse. . . . [The] psychiatrist diagnosed her patient's condition as post-traumatic stress disorder brought on by sexual abuse . . . some of the girl's claims were immediately discounted: She said that her grandmother flew about on a broom, that she had been tortured with a medieval thumbscrew device, that she had borne three children. . . . The family reconciled after their daughter told a judge in 1992 that she had made the whole thing up. . . ." Allegations against the psychiatrist included considering the daughter's statements as a certainty, not checking out anything else, failing to challenge claims, not considering that some of the claims were immediately discounted. *[Source:* Mental Health Law Reporter *(January 1995, Vol. 13, No. 1, p. 2).]*

This case offers lessons on the continued procedures after abuse has been reported (i.e., what takes place in treatment after the child abuse is reported as required by statute). If there is to be continued treatment by a therapist, whether in a public, private, or school setting, efforts should be made to establish corroborating evidence that verifies the allegations. If

If corroboration is not attempted, or corroborating evidence cannot be discovered, the evaluating and treating therapist should document this fact and qualify any report or findings accordingly.

parts of the story are discounted (the grandmother flew about on a broom; torture with a medieval thumbscrew, and so on), it may be time to question the abuse itself and revise the diagnosis, treatment plan, and prognosis.

If corroboration is not attempted, or corroborating evidence cannot be discovered, the evaluating or treating therapist should document this fact and qualify any report or findings accordingly.

Diagnosis and treatment of child abuse are difficult because very often there is no physical evidence to substantiate the allegations. The onus is on the professional to record and support each evaluation and treatment plan with, ideally, verifiable evidence. The purpose here is not to intimidate the therapist, but to raise a flag of caution. When abuse is alleged, it must be reported. When continuing treatment is indicated, there is an additional need to look beyond the client's words for corroboration or some other meaningful input.

Children sometimes make allegations that they later discount or deny. If litigation results, they might then join in the suit with their parents and pursue damage claims against the therapist.

In the case cited earlier in this section, a child made up a story that was accepted initially at face value by authorities. It was repeated to the psychiatrist, who visited with the child over 100 times in therapy sessions. Apparently, at no time did the authorities discount or disbelieve the child, nor did the psychiatrist, who seems to have taken the story at face value and did not determine independently whether parental sex abuse actually took place.

Later, the parents were reconciled, the child recanted and resides once again with the parents in an affluent suburb, and the mental health professional was forced to pay $272,000.

This type of dilemma can be faced by any mental health professional who treats sexually abused children. Child abuse may be revealed as incidental to family or marital therapy, play therapy, or even in a marriage enrichment seminar, and the same dilemma is present: Is the story true?

Videotaped sessions can be very effective in refuting allegations of implanted memories.

If the child is doubted, the therapist can be challenged as being unprofessional. If the child is believed and proves later to be unworthy of belief, the therapist can be sued. *If a complaint of this type is alleged, keep copious notes, document everything said and alleged, and, if possible, videotape the sessions.* Videotaped sessions can be very effective in refuting allegations of

Legal Lightbulb

- Suspected child abuse requires reporting to legal authorities.

- Civil and criminal immunity exists in most jurisdictions for good-faith reports or reports made on the basis of reasonable suspicion.

- Case precedent imposes a duty to attempt corroboration and independent verification of allegations made by a child.

- A therapist who lacks the experience and training to provide quality mental health services to an abuse victim should consult with another expert professional and make a referral to a therapist who has experience and training in treating victims of abuse. The suspected abuse must be reported, in good faith, to the proper legal authorities.

- Try to look beyond the words of a child, but if corroboration of the abuse victim's story is not possible, qualify any report or opinion to reflect this fact.

- Copious documentation, including but not limited to a videotape of the interview with the child, is critical.

- Take care not to influence the abuse victim's story and allegations.

- Avoid leading questions when interviewing the child.

- If in doubt about reporting abuse, err on the side of the safety of the child.

- Read the local child abuse statute. It's rarely more than a few pages.

implanted memories. If a lawsuit is brought for a misdiagnosis by the therapist, the clinical notes and taped sessions can be offered to support the diagnosis and treatment plan.

Documentation—followed by consultation, referral for specialized treatment, and testing—is the best procedure. One cannot, in the light of current research and litigation, assume a child's allegations to be true and devise a treatment plan based solely on the assumed truth of the allegations, especially if part of the story has already been discounted. When appropriate, qualify reports and opinions, and be wary of children who tell lies, exaggerate, or carry their imagination so far that they cannot distinguish fantasy from reality.

17

Child Custody and Consent-to-Treat Issues

Sam, age 7, was brought into Dr. Kline's office by a couple who introduced themselves as Sam's "father and mother," and was presented for play therapy. The office manager asked Sam's "parents" to fill out the usual intake form, and discovered that Sam's "mother" was actually his stepmother. Does this present a special situation?

~

Edgar, age 10, was reared by his grandparents since birth. Edgar's father deserted his mother before Edgar was born. His mother, unable to handle the child, left him with her parents, moved away, and married someone else. Edgar's grandparents have cared for the boy and have provided for his daily needs, but no custody papers have ever changed hands, and there were no court orders regarding legal custody. Edgar's grandparents decided to bring Edgar to Dr. Johnson for therapy. They agreed to sign Dr. Johnson's standard consent form. Do the grandparents have the authorization to consent for Edgar? Is their signed consent form valid?

~

Five years ago, when Jennie was seven years old, she went to Dr. Howard's office with her parents for family therapy. Each family member met with Dr. Howard individually as well as in the family group setting. Each session was documented, and Jennie's parents signed the standard intake and consent form. Therapy lasted a year or so and was terminated by agreement of all parties. Six years later, Jennie's parents were involved in a disputed divorce, and each wanted sole custody of Jennie. Jennie's mother requested a copy of the complete therapy record. Her father, however, sent a certified letter demanding that Dr. Howard not release any of the family's records.

Background

Children are often brought to therapy by a parent, a divorced parent with custody, a divorced noncustodial parent, a stepparent, a sibling, or a more remote relative—a grandparent. Depending on the circumstances, the therapist may or may not be able to obtain informed consent from the *legally appropriate person* to treat the child. Informed consent by a person without the authority to give consent, is no consent at all. This rule holds true in almost all nonemergency situations. The person presenting the child must have the legal authority to do so, and the therapist must determine who has this authority prior to taking on the child as a client.

Informed consent by a person without the authority to give consent, is no consent at all.

Most states have statutes that define the rights and duties of the custodial parent, but statutes have to be examined on a state-by-state basis. In one state, the general rights and duties of the custodial parent are:

1. The right to establish the primary residence of the child.

2. The right to consent to medical, dental, and surgical treatment involving invasive procedures, and to consent to psychiatric and psychological treatment.

3. The right to receive and give receipt for periodic payments for the support of the child, and to hold or disburse these funds for the benefit of the child.

4. The right to represent the child in a legal action and to make other decisions of substantial legal significance concerning the child.

5. The right to consent to the child's marriage and to his or her enlistment in the armed forces of the United States.

6. The right to make decisions concerning the child's education.

7. The right to the services and earnings of the child.

8. The right to act as an agent of the child in relation to the child's estate, if the child's action is required by a state, the United States, or a foreign government, except when a guardian of the child's estate or a *guardian* or *attorney ad litem* (appointed for purposes of a particular suit or action) has been appointed for the child.

In many jurisdictions, these rights of the custodial parent are shared by both parents as "joint custodians" or, in some states, "joint managing conservators." The joint control may come about either by order of the court or by agreement of the parties as approved by the court.

In some cases, when a divorce decree is granted, these rights are divided between the parties. For example, if one parent is a physician, the right concerning medical treatment may be assigned to a parent who is a physician; or, if one parent is an attorney, the right to represent the child in a legal action may be awarded to a parent who is a lawyer.

In almost all cases, the right to determine the child's primary residence is usually allocated to one parent, in order to provide the child with stability and to comply with school residence requirements.

Medical, dental, and surgical care, as well as psychiatric and psychological treatment, may be divided between the divorcing parents.

Legal Ramifications

Before treating a child, the therapist must determine whether the couple representing themselves as the child's parents are its biological parents and are married to each other. If so, either parent can consent to the treatment of the child.

Before treating a child, the therapist must determine whether the couple representing themselves as the child's parents are its biological parents and are married to each other. If so, either parent can consent to the treatment of the child. If the parents disagree and the therapist is caught in the middle, **the child should not be treated without a court order.**

If the parents are not presently, or have never been, married to each other, the mother usually has the right to consent to therapeutic treatment for the child.

If the parents are not presently, or have never been, married to each other, the mother usually has the right to consent to therapeutic treatment for the child. The biological father has no right to consent to treatment for the child until his paternity is established via a decree of paternity signed by the court. Request a copy of the paternity decree to determine whether the presenting parent is named as the legal father in the document. Make sure the nonmarried (to the mother) biological father has the right to consent to treatment, if he is the presenting parent.

If the parents are divorced, the rights of each parent are usually stated in the divorce decree in clear and unambiguous language.

If the parents are divorced, the rights of each parent are usually stated in the divorce decree in clear and unambiguous language. Read the decree and ask whether there have been any modifications since the decree was entered. If so, read the modifications; they sometimes change the rights of each parent in a significant manner. The latest modification will indicate parental rights. Divorce decrees can be modified until the child reaches majority.

All legal divorces have a written decree; a divorce cannot occur without one. Whenever a child of divorced parents is presented, demand a copy of the divorce decree and all modifications, and make a notation of your demand in the file. If the decree is not produced, do not commence treatment. Divorce and paternity decrees are public documents. They can often be ordered by fax and paid for by check. A lost decree can be replaced in a short time.

If an out-of-state decree is presented, contact a lawyer in the state where the decree was issued, and make sure you have the correct nomenclature and interpretation of the decree. Words and their meanings may differ from state to state.

A court order also exists when a party claims to be the guardian of the person of a minor child or an attorney ad litem or guardian ad litem. Demand to see, and take time to examine, the papers presented with the child. Court appointments usually state, specifically and clearly, the limits and responsibilities of the guardian or attorney. If you have a question, ask an attorney to examine the papers.

Children are often presented to therapists in real emergencies, when it is important to give them immediate help to improve their condition. They are also presented at times when the word "emergency" is a judgment call. A therapist who is asked to treat a child in an emergency should determine whether treatment is appropriate, document the emergency with a recitation of the facts leading to the conclusion, and then state the conclusion, "Emergency," and the rationale for the conclusion.

Remember, documentation *at the time of treatment* is critical. Should a suit be contemplated, the potential plaintiff/client may wait two years before filing. Then the court may take another few years before it brings the case to trial. At the time of trial, the therapist might not truly remember details of the incident, but a judge or jury will consider notes made at the time credible evidence of an emergency. A restored memory some years later, with no substantiating data to support the actions of the therapist, would be subject to question.

In rare instances, parents, acting on behalf of their children, have the right to sue a therapist for malpractice and to complain to the licensing board. Be careful. Although the child is technically the client, *everyone* is, in family systems therapy. The rights and obligations of the therapist should be carefully stated in the intake and consent form. The statute of limitations, which controls when a child can sue, generally extends to two years *beyond majority*. The child's records must be retained at least until this time period expires or until the time required by a state licensing board. Majority is generally reached when a child becomes 18 years of age; however, in some states, children reach majority when they marry or when they have their disabilities of minority removed (emancipation).

Some states have "mature minor" statutes that give minors, at ages 16 and 17, the right to receive therapeutic treatment without the consent of their parents, in the areas of drug and alcohol abuse, birth control, sexually transmitted diseases, and some other specific areas.

Some states have "mature minor" statutes that give minors, at ages 16 and 17, the right to receive therapeutic treatment without the consent of their parents, in the areas of drug and alcohol abuse, birth control, sexually transmitted diseases, and some other specific areas. When considering treatment for a mature minor, it is best to read the current statute. Mature minor statutes tend to be in a constant state of flux, depending on the opinions of state legislators and the interpretations of the law in court decisions. Mature minors are in a litigious area. Be very careful before you consult with the minor and before you inform or fail to inform the parents.

Although statutes vary, many states give the noncustodial parent the right to *consult with* a psychologist who is treating a child. Consultation is different from authorization to consent to the treatment of the child. Read the relevant documents carefully, and ask a lawyer for advice. One of the most difficult dilemmas a therapist can experience is being caught between the positions of two battling parents.

When children are presented by siblings, grandparents, friends in possession, or others, a genuine effort should be made to obtain the consent of the parent or other person authorized in the paperwork to consent to treatment of the child. If consent is unobtainable, have the presenting party sign a hold harmless agreement wherein he or she agrees to take responsibility for the child and for the consent being offered. Make a note in the file that you demanded the presenting person to obtain a court order giving authorization for consent to treatment on behalf of the child. In a technical sense, a stepparent is a legal stranger to the child. The fact that the stepparent and the child have the same name does not confer any legal authority on the stepparent. Have the stepparent obtain consent from the proper person.

When families are in therapy together, keep a separate record for each person in the family system.

When families are in therapy together, keep a separate record for each person in the family system. Each person can then receive, if requested, a copy of his or her record only, without the necessity of removing or concealing a portion of the record that pertains to another. The general rule is that each client has a right to a copy of his or her record only—not the record of a spouse or relative. Culling a multiple file is a nightmare. Avoid it by establishing separate records.

Usually, either parent has a right to a copy of a child's file. Where there are serious conflicts—for example, when one parent demands that a child's file be delivered, and the other demands privacy, confidentiality, and secrecy—seek a court order. Compliance with a court order removes from the custodian of the records the responsibility for sharing a file—or the possibility of serving jail time for contempt of court in preserving the secrecy of a file. When a judge rules, the file may be delivered or held confidential, depending on the judgment of the court.

One major exception to confidentiality is the mandatory reporting of child abuse. Every state requires that child abuse be reported. All clients must be told of this exception to confidentiality upon intake, and the

Legal Lightbulb

- Each state has different statutes concerning minors. Consult your state's statutes before treating a minor child.

- Obtain the protection of a court order before treating a minor child, if the parents are in positions of conflict.

- Guardianships, the appointment of attorneys and guardians ad litem, and paternity and divorce decrees (with modifications) are court orders that control the authority to consent to a child's treatment. Read them carefully and obtain the latest court order.

- In most divorce decrees, the statements concerning a child are subject to modification as long as the child is a minor. Any modification is as important as the decree itself.

- Minors can be emancipated by court decree or marriage.

- Minor children who are parents of children have the authority to consent to the treatment of their children.

- Generally, parents always have a right to be informed of the treatment of their minor children under 15. Only the mature minor provisions are exceptions.

intake form should indicate that child abuse will be reported. Although most statutes provide that the person reporting abuse has civil and criminal immunity from suit, the client should nevertheless be notified, to allow some discretion concerning the information shared with the therapist. This concept does not debate whether notice should be given; it only suggests that clients who believe that confidentiality will be maintained must be told that any abuse disclosed during a session must be reported to authorities.

Minors are indeed a special population. They have certain rights because of their status as children, but for the most part, the rights of children are controlled by parents, guardians, or other persons whose authority is contained in a court order.

When dealing with a child, it is imperative to review all legal documents that refer to the child in any way. Call a lawyer if you have any questions. Be aware that parents or guardians who are in conflict may place the child, and the therapist, in the middle of the dispute. When treatment for a minor is being contested, obtain a court order. Stay current on all the statutes that affect minors.

18

Children as Witnesses

Janie, age 4, was crying when her mother returned home from the supermarket. She pointed between her legs and said she hurt. Her mother examined her vagina and discovered bruises and abrasions. Janie's mother's boyfriend, Sam, was home at the time, as babysitter for Janie. Janie could describe some details, but was hazy when trying to explain exactly what happened while her mother was away.

~

Joshua, age 5, lived with his parents and was present when an altercation took place in the living room. He saw and heard the whole conflict and observed his mother hitting his father over the head with a frying pan. His father suffered permanent damage, sued for divorce, and sought custody of his son. Joshua, having remembered the incident, was afraid of his mother and cringed every time she entered the room. Joshua was able to narrate the incident clearly and with animated language.

~

Julie was looking out of a window as she waited for guests to arrive and celebrate her third birthday. She saw a big truck careen out of control and strike a friend's automobile just as the passengers were stepping onto the sidewalk. Three people were seriously hurt. The route of the truck and the location of the auto and passengers were at issue. Julie's testimony was critical for her friends to win their case.

Can a Child Be a Witness and Testify in Court?

Often, children are the only witnesses to a crime, an event, or their own sexual abuse. Before attorneys allow a child to testify, they will confirm that the following characteristics are present in their young witness:

1. The child has adequate mental maturity, intelligence, and articulation to testify about a case—what he or she saw, heard, smelled, felt, or otherwise experienced.

2. The child feels a duty to tell the truth because *to tell a lie is wrong*, and can separate truth from falsehood.

3. The child can separate fact from fantasy and can narrate the "facts."

4. The child observed, can recollect, and is able to narrate the facts in a meaningful way that provides to the judge and/or the jury valuable information that is not elsewhere available. The testimony of the child will yield truly significant input.

The View from the Bench

Any party to a suit can offer a child to the court as a witness. The child is under the same rules as an adult.

The characteristics above describe the capacity of a child to testify. Any party to a suit can offer a child to the court as a witness. The child can be sworn and is under the same rules as an adult, although, as a practical matter, children are handled more gingerly by cross-examining attorneys. If the judge, after talking to the child from the bench or in chambers, determines the child has reasonable maturity, intelligence, and capacity; knows it is wrong to tell a lie; can separate fact from fantasy; and can provide a narrative, the judge will allow the child to testify. Any thoughts concerning the child's testimony will then affect weight and credibility, not admissibility.

The Lawyer's View

There are some questions a lawyer must ponder, with the input of the mental health professional, before offering a child as a witness. A child is not just another witness. Children are less manageable, more volatile, and subject to more influences than adult witnesses. Also, they must be handled more gently, and they cannot be prepared for trial with the same intensity as adults or other more mature witnesses. Thus, the lawyer must review a bigger picture before calling a child as a witness, preparing the child for trial, or, especially, submitting the child to cross examination by opposing counsel. What should lawyers take into consideration when offering a child as a witness?

1. Children are vulnerable to having their memories and testimony distorted.

2. Children are suggestible.

3. Children can be led to get peripheral details wrong.

4. Children can be led to distort the central gist of events they experienced.

5. Children might distort or inaccurately recall events affecting their bodies—what something felt like; whether it hurt, and where.

6. The drama of the courtroom can affect a child long after the trial ends and the legal issues are settled or determined.

7. The pounding of the gavel, signifying the ruling of the court and the end of the trial, does not end the ordeal for the child. The memories of the trial experience, or the effects of the court's decision, will linger long after the trial is over.

8. A child should not be sworn as a witness if the primary evidence, or corroborating evidence, is available elsewhere.

In criminal or family law cases involving child abuse (sexual, physical, or emotional), the testimony of a child can be critical to the eventual outcome. The decision on whether to call a child as a witness is made by adults—parents, district attorneys, the contesting parties' attorneys, or, the judge. When considering a child as a witness, these adults must carefully weigh the possible outcomes of the trial, the effect on the child, the effect on future relationships between the child and any adult family members involved in the case, and whether the child's perception of events constitutes an accurate narrative.

The Therapist's View

When consulted by an attorney, a parent, a party to litigation, or a judge as to whether to put a child on the witness stand, the therapist must consider many factors, including the anticipated duration of the trial, and, because months, or even years, may pass between the event itself and the trial date, the anxieties produced in the interim. The therapist also needs to evaluate the personal, family, and posttrial therapeutic resources that are available to the child, and who might be responsible and available to offer future therapy.

The ultimate consideration is: What is in the best interest of the child? If two adults have a conflict and the child has been a bystander, should the child, usually a reluctant witness, be brought before the court, sworn, and subjected to examination and cross examination? Once the child takes the stand, the child can be protected only by the judge, and remains as a witness until dismissed. What must a therapist consider when consulted about the possibility of making a child a witness in a courtroom drama?

- When is the case set for trial, and can a series of postponements be expected?

- Is there a real possibility that the case will actually go to trial, or is an out-of-court-settlement being considered?

- If the therapist is engaged solely (or primarily) to prepare the child for trial, will this same therapist be available to the child for posttrial therapy? (Third-party payers and managed care companies rarely, if ever, pay for trial preparation or posttrial treatment if the client's difficulties were caused by the trial itself.)

- Will informed consent for the child to testify and to be prepared to testify be available from appropriate parties? If the child's parents are divorced, the therapist must read the divorce decree and determine from the decree who has the right to seek and consent to therapy for the child.

If the child's parents are divorced, the therapist must read the divorce decree and determine from the decree who has the right to seek and consent to therapy for the child.

Terminology differs in each jurisdiction. When a child is presented, demand a copy of the latest court decree and any amendments or changes. If the decree is not clear, seek a lawyer's advice to determine its meaning. If the decree is from a different jurisdiction (another state or nation), ask a local lawyer to engage a lawyer in that jurisdiction to educate the therapist regarding the meaning of unfamiliar legal jargon.

- Is funding or insurance available for posttrial therapy for the child, and perhaps for other parties involved? What are the limits?

- Will the parents (or significant others) participate in the child's therapy, if needed?

- Will a child witness be treated fairly or is the child a pawn in a bigger picture, and, if so, will the therapist be informed of the scope of the global machinations?

- Should an attorney ad litem be requested and appointed to protect the child's rights?

- Is the child willing to testify? Does the child know what processes and people are involved—a judge, the lawyers, and the contesting parties?

- Does the child have any idea of the ramifications of the outcome of the case?

- Can the therapist prepare the child for cross examination, and will the attorneys have protective orders in place to reduce the stress on the child?

- Can a possible conflict in loyalties be reconciled by the child?

- Will testifying in court make the child feel guilty? Can this feeling of guilt be handled in therapy, in a manner that serves the best interest of the child?

- Will the child be available, before and after the trial, to role play with parents, the therapist, and/or others?

- Is there an alternative to a court appearance to obtain the testimony of the child: audiotape or videotape; talking to a mental health professional, and having the professional report to the court; submitting written questions to the therapist, who then asks the child the questions in a private setting, with a court reporter present?

- How obsessed are the parents (or significant others) and the lawyer with the testimony of the child and the circumstances that are reported to have occurred? Before, after, and during the trial, are they going to pump the child for information or cajole the child into narrating certain testimony? How many times will the child have to tell the story to different people who may be interested and involved, or may be just plain curious? If the trial turns into a media circus, can the child handle reporters, with or without therapy?

- Will the child's testimony be transcribed and become part of a public record?

- Is the risk to the child as a witness greater than the risk to the parties if the child does not testify?

- If child sexual abuse or some other intimate circumstance is the pre-senting problem, and if the case is lost, will the court return the child to the alleged perpetrator or abuser?

- What will the posttrial reaction be in school, in church, in the neigh-borhood, and in relations with siblings, friends, family or extended family, or other important support groups?

- What will the effect of delay be on the child?

- How can the therapist insure the payment of a bill for services ren-dered if, after all is completed and done correctly, the party who en-gaged the therapist refuses to pay?

Legal Lightbulb

- Children of all ages, if they have the required characteristics set out above, can testify as witnesses.

- A judge determines whether a child is competent to testify. If a court finds a child com-petent, opinions about the information elicited go to weight and credibility.

- In forensic work, conventional wisdom would dictate that one therapist should be en-gaged for trial work and another for ongoing assessment and treatment. A conflict of in-terest might be charged if one therapist performs all tasks.

- Be cautious. Many losing parties blame the therapist, unjustly, for their loss. Some clients will not accept blame or responsibility for their actions. When their expectations concerning testimony or a trial outcome are not met, they may blame someone else—usually, the therapist.

- Judges try to protect children from overaggressive lawyers. Having an attorney ad litem and filing protective orders are often appropriate strategies, especially if the testimony is expected to be very damaging to one party. Cross examination of a child, even when presented gently, can be brutal.

- Preparing a child for court testimony is not the job of an amateur. If the problem arises, the therapist must gain competence by learning, training, education, or experience.

Children as witnesses present unique problems to the therapist, the judge, and the lawyers. Calling a child to be a witness because the child knows some simple fact is naive and unfair. Judges and lawyers ponder children's testimony seriously before deciding whether to call the child, and then whether to admit the testimony.

The mental health professional's duty involves more ponderable alternatives and circumstances, and transcends that of the lawyer, the judge, and the contesting parties. The therapist asks two questions: What will the child say? and What will be the consequences to the child after the testimony is given?

In forensic work, one therapist should be engaged for trial work and another for ongoing assessment and treatment.

19

Expert Witness

Six years ago, Dr. Jones saw a couple for marital therapy. He met with the father, the mother, and, on one occasion, their children. In family therapy, the daughter told Dr. Jones privately that she was apprehensive about her father, but gave no details. Dr. Jones recorded the remark in the file, but the remark was never clarified. Shortly thereafter, the couple stopped seeing Dr. Jones. Dr. Jones documented the file and, in accordance with state law, stored the file for the required maintenance period. Years later, the couple decided to divorce and each sought custody of their daughter. In light of the custody litigation, the daughter's remark, noted in the file, had taken on more meaning. Dr. Jones was served a subpoena duces tecum (his records were required as well as his person) for the custody hearing.

~

Dr. McCann, a therapist for child protective services, visited a child who alluded to child sexual abuse. Dr. McCann met with the child and concluded that no abuse had occurred. He reported his findings to the agent at child protective services. The agent dismissed the case and closed the file. Later, the mother and father were battling over termination of the father's parental rights after allegations of sexual abuse resurfaced. Dr. McCann received a subpoena to testify in court. Will Dr. McCann have to defend his conclusion in light of subsequent allegations of abuse?

The Big Picture

For many mental health professionals, the least attractive aspect of a therapeutic practice is responding to subpoenas or requests (actually, demands) to participate in litigation. A very small percentage of the mental health community makes a living offering forensic evaluation and testimony.

Most therapists get pulled into a lawsuit because they happened to have treated a client who is subsequently involved in litigation: a parent is divorcing a mate and is seeking custody of a child; or a defense attorney is attempting to reduce the damages (emotional distress; posttraumatic stress disorder) claimed by a former client after an accident. In many more scenarios, a therapist may be asked to "donate" time to individual's quest for justice.

Anyone involved in litigation knows it can be a very intrusive, time-consuming, unpleasant, and costly experience. The process can also be extremely intimidating for a mental health professional who ordinarily does not have contact with the legal system. There is no substitute for knowledge, preparation, and experience in alleviating the panic and fright that can set in upon receipt of a subpoena. This chapter provides information that can help reduce the anxiety of first-time recipients, as well as seasoned forensic experts, when an unwanted and unanticipated subpoena is served.

There is no substitute for knowledge, preparation, and experience in alleviating the panic and fright that can set in upon receipt of a subpoena.

Litigation is a stressful process. Lawyers are often stretched too thin to give adequate time and resources to processing a case. Occasionally, lawyers are ill prepared and make bumbling attempts at direct and cross examination. They do not have time to master the techniques and jargon of therapy, yet they must ask intelligible questions and seem knowledgeable. (Lawyers are constantly aware they are grandstanding for their clients—making a lasting impression.) However, most attorneys are bright, conscientious, and concerned about doing a good job for their clients. To match their skills, the mental health practitioner needs to be ready and fully prepared for the task of testifying in court.

Depositions and Courtroom Testimony: Any Differences?

There are generally two forums for offering testimony: an out-of-court deposition or courtroom testimony.

A deposition is a tool used by attorneys to discover any evidence that might be used at trial, or to preserve testimony to be introduced during a trial. Depositions generally take place in the office of one of the attorneys, or the office of the witness being deposed. A witness is sworn in by a court reporter, who records the proceedings and produces a typewritten

A deposition is a tool used by attorneys to discover any evidence that might be used at trial, or to preserve testimony to be introduced during a trial.

transcript for review and signature by the witness. The transcript is then filed with the court. Depositions are often called "fishing expeditions." The attorneys have wide latitude for the types and number of questions that can be asked of the witness. Virtually all questions, no matter how ludicrous, are permissible.

"Discovery," in a civil case, is defined as "the gathering of information that is relevant or likely to lead to relevant information." Thus, unlike courtroom testimony in front of a judge or jury, the witness may be asked to express opinions, speculate, relate hearsay, or reveal rumors.

Most objections, unless they challenge the form of the question (i.e., "Irrelevant," "Hearsay," "Calls for speculation"), are usually waived and not made in a deposition. Lawyers control depositions. There is no judge present and the witness does not have the protection afforded by a knowledgeable judge.

If you feel a question is vague, calls for speculation, or asks for hearsay, qualify your answer in those terms.

If you feel a question is vague, calls for speculation, or asks for hearsay, qualify your answer in those terms. In many respects, a deposition is a feeling-out process by all parties and counsel. Everybody is sizing up everyone else's strengths and weaknesses, and good lawyers will use the information learned in a deposition to their advantage.

Confidentiality is only a word used in a deposition. In view of all its exceptions, the concept has been reduced to the status of myth. Before you even open your mouth to answer a question about a client, you must be sure that an exception to the client's right to confidentiality exists. Prior to a deposition, you should seek the client's written consent to be deposed. If you do not have the client's written consent, or are not sure that an exception to confidentiality exists, do not answer until you see a court order authorizing or ordering you to do so.

Prior to a deposition, you should seek the client's written consent to be deposed.

A court order can be obtained only by filing a motion. Usually, a hearing is held, and then an order is issued by the court and signed by the judge. An attorney must be engaged to process the paperwork.

Do you, as a therapist, have a right to privacy/confidentiality? Unfortunately, in a deposition, your personal and professional background is fair game. One of the purposes of a deposition is to learn about you and to establish or attack your credibility.

Who will be your audience? All parties, as well as their attorneys and the attorneys' assistants, may attend a deposition. If people unrelated to the case are present (e.g., newspaper reporters), insist on a ruling from the court before proceeding. A deposition transcript is part of the official court record—a public record that can be viewed by anyone.

In court, you can assume the world is your audience. In high-profile, media-worthy cases, expect that every public document will be reviewed, and reporters will be camping on your doorstep. Before saying a public word, consult your lawyer.

Helpful Hints for Testifying in Court

1. Tell the truth: You have absolutely nothing to gain by lying. Lying can cost you your job, your license, your reputation, your right to vote (if convicted of perjury), and your freedom.

2. Testify from your own personal knowledge or observation, unless asked otherwise: Testify about what you know, and avoid using the word "we" (i.e., "We always do it this way," "We were told to . . . ") This usage tends to confuse jurors and could cause them to disregard your testimony because it sounds as if you are making it up or trying to shift blame.

Testify about what you know, and avoid using the word "we."

3. Listen to the question: Not listening is, without doubt, the biggest mistake witnesses make. Unless you listen carefully to each question, you will fall into verbal traps and give poor testimony. Focus your attention exclusively on the person asking the question, and try to block out your anxiety and other fears. Make sure you fully understand a question before answering it.

4. Answer only the question asked of you; if you do not understand it, ask that the question be rephrased: It is permissible to advise the questioner/attorney that you do not understand the question that is being asked. Ask for an explanation or rephrasing. Clarity is even more critical in a deposition because there is no judge present to rule on objections. You have a duty to be sure that you understand each and every question before you answer. Many lawyers will preface a deposition by stating to the witness that giving an answer to a question implies that the question was understood.

5. If you don't know an answer, say so: After their many years of undergraduate schooling, graduate and perhaps doctoral programs, professional licensing exams and licensing renewal, many mental health professionals have difficulty in saying, *"I don't know."* Trials are all about truth, and if "I don't know" is the truthful answer, it should be given. Your ego may be more severely bruised if you attempt to answer a question when you don't know the answer. Faking, overstating a position, bluffing, and getting caught in defending an indefensible position can be embarrassing and humiliating. Lawyers can ask interminable questions. A witness is not excused from the stand until the judge gives permission, and this usually occurs when the lawyers are finished with all of their questions.

6. Don't exceed your level of competence, experience, or training and qualify your testimony when necessary: If you are not qualified or do not have the experience and training to answer a question or give an opinion, do not offer one. Do not let yourself be badgered and forced into responding, no matter how much ridicule the lawyer directs at you. If you do not have sufficient information, or if there are extraneous or contingent facts or events that could influence your opinion, qualify your answer or opinion. You will be called on to defend every opinion you express.

If you are not qualified or do not have the experience and training to answer a question or give an opinion, do not offer one.

7. Avoid being specific about dates, times, and empirical statistics unless you personally recorded them and are certain they are correct: Use phrases such as "on or about," or "estimated to be" when testifying. Mistakes about dates and numbers invite heavy cross examination. If you are not absolutely positive about a date or time, or empirical data, do not be specific. There is often a long lag time between a deposition and a trial. If you testified in your deposition that a client made a statement to you on March 3, 1995, and two years later, at trial, you testify that the statement was made May 13, 1995, you would certainly be challenged on cross examination. By using the phrase "on or about" each time, a small discrepancy is a lot easier to handle. Never guess; if you are approximating, be sure to say so. Use the phrase "I would estimate. . . . "

8. Be prepared, and never testify without reviewing your records and any prior depositions you have given in the case: Sometimes, the only favorable evidence an attorney has is the inadequacy or inconsistency of records or reports in the files that were furnished to him by potential witnesses or that were buried deep in a client file. If you are unable to recall details of your own records or your prior testimony, you will make a terrible impression on the judge or jury. Look over your records very carefully;

Look over your records very carefully; if necessary, memorize them.

if necessary, memorize them. If you are aligned with an attorney in the case, ask him or her to review your records with you beforehand. Look for problem areas, weaknesses, inconsistencies, and points of direct and cross examination.

Ask the attorney whether other documents have been delivered about which you could be asked to comment. Review those documents as well, to avoid surprises.

Be sure to review the transcript of any deposition you have given. You may be asked whether you reviewed any documents, pictures, or files in preparation for the deposition. If you did, the questioning lawyer is entitled to review them and to question you about them.

If you are providing documents as the basis of your testimony, make sure they are marked for the record, and refer to them as "marked exhibits." This designation will prevent confusion later on, when memory of the deposition has faded.

Prepare a chronology of significant dates so that you can testify crisply about when events took place. Prepare an index and table of contents so that, during interrogation, you can find specific notes more easily. The client file should be in a loose-leaf notebook or a securely fastened file. (The only thing more disconcerting than having a witness shuffle pages frantically, looking for a notation in a file, is having the whole file spill on the floor.)

Prepare a chronology of significant dates so that you can testify crisply about when events took place.

Visit a courtroom; observe and sit through a trial. A wise man once said, "The learned are educated by the experience of others; a fool learns only by the fool's own experience."

The Bottom Line

1. Remember the four c's—be cool, calm, courteous, and consistent in your demeanor: The best witnesses are those who respond in the same manner to each attorney asking the questions. The best witnesses and deponents are those who are equally helpful and concerned when questioned by the opposing attorney as when questioned by their own attorney.

Before giving a deposition, ask for the identity of each person in the room. Know which lawyer represents which party in the case. This will help you understand where an attorney may be coming from in framing and directing questions.

A deposition is an opportunity to preview a witness for testimony at trial. Attorneys will probe to see what upsets, angers, or frightens a witness.

An attorney may try to wear you down by prolonging the length of the deposition. Depositions are scheduled to continue from the time they are set to begin until they are finished, excluding holidays, weekends, and non-business hours. An attorney can ask you the same question several times. "Asked and answered" objections are generally waived, and no judge is there to rule against repetition.

Avoid sarcasm and argumentative responses. They will generally only invite tougher and more numerous questions from the attorney and greatly reduce your effectiveness as a witness.

Avoid sarcasm and argumentative responses. They will generally only invite tougher and more numerous questions from the attorney and greatly reduce your effectiveness as a witness.

2. Do not volunteer unnecessary information: Respond with "Yes" or "No" to a question whenever appropriate, and do not expound on your answer unless specifically asked to do so. Volunteering information has been the downfall of many witnesses, especially during cross examination. If you absolutely feel the need to explain your answer, make the explanation brief, thoughtful, and responsive to the question.

Respond with "Yes" or "No" to a question whenever appropriate, and do not expound on your answer unless specifically asked to do so.

In a deposition, there is absolutely no reason to volunteer information. Often, at the end of a deposition, an attorney will ask whether a witness would like to add anything for the record. In trial, this question would be met with an objection ("Calling for a narrative"); in depositions, objections are generally waived and there is no judge. You should respond by advising the attorney that, to the best of your ability at this time, you have answered all the questions propounded to you.

3. If in court, seek help from the judge when needed: If an attorney bombards you with a series of quick questions and you feel you are not being given ample opportunity to consider and respond appropriately to each question, turn to the judge and let him or her know you are having trouble with the questioning.

If you don't understand a question and the attorney is causing you difficulty, advise the judge that you really don't understand the question, and ask whether you still must respond. Most judges will assist you under these circumstances.

4. Rely on your attorney for help in a deposition: During a deposition, breaks may be taken at any time. (In a courtroom, the judge will schedule them.) If you are having difficulty with a line of questioning, plead the necessity of a rest-room break, or the need to respond to a page signal, and then consult with your attorney outside the deposition room. Try to avoid stopping the record merely to consult with your attorney. But if it is unavoidable, it is better to stop the record and discuss the matter with your attorney rather than stumble into a trap.

If your attorney instructs you not to answer a question, do not answer it. If opposing counsel is particularly aggressive, he or she may try to pressure you into responding by saying that if you don't answer, you will be brought before a judge who could not only compel you to answer but could also make you pay attorneys' fees and court costs. It would be appropriate for you to advise the opposing lawyer that any further attempts to get you to respond to the question will be considered unethical interference with your attorney–client relationship, and will be reported to the bar association.

5. Don't assume your attorney knows anything about you or the subject matter of your testimony: Not all attorneys are well prepared or knowledgeable regarding the subject matter at issue. Force your attorney to take the time to visit with you about matters or evidence you would like to be asked about, and what you view to be significant problem areas. You may have to educate your attorney. Remember, you will generally know more about the subject matter in the case than the attorneys will.

In evaluating witness testimony, the law allows certain criteria to be used to weigh credibility. It is helpful for you to know the basis on which you will be reviewed and judged when testifying.

You should understand the general goals of the attorneys in both direct and cross examination, and the legal criteria and goals used by the judge and jury. Knowing and understanding them can better prepare you for offering testimony.

Being prepared—understanding attorneys' goals, and the criteria on which the therapist's testimony will be judged—should be helpful in alleviating anxiety when testifying. Take the time to review the helpful hints in this chapter every time you are subpoenaed. Having your memory refreshed can help to reduce your anxiety.

Legal Lightbulb

Criteria Used by Judge and Jury to Evaluate Witness Testimony

- Conduct, attitude, demeanor, and manner while testifying.
- Ability to recollect, remember, and relate the facts about which the witness is testifying.
- Prior/subsequent consistent or inconsistent statements.
- Consistent or inconsistent testimony, compared with other witnesses' statements.
- Bias, interest, motive not to tell the truth.
- Character or community reputation: honesty and veracity, or dishonesty.
- Admission that the witness did not tell the truth.
- Prior conviction of a felony.

Additional Criteria for Evaluating Experts' Testimony

- Education, training, and experience.
- Truth of the basis of the expert's opinions. Is the foundation for the opinion of the expert witness sound?
- Are opinions supported by sound scientific criteria?

Goals of the Attorney

Direct examination

- To establish the witness's credibility via credentials, objectivity, reliability, and training.
- To discredit the opposing witnesses (or party) by attacking their credentials; lack of objectivity, reliability, and training; and their actions, conditions, and motives.
- To elicit favorable testimony.

Cross examination

- To attack the opposing witnesses' credibility by casting doubt on their credentials, objectivity, reliability, and training.
- To discredit the opposing witnesses' testimony by attacking their actions, conditions, and motives.
- To elicit favorable testimony.
- To show that the expert's opinion is not based on sound scientific criteria.

20

Forensic Evaluation

Kate, a social worker, was appointed by the court to prepare a custody evaluation in a divorce case. At the trial, she offered testimony adverse to the father. As a result, the mother was awarded custody of the two children. The father, unhappy with the outcome of the trial, was upset with Kate. He filed a complaint with the licensing board alleging gross incompetence against Kate. His comments included the fact that his ex-wife suffered from a manic depressive disorder, but no home visits were ever made and his ex-wife's psychiatrist was not consulted. Furthermore, he alleged Kate was biased against him because, in contested divorce proceedings, Kate had just lost custody of her own teenage son to her husband.

~

Eric, a divorced father of a two-year-old girl was convicted of sexual abuse, due in large part to the testimony of Dr. Schmidt. Dr. Schmidt testified that, in his opinion, the girl had been sexually abused. His conclusions were based on two interviews with the child, four interviews with the ex-wife, and one half-hour session with Eric. No psychological testing of Eric was performed. Six months after Eric was sent to the state penitentiary, his ex-wife admitted she contrived the whole case because she was upset that Eric had been having an affair. Upon release from prison, Eric filed a complaint against Dr. Schmidt.

Crucial to the proper administration of justice are mental health forensic experts, who, by virtue of their education, training, and experience, testify and offer to the judge or jury in a lawsuit opinions concerning ultimate issues of fact: mental competency, mental health or condition, best interest of a child, sanity, competency to perform certain acts, capacity to make a will, characteristics of "date rape," or psychological profiles of mass murderers. In any courtroom on any given day, a mental health professional will be assisting in a court case.

Criteria and Guidelines

Mental health practice is as much an art as a science. Many opinions and diagnoses are based on subjective interpretation of (sometimes limited) objective criteria. The education, training, and experience of mental health forensic experts are of vital concern to the courts, the contesting parties, and the attorneys who rely on their opinions, analysis, and testimony.

Each state has established criteria for professionals who are qualified to offer forensic mental health testimony.

Many mental health experts have had problems because they offered forensic opinions even when they lacked sufficient training and experience regarding the issues. Each state has established criteria for professionals who are qualified to offer forensic mental health testimony. In addition, national and state mental health organizations publish guidelines for giving forensic testimony. In Texas (40 Administrative Code, Chapter 725), the minimum qualifications for a person who wishes to conduct a court-ordered social study in a custody case are:

> Licensed or certified in an appropriate professional field, and possess a master's degree from an accredited college and have 2 years of professionally supervised full-time experience that includes evaluating physical, intellectual, social, and psychological functioning and needs and the potential of the social and physical environment (present and/or prospective) to meet those needs; or, at least 10 court-ordered social studies under the supervision of a person meeting the minimum qualifications,
>
> or, Possess a bachelor's degree from an accredited university or college and five years of professionally supervised . . . or at least 20 court-ordered social studies under the supervision of a person meeting the minimum qualifications.

The person conducting the study must meet the following requirements:

- If the investigator has a conflict of interest with any party or if he may be biased by previous knowledge, he must disqualify himself.

- If the investigator needs to discuss substantive issues about a case with an attorney representing a party, he must communicate with all attorneys in the case.

- The investigator must verify, to the extent possible, all statements of fact pertinent to the study. Sources of information and verification must be noted in the report.

- The basis for the investigator's conclusions must be stated in the report. If only one side of the case has been investigated, the investigator must refrain from making a custody determination but may state if the party investigated appears to be suitable for custody.

The Texas statute goes on to require that, unless the court directs otherwise, the social study must be conducted according to the "Guidelines for Court-Conducted Child Custody Evaluation," published by the Association of Family and Conciliation Courts. Many other similar guidelines are published by national mental health associations.

The American Psychological Association, in its *Guidelines for Child Custody Evaluations in Divorce Proceedings* [*American Psychologist, 49,* 677–680 (1994)], requires in part:

- The psychologist gains specialized competence.

- The psychologist is aware of personal and societal biases and engages in nondiscriminatory practice.

- The psychologist avoids multiple relationships.

- The psychologist obtains informed consent from all participants.

- The psychologist informs participants about the limits of confidentiality.

- The psychologist uses multiple methods of data gathering. (Important facts and opinions are documented from at least two sources whenever their reliability is questioned.)

- The psychologist does not give an opinion regarding the psychological functioning of any individual who has not been personally evaluated.

- The psychologist clarifies financial arrangements before commencement of the evaluation.

- The psychologist maintains written records.

Failure to follow such published guidelines can result in suits for professional negligence (malpractice), licensing board complaints, and expulsion from professional associations.

Failure to follow such published guidelines can result in suits for professional negligence (malpractice), licensing board complaints, and expulsion from professional associations.

Suggestions to Consider

A review of the requirements and guidelines embodied in state statutes, or found in association guidelines, bring to light certain basic concepts regarding forensic testimony:

1. Do not give forensic testimony without first acquiring the appropriate knowledge, skill, training, and experience. Just because Dr. X has a PhD in psychology and fifteen years' experience, he is not necessarily qualified to offer forensic testimony in a particular case. If a seasoned therapist who has little experience in evaluating sexual abuse cases stumbles into sexual abuse allegations while involved in a custody evaluation, he or she would be required to defer to another professional who has sufficient experience in that specific area.

It is important to know one's own level of competence and not reach beyond it. Learn the criteria required by your jurisdiction with respect to becoming qualified to testify, and how evaluations are to be conducted. Find out what particular judges want, and how the expert can best serve the court as well as the parties.

The opportunity to earn a fee has clouded the judgment of therapists who, when asked to make an evaluation they really are not competent to render, accept the offer. Know your limits and professional levels of competence in different areas. Can your testimony withstand rigorous cross examination?

2. Do not do an evaluation if there is any possibility of bias, dual relationship, or conflict of interest. We all have biases or prejudices, however slight they may be. The court and the parties deserve as objective an evaluation as possible. Failure to disclose a prior relationship with a party, a personal prejudice, or an experience that could cloud judgment, invites fertile cross examination when uncovered by an attorney or other party; it can be the basis of a complaint for malpractice or disciplinary action. Attorneys will probe for even the slightest hint of bias, prejudice, or conflict, and will usually discover facts that impair clinical objectivity.

3. Do not be the treating therapist and the forensic evaluator. This dual relationship poses a problem. Many therapists have contracts with governmental agencies to perform evaluations and offer treatment to sex offenders or other criminals. The treating therapist should always have the client's best interest in mind, but having to be an objective and impartial evaluator can create conflict. A treating therapist may also be put in the position of breaching confidentiality. The therapist should clarify the relationship with the client and then wear only one hat throughout the professional relationship with that client.

If the therapist chooses to provide treatment and court-ordered evaluations, this dual role should be carefully and clearly disclosed to the client. Informed consent should be given to the therapist. It is imperative to clearly document both the disclosure and the consent. Licensing boards are becoming ever more sensitive to the "informed" part of informed consent.

If the therapist chooses to provide treatment and court-ordered evaluations, this dual role should be carefully and clearly disclosed to the client. Informed consent should be given to the therapist.

4. Do a thorough evaluation and verify important facts and information. Get as much verified information as is required to allow you to render a meaningful opinion. Verify from more than one source the critical facts or information in the case. Do independent investigation. In therapy, a mental health professional can accept a client's view of the universe, but this is definitely not the case with forensic evaluations. Do not accept at face value all the information provided by participants. If you are unable to satisfactorily verify important facts, state so in your report. A major question: If one fact proves to be incorrect, how reliable is the rest of the information?

5. Qualify the report when in doubt, when information is not received or verified, or if a participant was not evaluated. Lawyers and litigants want you to tell the court information and opinions that will advance their side of the case. They may even be paying you with the expectation of favorable testimony. The mental health expert is obligated, however, to be scrupulously honest and must avoid misleading courts and parties with their reports and testimony. It is better to admit a weak area in the evaluation report than to have it forcefully (and often sarcastically) drawn out during cross examination.

6. Keep thorough records of all that transpires during the evaluation process, including all information gathered, a list of all sources, a list of all records used to attempt verification of information, a list of all recommendations and requests made, and a list of all the relevant times and dates of the material. Document as if a complaint was going to be filed against you.

7. No matter what the circumstances, do not be pressured into stating an opinion if you are not qualified and have the backup data to give one.

8. Stay current and well informed concerning developments and changes in the mental health field. What is common and acceptable in one month may be obsolete and not recognized as valid in the next.

9. Clarify any fee arrangements up front, and disclose fee arrangements readily. Lawyers often question an expert witness about his or her fee in lieu of "expertise." State the fee arrangement at the inception of the report, for example:

> I, Dr. Q, was engaged by Party Y to perform an evaluation of the parties and their children and to render an opinion on which parent should be named the primary caretaker of the children. The fee agreed upon was $125.00 per hour with a $2,500.00 retainer fee paid in advance. . . .

Consult with judges and lawyers in your jurisdiction regarding expectations of forensic mental health experts and testimony in their courts.

10. Consult with judges and lawyers in your jurisdiction, regarding expectations of forensic mental health experts and testimony in their courts. Knowing what is expected can help you do a better job of evaluating and rendering your opinions.

Nothing can absolutely eliminate the unsavory experience of vigorous cross examination by an attorney for the party against whom you have rendered an unfavorable opinion. However, by following these suggestions, you can eliminate the possibility of a personally adverse decision being rendered against you in a malpractice case or in a licensing board investigation.

21

Involuntary Commitment

A psychologist, Dr. Anthony, had seen a patient, Justin, in therapy for six months. The patient had been diagnosed several years earlier as schizophrenic, and was living alone. Justin was also seeing a psychiatrist, Dr. Barnett, who monitored his medication.

When it became apparent that Justin was not taking his medication, Dr. Anthony consulted with Dr. Barnett about the symptoms he was observing. Justin was hearing voices again and was threatening to "blow away" the voices as soon as he identified where they were coming from and whom they belonged to. Drs. Anthony and Barnett agreed that inpatient care was required to stabilize Justin. Dr. Anthony signed an affidavit and submitted a mental health warrant to the County Mental Health Department so a 48-hour commitment order could be entered by the Probate Court.

Justin was subsequently taken into custody by the county sheriff and transported to County Hospital for observation and evaluation. He was released after 48 hours; the County Hospital psychiatric staff determined that Justin was not a danger to himself or others. Justin filed a licensing board complaint and a lawsuit alleging wrongful diagnosis by Dr. Anthony and false imprisonment.

∼

A family applied to the probate court for an involuntary commitment order for their daughter, Jennifer. Jennifer's psychiatrist recommended admission to a local facility where she had staff privileges. The court issued a commitment order confining Jennifer to the recommended hospital. While hospitalized, Jennifer was sexually abused by two attendants. Unknown to the family, the hospital had been investigated twice by state authorities within the past year. Complaints by prior patients or their families cited sexual abuse and neglect. The investigations were closed when the families and the patients allegedly refused to cooperate. Jennifer's psychiatrist had been aware of the allegations but assumed, when the investigation was closed, that the complaints were meritless. Does Jennifer's psychiatrist have anything to worry about?

~

Susan, a licensed professional counselor, provided postdivorce therapy. One of Susan's patients, June, a divorced mother with one daughter, was having a difficult time dealing with her divorce. She was depressed and occasionally mentioned the difficulties of raising a child alone. She said she wished that her daughter would just disappear so that she would be spared the pain of child rearing. June met with Susan irregularly; she canceled appointments at the last minute, or forgot about them entirely. One day, Susan received a phone call from June's sister. She described to Susan her concerns about June, who was exuding strange behavior patterns; she felt that June's behavior was so extreme that June's daughter might need some protection. Susan offered her services to facilitate an inpatient admission at an excellent facility. After a few more calls to discuss inpatient admission, June's sister stopped calling. No action was taken to admit June to a mental health facility. A few weeks later, Susan picked up a newspaper and read that June had stabbed her daughter to death and then had killed herself.

The problems presented by an involuntary admission of an angry, unstable, or borderline patient can create havoc for a mental health professional's peace of mind. A therapist could face a "damned if you do and damned if you don't" situation. A balancing of risks must take place. One could correctly assume that the damages that could be awarded in a suit for improper diagnosis and a brief involuntary admission would be far less than the damages assessed for inaction, no admission or police investigation, and then a resulting suicide or homicide.

Every state has an involuntary commitment law that details the steps and criteria to be followed and applied before a person can be involuntarily admitted for inpatient mental health care.

Legal Mandates and Safeguards

Every state has an involuntary commitment law that details the steps and criteria to be followed and applied before a person can be involuntarily admitted for inpatient mental health care. Most require a legal finding of "imminent physical danger to self or others" before a court can deprive a person of his or her liberty and order confinement to a mental health facility. (One must keep in mind that no crime has been committed, and deprivation of liberty is usually associated with criminal acts and criminal law.) State statutes stagger the length of confinement for an initial evaluation period from 24 to 76 hours. Lengthier commitment terms apply, upon appropriate legal, medical, and/or psychiatric findings.

Consumer activism in all parts of the country has resulted in tremendous changes in the law regarding commitment for mental illness. The federal government has mandated that each state must establish a protection and advocacy system for mentally ill persons, to safeguard against abuses. Many states specifically set out by statute the rights of an inpatient when committed (involuntarily or voluntarily) to a mental health facility. Usually, a finding of "danger to self or others," by itself, will not constitute a finding of mental incompetency. The patient must be consulted on all aspects of his or her diagnosis and treatment, and an informed consent must be obtained. Until a guardian or conservator is appointed by a court, the therapist must provide services only with the consent of the patient or by court order directing the treatment.

Patients' Rights

The patient, until adjudged by the appropriate court to be mentally incompetent to manage his or her own affairs and personal health, retains all constitutional and civil rights, including the right to sue. A person who is confined to a mental hospital but has not been declared incompetent can bring a suit for habeas corpus and obtain release. Of even greater concern, the person can sue his or her "captors" (mental health professionals) for negligence and false imprisonment.

A person who is confined to a mental hospital but has not been declared incompetent can bring a suit for habeas corpus and obtain release. Of even greater concern, the person can sue for negligence and false imprisonment.

Specific state statutes often set out a precise list of additional rights a person has while an inpatient at a mental health facility. These specific rights may include:

- Right to receive visitors.

- Right to communicate with a person outside the facility.

- Right to communicate by uncensored and sealed mail with legal counsel, courts, or the state attorney general.

- Right to be notified, upon admission, of the existence, purpose, address, and telephone number of the protection and advocacy system for mentally ill persons, as required by federal law.

- Right to appropriate treatment for the mental illness, in the least restrictive setting that is available and appropriate.

- Right to obtain an independent medical or psychiatric examination or evaluation.

- Right to an individualized treatment plan and to participation in developing the plan.

- Right to humane treatment and reasonable protection from harm.

- Right not to receive unnecessary or excessive medication.

- Right to be informed of these rights upon admission. (In some states, communication in a language understood by the patient is required.)

With the nationwide concern for patients' rights and protection from abuse, the deck seems to be stacked against the mental health professional. Compared to even a decade ago, it is much more difficult to involuntarily commit mentally ill persons and keep them in an inpatient facility. What can a therapist do when a client does not clearly present an imminent physical danger to self or another party, but is knowingly or unwittingly not taking necessary medication or following treatment recommendations? What can a therapist do when a client refuses to stay in treatment or counseling when, in the therapist's opinion, it is badly needed?

In most instances, all the therapist can do is provide the client, or significant third parties, with warnings as permitted by law. The therapist can also give the client, in writing, treatment recommendations and potential resources. The client's file should clearly document, with date and time of day, all information provided directly to the client or sent to the client's authorized mailing address. Certified mail is not always recommended, since a client may refuse a certified letter while regular mail is delivered. Until legislation is passed that will allow for court-ordered outpatient treatment for a mentally ill person before the person or another party is in imminent physical danger, not much else can be done.

Clinical Records as Documentation

Before seeking or supporting an involuntary commitment, a therapist must be sure the clinical record reflects findings consistent with the state's burden of proof for involuntary commitment. If, as in most states, the standard applied by the court is the "imminent physical danger test," the file should reflect adequate evidence to support the therapist's conclusion that someone (a third party) is in imminent physical danger from the client, or that the client is personally in imminent physical danger. If in doubt, consult often with colleagues using de-identified information about all observations and concerns. Document all consultations and the advice or conclusions received from colleagues. Colleagues need not identify the client, only the problem.

Contact a lawyer and become familiar with commitment procedures and law in your jurisdiction. Learn what the burden of proof will be and what findings a court must make before ordering commitment. Create a record that leaves no doubt about the reasonableness of your conclusion, and proves the imminent physical danger existed. Consider whether your clinical record will hold up in court, and under close scrutiny by other experts.

If the client has authorized you to contact family members, recommend, to each person contacted, that involuntary commitment proceedings be pursued. (Do not initiate this action yourself.) Provide the family with information on how to secure a commitment order. An angry client is less likely to sue a family member than a therapist.

Before contacting family members, however, urge the client to voluntarily commit to inpatient care. You can then either arrange the admission or provide the client with written information regarding the steps to take for admission. Document your concerns and your recommendations to the client.

The duty to warn issue is discussed in Chapter 22; but the issue to consider here is whether it is enough to warn as permitted by law. Does a therapist have a further obligation to seek involuntary commitment when inpatient care is indicated? To date, statutory and case law does not impose on the therapist the duty to seek involuntary commitment of a client. However, a therapist does have the duty to advise the client of all treatment that the therapist believes is needed. If the therapist cannot provide the type or quality of care needed, an appropriate referral must be made. Beyond recommending inpatient care and quality sources and resources, no further action is required of the mental health professional at this time.

To date, statutory and case laws do not impose on the therapist the duty to seek involuntary commitment of a client.

Clients Who Live Alone

A client who lives alone, without family or friends who can be identified, poses a unique concern for the therapist. The person may present a situation in which, after balancing the risk and reward, a therapist chooses to initiate and secure a mental health commitment order for the client. This action may be taken even though the therapist recognizes there is no legal duty to do more than provide mandated warnings or recommendations as to needed care and sources of care and other resources. As with other challenges in professional mental health practice, a thoroughly documented file can help reduce and manage risk. At a minimum, it provides some comforting backup when taking on a duty one is currently not obligated to assume.

Negligent referral to another therapist or to a treatment facility can be the basis of a lawsuit and the award of damages.

If a therapist plans to recommend a treatment facility, or to secure commitment of a client to a particular facility, the therapist is obligated to have that facility thoroughly checked out and to know the quality of mental health treatment available. Not only must the facility be of high quality, but it must also be able to serve this specific patient adequately. Negligent referral to another therapist or to a treatment facility can be the basis of a lawsuit and the award of damages. Know your referral sources. Do some detailed homework. Call the state board, or appropriate state agencies, and inquire about complaints and the licensing status of the facility. Document the calls. Consult with colleagues—and again, document all findings.

Among the many risks presented to a mental health professional, some can and must be faced, and others are pitfalls that can be stumbled into. Risks are unavoidable, but foresight, defensive practice, and good record keeping can steer you away from the pitfalls. This is true in every area of your mental health practice, not just in your decisions on commitment.

Legal Lightbulb

- All states have legislatively advanced the protection and rights of mentally ill persons, and protection and advocacy systems are in place.

- Contact a lawyer, and learn about the commitment process and laws in your jurisdiction. Know where the burden of proof rests, and what findings a court must make before ordering commitment.

- As a first effort, try to get the client to self-commit to inpatient care.

- If the contact is authorized by the client, involve family members and urge them to pursue involuntary commitment.

- Document all your recommendations, findings, and observations. When seeking or assisting in involuntary commitment, your clinical record should leave no doubt as to the reasonableness of your conclusion that the client, or another person, is in *imminent physical danger.*

- Consult early and often with colleagues if you are unsure about a client's condition or about what action you should take. Document each consultation. The right to consult with colleagues should be in the initial intake form.

- Keep a current list of referral sources, individual mental health professionals, and reputable mental health facilities. Contact licensing boards, state agencies, and colleagues, and document your inquiries and findings. Recommend only excellent-quality care providers.

- Make sure every person or entity to whom you make a referral has adequate, current, and appropriate mental health liability (malpractice) insurance.

- As of early 1998, you have no legal duty to directly seek commitment of a client. However, there may be a duty to warn in your jurisdiction. There also may be a duty to refer a client to the best available source of care if you cannot provide it. Check your local statutes regarding commitment.

- If circumstances and conscience compel you to directly seek involuntary commitment of a client, do so only if you are sure it is absolutely necessary to protect the client or another party. Get competent legal and professional mental health advice before seeking involuntary commitment.

22

Threats of Violence

Mark, a junior varsity star athlete, was scheduled to meet with his school counselor to discuss possible college opportunities. But instead of discussing college options, Mark was enraged by a minor confrontation he had had with his general manager at McDonald's the previous day. He was absolutely furious with her and told his counselor he was going to "blow her away." The general manager, who had already dismissed the confrontation from her mind, did not know of Mark's anger and was unaware of any possible danger.

~

Beth, in the midst of a hotly and bitterly contested divorce, met with her therapist frequently and displayed inordinate and inappropriate anger toward her lawyer. In each session, she became irate over what she considered her lawyer's incompetence and lack of understanding. She complained, with ever increasing hostility, that her lawyer might cause her to lose her children in the ongoing custody fight. In one conversation with her therapist, Beth was so agitated and angry, she blurted she would do "something" to her lawyer if she did not gain custody. Her lawyer, aware of the tension but not realizing the depth of Beth's hostility toward him, continued representation in the case, with no change of approach or strategy.

~

What should the counselor and the therapist do—notify the general manager and the lawyer? Should the lawyer and the general manager dismiss the verbal threats as part of the normal risk of their job, or take serious precautions?

Determining whether an upset person is potentially dangerous is a clinical quagmire, and what to do about it is a complex dilemma that presents a real challenge in the area of clinical judgment. Unfortunately, there is no clear-cut method for evaluating verbal threats, but there are guidelines.

A serious threat is not to be taken lightly, nor is it to be shrugged off as benign, without complete documentation explaining why the threat has been discounted. Correct treatment for a client who is belligerent, or who threatens violence, is not the aim of this chapter. The purpose here is to encourage every mental health professional to take even the slightest threat seriously.

As a precaution, check your local statute. Some statutes (and related case law) indicate that a therapist can warn an identifiable intended victim. Other statutes (and case law) indicate that the therapist *may* call only police or medical authorities. In some states, laws are not definitive and the legal future of the duty to warn is yet to be determined. Local statutes (and case law) are supplemented by rules of licensing boards, which often contain conflicting requirements, rights, and duties when a client or identifiable potential victim is threatened (i.e., there is danger to self or others). Typically, the rules state that the therapist shall use "reasonable steps and procedures" to prevent harm.

A serious threat is not to be taken lightly, nor is it to be shrugged off as benign, without complete documentation explaining why the threat has been discounted.

Duty to Warn

The duty to warn potential victims of a possible attack or homicide so they can take steps to protect themselves, or the duty to warn family members that a client has threatened suicide remains one of the developing areas of law and varies from state to state. Here are some conflicting examples from different jurisdictions:

1. There is an affirmative duty to warn an identifiable potential victim of a plausible homicide.

2. There is no duty to notify anyone. Therapy is not such a science that the danger to self or others is so clear-cut as to impose a duty on the therapist to recognize potential homicide or suicide and then to warn the victim (homicide) or the family (suicide).

3. A professional **may** disclose confidential information only to medical or law enforcement personnel, if the professional determines that there is a probability of imminent physical injury by the client to the client or to others, or that there is a probability of immediate mental or emotional injury to the client.

4. Where the therapist feels the client presents a danger to self or others, the therapist shall take "reasonable steps" to prevent the anticipated harm. (This is the wording in the guidelines of most ethical canons.)

Some state statutes imply that because a therapist can rarely determine, with a reasonable degree of certainty, whether a client is a danger to self or others, there is no duty to warn family, friends, or potential victims. What-ever is done must be documented thoroughly, to protect the therapist.

When danger to self or others becomes part of the therapeutic facts, a warning signal should appear. Doing nothing is not acceptable; it is actu-ally acting by inaction. The therapist must make an immediate investiga-tion to determine the best course of action. Several sources of information should be contacted:

1. A lawyer.

2. The malpractice insurance carrier. Give notice of a potential homi-cide or suicide and ask for information concerning the problem. (An insurer would rather prevent a lawsuit than defend one, even successfully).

3. The licensing board. Ask whether a knowledgeable person on staff, or a competent staff attorney, is available to share information. Some boards are very helpful and offer the latest law, the current board rules, and suggestions regarding the best solution to the problem. Other boards just bounce the problem back to the therapist. They declare the problem "legal in nature" and say a lawyer must be consulted.

4. A colleague who is knowledgeable in therapeutic ethics, or a profes-sor who teaches such a course at a local university.

Wording on the Intake Form

Many states require the therapist to notify each client concerning the limits of confidentiality. These limits apply if the state requires the therapist to warn potential victims of harm or to notify families in the event of a potential suicide.

Review your intake and consent form before any incident happens. Most confidentiality statutes provide that the client can waive confidentiality in writing. Many states require the therapist to notify each client con-cerning the limits of confidentiality. These limits apply if the state re-quires the therapist to warn potential victims of harm or to notify families in the event of a potential suicide. On the intake form, the client should authorize the therapist in advance to breach confidentiality if there is a reasonable danger to self or others, and if there is a possible way to protect the life of the client or some other person who is assumed to be in danger. The therapist customarily uses the same form when releasing any information to a third party.

The therapist has some protection if, on the intake and consent form, there is a specific, written waiver of confidentiality when the client or another person is in danger. A defensive intake form will provide that if, in the therapist's opinion, the client presents an imminent danger to self or others, the therapist may breach confidentiality by notifying persons who, in the therapist's opinion, might be in a position to prevent the harm. Confidential information is only released when the client waives the right to privacy in writing. The therapist is then permitted to share information with third parties.

A waiver contained in the intake and consent form, which is signed when therapy commences, does not allow the therapist to share information inappropriately, but it does grant permission to breach confidentiality when danger to self or others is a reasonable therapeutic possibility, and then only on a "need to know" basis.

The therapist has some protection if, on the intake and consent form, there is a specific, written waiver of confidentiality when the client or another person is in danger.

The Homicide or Suicide Scenario

Kathy had been visiting a therapist for about six months. Accurate records were maintained for each session, in accordance with the legal and ethical guidelines of the profession. They were completed and up to date. Suddenly, Kathy committed suicide. Her family demanded all the records and, as part of the litigation, desired a deposition by the therapist, complete with a subpoena duces tecum (in person, with all the case records).

A subpoena, in these circumstances, is the nightmare of every therapist. Review the potential allegations that might be filed in the complaint or the petition for damages. Each of these as yet unproven allegations is filed in court papers, made a part of the public record, and accessible to reporters, the licensing board, or any curious citizen. Charges might include:

- Deficient or negligent diagnosis, assessment, or evaluation.
- Deficient or negligent treatment, history or file review, or prognosis.
- Negligent deviation from accepted standards.
- Failure to formulate a comprehensive and interdisciplinary treatment plan.
- Failure to have the client undergo a physical examination.

- Failure or inappropriate reluctance to refer for further treatment or for psychotropic medication.

The above allegations will be made, with some modification, in most malpractice suits when a suicide or homicide has occurred and a therapist is named as a defendant. Therapists, armed with the knowledge of what can go wrong, have the opportunity to protect against the problem by documenting, during therapy, that none of the allegations is true. These are the recommended practices, in dealing with every client:

- Thoroughly document every diagnosis, assessment, or evaluation.

- Document the reason for a treatment; review the file often, and change the prognosis (when indicated) by updating your evaluations and assessments.

- If a past therapeutic history is available, review it. Insights regarding the client may have been uncovered and recorded by previous therapists.

- When deviating from accepted or common standards, document, as substantiation for the deviation, the recommendation of a learned minority or of some legitimate mental health authority, to depart from common treatment modalities.

- Consult with other professionals, and document the consultations. Other therapists, rehabilitation counselors, lawyers, physicians, and other specialists can be very helpful.

- Adopt the sensible procedure of requesting that the client take a full physical exam, to rule out physical illnesses that can be treated with medication, or the need for a prosthesis such as a hearing aid.

Homicide or Suicide: The Aftermath

At the first inkling of the suicide of a client, or at the first notice that a client has hurt another person (or self), or has killed someone, the therapist should call his or her malpractice insurance carrier.

At the first inkling of the suicide of a client, or at the first notice that a client has hurt another person (or self), or has killed someone, the therapist should call his or her malpractice insurance carrier. Every therapist in private or public practice has some exposure to a malpractice suit, and the best self-protection is a substantial malpractice policy, which can be obtained privately or through a national organization at reasonable cost. Malpractice insurance carriers have risk management experts who can guide a therapist through the steps suitable for self-protection. Keep in mind that each policy contains directions in the event an actual or perceived loss occurs, and, to remain protected under the policy, the terms of the policy must be scrupulously honored.

This is also the time to consult with a private attorney who is knowledgeable in mental health law. Generally, the interests of the malpractice insurance carrier and the therapist are identical, but, in some cases, especially if the claim exceeds a policy's limits, their interests may conflict. Collect all the client records and make copies for the lawyer, the insurance carrier, and, perhaps, a learned colleague. Review the paperwork and all client documentation. Should there be litigation, the clinical record will be the first item reviewed. Study the record, make any corrections in the appropriate manner (see Chapter 3), and be sure the file is ready for review by third parties, if necessary.

Advisable Actions

1. Make sure clinical notes and records are current and reflect recognition of all presenting problems via a diagnosis, a treatment plan, and a prognosis.

2. Make a referral when a problem exceeds your level of competence. Recommend a physical exam where warranted, and note the recommendation in the record. Coordinate with other health care providers as an interdisciplinary team. Note when a client fails or refuses to follow your suggestions, and quote the reason the client gives for such failure or refusal. Has the client assumed a risk of any damage by failing or refusing to follow legitimate suggestions such as attending certain classes, obtaining a physical exam, or other recommended helpful actions?

3. Indicate in the records that the facts and notes support the treatment plan and are not recorded for insurance reimbursement purposes.

4. Follow all protocols where an agency, entity, organization, or school has published procedures concerning the danger to self or others. Document your compliance.

5. Consult with a colleague(s) whenever a suicide or homicide is a possibility. Make sure no preventive stone is left unturned.

6. If a suicide or homicide occurs, consult at once with your malpractice insurance carrier. Say and do nothing unless the insurer advises you

In the intake and consent form, have a waiver of confidentiality in the event of a threat of harm to self or others.

to do so. A slip at this time might waive the protection offered by the insurance policy.

7. Take every threat of suicide seriously, even if it is constant and repetitious. If possible and authorized, involve family members. In the intake and consent form, have a waiver of confidentiality in the event of a threat of harm to self or others.

8. Establish office protocols for suicide or violence prevention.

When danger to self or others is a possibility, notify the police if permitted in your jurisdiction. Calls to 911 are recorded, providing good evidence that a preventive call was made. A report on the call must be entered in the clinical record.

Should the problem of homicide or suicide arise, review the latest state mental health code and the latest ethical canons of your licensing board. Notify your malpractice insurance carrier and your lawyer. Homicide and suicide are serious and tragic events, and input from all sources is critical to a sensible assessment of the problem and future decision making.

There is no definitive legal yardstick indicating exactly when a therapist has a duty to warn of potential homicide or suicide.

An angry client who makes threatening remarks should be taken seriously at all times. The client may mean it. Although the duty to warn statute varies from state to state, the risk of having a possible suicidal or homicidal client is significant enough to take the necessary precautions. Violent threats of homicide or suicide expose the therapist to many issues, including malpractice, ethical complaints, pecuniary damages, public scrutiny, and/or queries of competency.

The guidelines in this chapter will be helpful when the unthinkable occurs. A therapist can't look for a rule of thumb or a set of procedures to be followed in all cases, but case-by-case awareness will minimize risk.

Legal Lightbulb

- States have statutes or ethical canons or case precedents that control the duty to warn intended victims of danger, or to warn others about a client's own safety. Check the current state requirements each time there is a potential problem.

- There is no definitive legal yardstick indicating exactly when a therapist has a duty to warn of potential homicide or suicide.

- Whether the therapist elects to warn or to not warn, clinical notes should document the rationale for the decision.

- A threat to commit violence in the future is not always an indication that violence will occur.

- Every graduate therapist knows the *Tarasoff* case,* a California decision with duty to warn implications. Is *Tarasoff* the law in your jurisdiction? Fifty independent determinations have to be made—one in each state—and even then, nothing will be really known until the first state supreme court case is decided in each jurisdiction. There is no federal case.

- Call the state chapter of your professional organization. Most national organizations have taken a stand on the duty to warn situation, but the positions change occasionally. Get a current reading.

- Ethical canons and guidelines, as well as published materials, are admissible evidence to show the minimum standards of conduct required by therapists' duty to warn.

- In almost every homicide or suicide case, a lawyer is consulted to determine therapeutic liability.

- Take threats seriously. If you hear of a client homicide or suicide, take immediate steps toward damage control.

- Document every potentially harmful comment and how it was handled.

*Tarasoff v. Regents of The University of California, 551 P. Td. 334 (Cal. 1976).

SECTION SIX

PRACTICE MODELS

23

Groups

The prospects for the average mental health practitioner in today's competitive and cost containment environment are threefold:

1. Continue in solo practice with a shrinking client base.

2. Become a contract panel provider and accept increasingly reduced fees for services.

3. Become entrepreneurial by enlisting the support of a group of other like-minded professionals and becoming a "Group without Walls."

Too often, solo practitioners settle for an expense-sharing or office-sharing arrangement. They share office space, employees, supplies, billing, and scheduling. They may even share publicity, public speaking engagements, advertising, stationery, business cards, and other common expenses. Such arrangements have always been attractive for key reasons—the ability to maintain individual practices, reduce overhead, and gain vacation and emergency coverage and cross referrals of clients and patients.

The principal disadvantages in today's mental health care market are the inability to contract independently for group managed care, and the potential for joint liability if clients perceive the "suitemates" as partners. In addition the members may face antitrust issues if they implement a common fee structure.

Group without Walls

An attractive and increasingly popular way to eliminate these disadvantages is by formalizing a Group without Walls—a single legal entity, usually a professional corporation (PC), in which participants share a common license; for example, all members are licensed professional counselors (LPCs). If the group consists of a mix of LPCs, social workers, and psychologists, a general business corporation or partnership can be established. This model differs from a preferred provider organization (PPO), which is usually established by a single investor corporation or group of corporations rather than a group of individual practitioners.

When a group creates a legal entity, each member may continue to maintain his or her own individual practice at a different location.

When a group creates a legal entity, each member may continue to maintain his or her own individual practice at a different location. By combining specialties and offering a broad range of services of multiple providers at different locations, the group is more attractive to employers, hospitals, health maintenance organizations (HMOs), insurers, and payers. Operating as a single entity, the members will clearly be in a better position to negotiate financially rewarding managed care contracts.

The legal entity created by the group acts as a centralized vehicle for contracting, billing, purchasing, scheduling, marketing, and quality assurance. The entity will be responsible for developing the practice standards, quality controls, and outcome studies that are critical when applying for managed care contracts.

The greater the degree of integration, the lower the potential for antitrust violations.

However, the concept of multiple independently operated offices raises price-fixing issues. It is crucial to retain the services of an attorney and an accountant who have experience with issues faced by the health professions to avoid potential antitrust and federal regulation violations and typical management issues. The group must resolve compensation issues, conflicts between participants, the potential for inefficiency, and the loss of economies of scale due to multiple locations. Generally, the greater the degree of integration, the lower the potential for antitrust violations.

Alternative Group Arrangements

Some groups have preferred complete integration, with all sites owned and operated by the group and all revenues and expenses flowing through the common legal entity. Others, preferring partial integration, have followed the independent practice association (IPA) model, in which participants maintain independent practices and compete against each other for all non-IPA business. The group shares the risk associated with (1) the managed care contracts negotiated by the IPA and (2) the individual participants who have entered into provider agreements with the

IPA. A complete set of bylaws for an IPA is reproduced in Appendix A, on page 233.)

Partially integrated groups are generally not as efficient as fully integrated entities; the expense sharing is not as complete, and they face antitrust issues. They can negotiate capitated rates and fees-for-service rates with the payer, but cannot maintain a common fee schedule for discounted fee-for-service work among the participants. In theory, the IPA must negotiate the fee that will be paid to each provider for services to enrollees under the managed care contract. The IPA profits when providers are paid less than the amount the IPA will receive from the payer. Providers in independent practices are prohibited from establishing a common fee schedule. This practice, called *price fixing*, is illegal.

Providers in independent practices are prohibited from establishing a common fee schedule. This practice, called price fixing, is illegal.

Pros and Cons

Before deciding on whether to participate in a group or a Group without Walls, a practitioner should answer these questions:

- Who are the other participants? Can I trust them? Are they competent and ethical practitioners? Can we work together?

- What are my objectives? Do they align with those of the other participants?

- Does the group as a whole have enough management experience and business acumen to successfully operate the entity and negotiate favorable contracts?

- Do I want to completely integrate my practice with the group, or do I want to maintain an independent practice and share only clients, revenues, and losses flowing from the managed care contracts the group negotiates?

- Am I willing to devote, each week, the extra hours necessary to the successful operation of the group entity? (Often, individual practitioners lose sight of the time necessary to manage, control, and operate a group. Meetings can drive some practitioners "nuts.")

- What is the condition of my practice? Am I comfortable with my income and workload, and should I risk capital and independence for participation in a group entity?

- How far can I peek into the future of the "business" of providing mental health services?

- Will the group be able to raise enough capital for start-up? Prudent capitalization requires sufficient capital to meet costs for the first two, or perhaps three, years.

- Am I prepared to share management and decision-making authority?

- Am I willing to abide by decisions made by others when they affect my income and my future?

The Professional Corporation

After a group has decided to establish a legal entity to promote managed care contracting, the participants must select the most effective type of entity to form. (Subsequent chapters in this section describe the various entities.) As previously stated, the most common entity is the professional or general business corporation. Once the articles of incorporation have been approved by the state and the corporation's charter is issued (both steps are the responsibility of the corporate attorney), careful thought must be given to day-to-day management and operation of the entity. This phase begins with the drafting and adoption of the corporation's bylaws—the rules by which the corporation must operate.

A common method of operation uses an executive committee, of which all participants are members. Regular meetings are usually scheduled. They may be more frequent during the initial start-up period and become less frequent as the entity becomes established. Contracts can be reviewed, adopted, rejected, or modified at these meetings. Duties can be delegated and offices rotated.

Credentialing should be a process in which all participants are involved. The bylaws can provide for the establishment of a credentialing committee, of which all participants are members.

The company bylaws are the most critical document prepared during an entity's formation. They should be reviewed carefully and must be clearly understood by all participants in the group. Considerable time and money can be saved if the participants review and consider the bylaws prior to visiting with an agreed-on attorney. If each issue has to be discussed and decided with an attorney present, the hourly charges will be very high. The final draft of all legal instruments must be prepared by an

attorney, who will coordinate business, legal, and professional requirements into the final legal vehicle.

Many groups flounder under the weight of disputes over (1) unexpected
or higher than anticipated costs and expenses, and (2) real or perceived
inequitable workload distribution. It might be prudent for the entity to
consider leasing equipment for greater flexibility and cost savings, in
light of the fast pace at which technology is advancing. Outsourcing
such needed tasks as marketing and utilization review could also lead to
time savings, flexibility, and long-run cost savings.

Internal conflicts can usually be avoided by thoughtful communication
and planning. An inherent risk in any group activity, however, is an unpleasant association with people who prove to be problematic for reasons
of temperament, character, and ability. The entity will only be as strong or
as successful as the people behind it, so choose fellow participants well. At
a minimum, check references, community reputations, and professional

Legal Lightbulb

- To be a player in the game for managed care contracts, group formation is necessary.

- Improperly established groups can lead to liability for negligence, faulty contracts, and antitrust and regulatory violations.

- The group will only be as strong and as successful as the people who comprise the group.

- Competent legal advice should be obtained by each participant prior to formation, and by the group upon formation.

- The articles of incorporation, bylaws, contracts (leases, purchase documents, debt in-struments), and other documents are all legally enforceable instruments. They are to be drafted by a professional, but not signed without careful review and detailed explana-tion as needed.

- The sample bylaws in Appendix A are only a sample and are not to be copied or used verbatim. They will be most helpful if used as an agenda for discussion prior to consult-ing with the lawyer who will draft the final documents.

histories. Then check to determine whether there is malpractice insurance in force and no pending complaints before the licensing board.

Choose advisors well also. As with any legal entity, it is imperative to obtain competent legal advice on structuring and operating the company and on statutory and regulatory issues. Given the right participants and the right structure, there can be greater success in numbers and participants than one might achieve as a solo practitioner. One thing is certain: Negotiating a managed care contract with a health plan or an employer is almost an impossibility for a solo practitioner.

24

Partnerships

Kevin and Don, two marginally successful mental health professionals practicing in the same building, decided to combine their practices and talents and form a partnership. They agreed to co-sign a lease for new space in the same building where they had maintained their individual practices for several years. They agreed to share all profits and losses fifty–fifty, and they even created a new name: "The Healing Behavioral Health Center." However, they never got around to putting together a written partnership agreement. Twelve months later, in the midst of an afternoon of bickering over teaching income, vacation time, and disproportionate revenue generation, Kevin was served with a citation in connection with a lawsuit filed against him by an unhappy client with whom he had had an inappropriate sexual relationship. Don was stunned. He immediately went to his lawyer and asked if it was too late to back out of a verbally agreed on partnership. Or was he also liable?

For decades, a partnership has been the most common and preferred business entity for two or more professionals. There is presumed safety in numbers, and it is comforting to have someone with whom one can share risks and losses, and who can cover a practice when an illness occurs or a well-deserved vacation takes place.

When properly conceived, drafted with the appropriate and necessary detail, signed, and implemented, the traditional partnership is a sensible and useful legal entity. When improperly conceived and structured, a partnership can be fraught with peril.

A Handshake Is Enough

A partnership is a basic legal entity that simply requires an agreement, which can be expressed or implied, between two or more persons, to carry on a business for profit. It does not require a formal, written partnership agreement. Two professionals, by their conduct and course of

A partnership is a basic legal entity that simply requires an agreement, which can be expressed or implied, between two or more persons, to carry on a business for profit. It does not require a formal, written partnership agreement.

Partnerships have fewer legal requirements for their operation and management than corporations do.

dealing, can create a partnership by implication. Many partnerships and individual business ventures began with a handshake and still are in existence today.

Once a partnership is established, each partner has a fiduciary duty to the partnership and has the right to use partnership property for conducting partnership business. Unless specifically negated in a partnership agreement, each partner has an equal right to participate in the management of the partnership, including the hiring, firing, and supervising of employees and staff.

The attraction of a partnership entity has always been the simplicity of its creation and operation. Partnerships have fewer legal requirements for their operation and management than corporations. There are usually no state filing fees for general partnerships. They have unlimited flexibility, and partners are free to structure compensation, management, ownership, operations, dissolution, and responsibilities any way they wish.

Partnerships, like a sole proprietorship, result in only one level of taxation. All income and expenses flow through the partnership to individual partners in accordance with the percentages established in their partnership agreement. For federal tax filing, each partner would receive a K-1 form from the partnership, reflecting his or her share of partnership income and expenses. Partnerships are generally not subject to state franchise taxes.

Disadvantages

As with any entity, there are disadvantages to partnerships, as Don found out when he finally sought legal advice regarding his partnership with Kevin. Partnerships feature shared responsibility and authority, and, unless limited by the partnership agreement, each partner has an equal voice in the management of and liability for the partnership.

In a general partnership, each partner has joint and several liability for the obligations of the partnership and for each partner's malpractice, as well as for negligent acts of agents, servants, employees, and staff members. When Kevin was sued for inappropriate acts with a client, Don could be held personally liable, as Kevin's partner. By registering the partnership as a limited liability partnership under appropriate state law, Don could have avoided personal liability for the negligent acts of the other partner (Kevin) or of representatives of the partnership, unless he was directly involved in the activity or had notice of the wrongful activity at the time of the occurrence.

In one case, an intern was under the supervision of a licensed therapist. The intern, unknown to the supervisor, had carried on an inappropriate sexual relationship with two clients. The supervisor's clinical notes did not reflect that the subject of sexual relationships was ever discussed, although the intern did pass an offhand remark that each of his clients was very "sexy" and he had fantasized about them at different times.

The supervisor was disciplined by the licensing board and liable in a malpractice suit. Had the supervisor been a partner, and had the partner acted as the intern did, there would have been "partnership liability" and partnership responsibility.

Limited Liability Partnerships

Generally, states will allow partnerships to register as limited liability partnerships by filing an application with the Secretary of State. A partnership will be required to carry a minimum amount of liability insurance or provide minimum funds designated and segregated for the satisfaction of judgments against the partnership. Because these insurance or fund requirements are generally much lower than policy limits on the average malpractice insurance policy carried by mental health professionals, they are not a prohibitive financial burden when securing limited liability registration. A partnership will also be required to include the phrase "registered limited liability partnership" or the initials "LLP" in the partnership name.

States will allow partnerships to register as limited liability partnerships by filing an application with the Secretary of State.

Partnership laws vary from state to state. A therapist contemplating a partnership entity should seek competent legal advice well before any agreement is reached or action is taken.

Many diverse factors need to be weighed carefully before entering a partnership agreement, but, with careful consideration and good legal advice, a partnership agreement can be crafted to eliminate most problems before they occur. A brainstorming session to discuss possible areas of conflict is always helpful. Remember, never enter into a partnership agreement that is not well thought out, reduced to writing, reviewed by a lawyer and an accountant, and signed by each partner.

Legal Lightbulb

Considerations for a Partnership Arrangement

1. **Liability:** Limit liability by registering as a limited liability partnership.

2. **The number of partners:** Having just two partners almost always guarantees deadlock when a genuine disagreement occurs. Two competent individuals can reasonably disagree with each other, but some disputes can be profound (i.e., each can feel deeply about his or her point of view).

3. **Ownership percentages:** When deciding income and expense allocations, what income shall be considered partnership income as opposed to separate income of each partner (book royalties, honoraria, lecture fees, teaching income)?

4. **Partnership management:** Should the partners alternate such titles and terms as "managing partner"? What issues should be submitted for majority vote of the partners? All? Should the agreement provide for "alternative dispute resolution" methods such as arbitration, mediation, conciliation, and negotiation? Under whose auspices? How often, or seldom, should meetings be held?

5. **Operational expenses:** Should a partner's right to obligate the partnership for operational expenses be limited? Should any expense in excess of $150 require approval of a majority of partners? If there is a monetary limit, what should the limit be?

6. **Maintenance of client files and records:** How should the files be maintained, distributed, destroyed, or preserved when a partner withdraws from the partnership or if the partnership is dissolved by law, consent, death, or termination? Who is allowed access to the files and records? (Each partnership requires a comprehensive plan for disposition of a file if either the therapist or the client dies.)

7. **Office hours:** How much time should each partner be expected to devote to the partnership?

8. **Vacation days:** How many vacation and sick days should each partner be allowed?

9. **Insurance policies:** How much insurance (life, major medical, income disability, malpractice, personal property) should the partnership carry for the partnership and for each partner?

Legal Lightbulb

(continued)

10. **Signature authorization:** Should all partners have signatory authority on bank accounts or should more than one signature be required for checks or withdrawals? Who should sign contracts with managed care or insurance companies; sign as lessors of equipment; distributors of tests; purveyors of personal property; or subcontractors?

11. **Storage of records:** Where will financial records of the partnership be maintained, and what financial records will the partnership generate? Who will retain the CPA, lawyer, banker, insurance adviser, or other service providers, if appropriate?

12. **Background check of partners:** Learn who your partners are. Call the licensing board and inquire about complaints or disciplinary actions. Require each potential partner to submit a credit report for review by the other potential partners. Consider mandating instant termination for any partner whose malpractice insurance is terminated or denied.

13. **Legal counsel:** Secure your own independent legal adviser. Conflicting views and interests may exist among partners, and one lawyer cannot appropriately advise and represent each partner when conflicts arise.

14. **Financial losses:** If there are financial losses, can each partner pay a fair share? For example, suppose a partner dies or the partnership terminates and the partnership has outstanding obligations such as leases, purchase agreements, or long- and short-term debt. Should each partner place a sum in escrow to ensure the fulfillment of partnership financial obligations?

15. **Debt:** Can any partner guarantee the debt of any third party for any reason? Or is this a prohibited act?

16. **Termination:** Detail the procedures for terminating the partnership for any reason.

An example of an application for registration of a limited liability partnership is shown here. The format in your jurisdiction will vary. Familiarize yourself with the basic content, and then bring your comparable data to a competent attorney for review, preparation, and filing.

An example of a complete partnership agreement appears as Appendix B, on page 251.

Sample Form

APPLICATION FOR LIMITED LIABILITY PARTNERSHIP

The following named partnership applies to become a registered limited liability partnership pursuant to the Texas Uniform Partnership Act.

1. The name of the partnership is 3P Wellness Center, LLP.

2. The federal tax identification number of the partnership is 98–123568.

3. The street address of the principal office of the partnership in Texas is 4635 Main Street, Richardson, Texas 75064.

4. The number of partners in the partnership at the time the application is submitted is three.

5. The partnership engages in the following type of business: mental health counseling.

6. The undersigned partner has been authorized by a majority in interest of the partners in the partnership to execute this application.

    Signed this 30th day of February, 20__

3P Wellness Center, LLP

By: _____

James Hathaway, Managing Partner and Attorney-in-Fact, authorized to execute this application for a majority in interest of the partners

25

Solo Practitioner: Incorporate or Not?

Henry James, PhD, a newly licensed psychologist, moved to a small community in order to enter private practice. He expected referrals from two local physicians and the local school district. In the central business area, he located a small commercial building that was available for lease and was perfect for his needs. He anticipated hiring a part-time clerical person to help with billing, correspondence, filing, and scheduling. His brother-in-law, an in-house accountant for a small manufacturing company, advised him to incorporate right away. Should he?

The vast majority of mental health practitioners in private practice are solo practitioners who operate their practices as sole proprietorships. Operating out of one or more leased offices, a solo practitioner enjoys complete autonomy and is responsible for all decision making. The success of the practice rises and falls on his or her talents and efforts. Having a small support staff often allows for improved cohesiveness, loyalty, and congeniality in the workplace. The solo practitioner has absolute personal responsibility for compliance with all local, state, and federal regulatory requirements, as well as for his or her own acts, negligent or otherwise, and those of the support staff.

Advantages of a Solo Practice

- Complete autonomy; perfect for the self-reliant, independent practitioner.

- Flexibility regarding hours, working conditions, operational practices, services, and so on.

- Easy to start; can be owed and operated with no formal or burdensome structure.

- Single layer of taxation; all income and expenses reported on Schedule C of the federal income tax form.

- Responsible only to the licensing board, to national, state, and local organizations, and to persons with whom a contract exists.

- Minimal or no start-up legal fees.

Disadvantages of a Solo Practice

- **Personal liability:** All of the practitioner's assets, personal or practice-related, are at risk for negligent or wrongful acts of the practitioner and staff members, and are subject to both general and professional liability claims.

- **Complete financial responsibility:** No one else shares in the risk and losses, or covers during downtime for illness or vacations.

- **Limited financial and professional resources:** All capital and income are dependent on one person.

- **Limited professional support:** The workweek has longer hours, especially at night and on weekends, and the practitioner is "on call" all the time.

- **Limited staff support:** A small number of employees must fill a variety of roles.

- **Divided duties:** The practitioner handles business and management responsibilities as well as the practice of mental health. The *business* of a practice is as important as the *practice* of a practice.

- **Reduced competitiveness:** There is little possibility of securing managed care contracts.

- **Limited cost sharing:** No scale economies for library, common waiting room, receptionist if needed, stationery, and networking.

A serious drawback to the sole practitioner model is the risk of personal liability for negligent or wrongful acts and contracts. Many mental health practitioners incorporate to protect themselves from malpractice claims. A common, but false, belief is that if a practitioner incorporates a practice and later is sued for malpractice, his or her personal assets will be protected from a successful litigant's reach.

Comparison with a Corporation

A corporation will *not* shield a practitioner and his or her personal assets from a claim of personal negligence. A professional person is always personally liable for his or her own acts of negligence. If Doctor James negligently breaches a client's right to confidentiality and is sued, it does not matter whether he is an employee of a corporation that he may or may not own, or whether he is associated with a corporation. He will be sued in his individual professional capacity and, if found to be negligent, will be individually liable for the damages assessed. His personal assets would then be at risk to satisfy the court judgment.

A corporation will not shield a practitioner and his or her personal assets from a claim of personal negligence.

A corporation can shield a practitioner from liability for the negligent or wrongful acts of other employees of the corporation only if the mental health professional is free from personal negligence or wrongdoing. If a staff worker's negligent acts were committed in the course and scope of his or her employment, then the corporate employer and the staff worker would be named as defendants in the lawsuit. When a small office is the defendant, however, it is unrealistic to think that the plaintiff's attorney will not assert a theory of negligence (i.e., failure to properly supervise) in an attempt to impose personal liability on the shareholder professional.

Dr. James was notified that his regular part-time office helper was involved in a motor vehicle accident and would be out for six weeks. Desperate for assistance, Dr. James called a local temporary-employment agency. The agency sent Shirley to Dr. James, but she arrived forty-five minutes late. Dr. James had a full schedule that day, and had little time to acquaint Shirley with office procedures. Later in the day, Shirley took a break to use the rest room, and left a client's file on the counter. While she was away from the front desk, a client's husband came in unannounced to discuss with Dr. James his concerns over his wife's depression. He noticed that the file on the counter was his wife's file. She had had an appointment earlier in the day with Dr. James. When she left, Dr. James gave Shirley the file and instructed her to put it in the file cabinet in the adjoining room and lock the cabinet. The husband opened the file and read several pages of notes before Shirley returned. The notes revealed that the wife had had a two-year affair with a coworker. The affair had ended a while back, but the wife was depressed and guilty over the episode. The husband confronted the wife and filed for divorce.

In the event a lawsuit is filed, Dr. James would face accusations of negligent supervision and training of Shirley regarding confidentiality, because he did not personally ensure that the file would be secured from prying eyes. Even if Dr. James had incorporated his practice, that fact would not shield him from personal liability. His corporate and personal assets would be at risk. Professionals are always responsible for their own professional negligence.

By incorporating, a therapist could create the possibility of contracting for services, space, loans, and other practice needs in the corporate name. When a legal instrument is signed, for example, "Dr. Henry James, President, ABC Behavioral Health Center, Inc.," a corporate obligation is created, as opposed to a personal obligation. If the practice is unable to generate enough revenue to make loan or lease payments, the lender and landlord could only sue the corporation. The personal assets of Dr. James could not be garnished or attached ("subject to reach") by the creditors. Should the corporation default on a debt, such default would not become part of Dr. James' personal credit history.

As a practical matter, most landlords and lenders will require personal guarantees from the principal shareholders in a corporation. If the business falters and money is owed, they can then look to the guarantors, as well as the business and its assets, to recover funds due. If possible, it would be wise to contract only as "President [or other title] of _____ Corporation."

Advantages of Incorporating

If a corporation makes a profit after all expenses, including salaries, are paid, it must pay corporate income tax.

There are certain tax advantages to incorporating, but, in recent years, these advantages have been tremendously diminished. In theory, a corporation establishes multiple layers of taxation. Both the corporation and the individual employees are subject to federal income taxes. If a corporation makes a profit after all expenses, including salaries, are paid, it must pay corporate income tax. Employees pay taxes on the salaries paid to them. After corporate taxes are paid, some portion of any excess profit may be distributed as dividends to shareholders, who must pay federal income tax on the dividends. By electing Subchapter S status, however, a corporation can avoid the multiple tax layer problem. All income will flow out, and only the recipients will be taxed. To elect Subchapter S status, the shareholders—and their spouses—must file IRS Form 2553. There are eligibility restrictions, so competent legal tax advice should be sought.

The cost of incorporating a practice may run from five hundred to several thousand dollars, depending on the state of incorporation. Over the course of a career, these incorporating expenses may be trivial, but they are often very significant to a practitioner who is just starting out. Incorporation costs include legal fees, minute book, incorporation fees, and state franchise taxes.

Faced with the cost of establishing a corporation, the lack of a shield for one's own personal acts of negligence, and the multiple tax layers, why would a practitioner choose to incorporate? Three reasons are often cited:

1. Limited liability (a shield from employees' negligence and corporate debts) is better than total liability.

2. A corporation has continuity of life; it will survive the death, incompetency, retirement, withdrawal, termination, or resignation of any officer or employee because it is a separate legal entity.

3. The transfer or issuance of stock makes it easier to transfer ownership or to allow others to participate in ownership.

When a solo practitioner dies, so does his or her practice. It is much easier to pass on a practice that is incorporated; the corporation itself owns the assets, including the location, telephone number, and goodwill (reputation). The heirs of the shareholder/practitioner who passes away can negotiate to sell the practice in one neat package: they sell all their inherited stock in the corporation.

If an incorporated practitioner wants to bring in a partner, it is not necessary to establish a new legal entity. Only one event would have to occur: The issuance of additional shares of stock to the "partner," now a shareholder. Special kinds of corporations can be created in each state, but most states allow for "like kind" licensed professionals to incorporate under professional association or professional corporation statutes. These statutes allow people who hold the same professional license to

The corporate shield can prevent personal liability if another therapist is sued and you have had no contact with the suing client (plaintiff, complainant, or petitioner) and no responsibility for training or supervising the guilty or liable therapist.

establish a corporation in which ownership will always be limited to holders of that same professional license. These special corporate vehicles are not available for integrated mental health group practices, where practitioners hold different licenses and are involved in different mental health disciplines.

In any arrangement to practice with other professionals, it is critical to limit liability for another professional's negligence through incorporation or another limited liability vehicle (i.e., Limited Liability Professional Partnership, or Limited Liability Company). The corporate shield can prevent personal liability if another therapist is sued and you have had no contact with the suing client (plaintiff, complainant, or petitioner) and no responsibility for training or supervising the guilty or liable therapist.

Disadvantages of Incorporating

- **Possibility of ownership restrictions:** For licensed professionals' corporations, Subchapter S status requires thirty-five or fewer shareholders for special tax treatment.

- **Possibility of corporate and dividend taxation:** Unless Subchapter S status is secured, multiple layers of taxation can occur and the sale or dissolution of the corporation can trigger capital gains tax liability.

- **Corporate formalities:** Board/shareholder meetings, payment of annual state franchise taxes, maintaining the corporate minute book are only some of the protocols that must be observed.

For most individuals who will practice alone, with limited or no support staff, incorporation does not make much sense. If continuing the life of the practice, or attracting additional ownership or capital, or fulfilling some compelling state tax requirement is not a relevant consideration, the additional cost of establishing and maintaining a corporation, and the additional burden of observing corporate formalities would convince a sole practitioner to remain unincorporated. If any of these reasons do exist, or if a group practice is anticipated, incorporation certainly should be considered, but only after careful consideration of advice from legal and financial advisers, usually including an accountant, a banker, an insurance representative, and, if possible a financial planner.

Legal Lightbulb

- There is no shield from liability for one's own personal acts of negligence or misconduct, but a corporation can shield you from the negligence and malpractice of others.

- Having employees or other professionals in the practice usually is sufficient reason to incorporate.

- Corporations have continuity of life. If you wish to pass on your life's work, or sell out and live comfortably in retirement, incorporating makes sense.

- Corporations can result in multiple layers of taxation (without Subchapter S election).

- Incorporating allows for the possibility of entering into contracts in a corporate, as opposed to a personal, capacity, creating corporate, rather than personal, liability.

- Incorporating requires start-up money for attorney fees, state incorporation fees, and first-year state franchise taxes.

- Incorporating requires adherence to corporate formalities—meetings, maintenance of a minute book, payment of annual franchise taxes.

- Secure competent legal and financial advice before deciding to incorporate in your jurisdiction.

Examples of articles of incorporation for a professional corporation and a general corporation are presented in Appendixes C and D, respectively (pages 256 and 260). Because incorporation statutes and requirements vary from state to state, these models from the authors' home state should not be used without competent legal advice from an attorney in your jurisdiction. They serve as an agenda for discussion and consideration during the decision-making process.

SECTION SEVEN

HOW TO AVOID
MALPRACTICE CHARGES

26

Acts of Commission

Dr. Smith, a psychologist, primarily worked with couples in therapy. One particular couple, thankful for Dr. Smith's help and inspiration in therapy, wanted to create a foundation focusing on widowhood and remarriage. They approached Dr. Smith and asked if he would be the clinical director, as well as business manager and chief operating officer, of this foundation. Can Dr. Smith take this job?

~

Susan, a social worker employed by a church foundation in Los Angeles, helped a child of a minister and his wife, in play therapy. After a year, therapy concluded satisfactorily, and Susan had no more contact with the family. One day, Susan unexpectedly met the minister again. He was now divorced, and he invited Susan to visit, and perhaps join, his congregation. Later, Susan began taking lessons from the minister, in an effort to integrate social work with religious values. Gradually, their relationship became closer. One evening, they were kissing and were seen by a friend of the minister's former wife, who reported the incident to Susan's agency. Is Susan's conduct a violation of professional boundaries?

~

Seven years ago, John, a professional counselor in private practice, terminated therapy with a client, Samantha, by mutual agreement. John did not see or hear from Samantha for years afterward. He had relocated from San Francisco and was practicing in Massachusetts. Samantha also had relocated to Massachusetts and happened to discover that John was practicing in the area. She called to make an appointment for therapy. When she came for her appointment, both decided they would rather date than become involved professionally as patient and therapist. John referred her to another therapist, and they began dating. Can John date Samantha?

What Is a Malpractice Action?

A malpractice action is a civil action that seeks money damages. A civil action is distinguished from a criminal action, where conviction results in a fine or a jail sentence, and from an ethical violation, where the therapist's license is jeopardized.

In a malpractice action, the plaintiff is usually a client and the defendant is the therapist. The suit is filed in the civil justice system and the decision, if won by the plaintiff, results in money damages. The money damages are paid by the defendant therapist, or the therapist's malpractice insurance company, to the plaintiff.

Most therapists have malpractice insurance. Most insurance carriers will provide the therapist with a defense attorney; make experts available; pay damages if assessed by the judge or jury; pay for a transcript of the trial if needed; appeal if necessary, and pay the premium on an appeal bond; and settle, and pay the settlement costs if appropriate. (For the limits and benefits of your malpractice insurance, read your policy carefully.)

Elements of Malpractice

To recover damages in any malpractice action, the client/plaintiff must prove four historical elements:

1. The therapist owed the client a *duty to conform to a particular standard of conduct* (i.e., what a reasonable therapist would have done under the same or similar circumstances).

2. The therapist was derelict because the therapist *breached the said duty* by some act of commission or omission.

3. Because of the dereliction or negligence, the *client/patient suffered actual damage*.

4. The *therapist's conduct was the direct or proximate cause* of the damage.

A breach of duty forms the basis of malpractice suits. The therapist must keep duty, standard of care, and negligence in mind at all times.

A breach of duty forms the basis of malpractice suits. The therapist must keep duty, standard of care, and negligence in mind at all times. In determining the appropriate standard of care, there is a "battle of the experts." Each side calls expert witnesses to testify, and each side, in testimony, offers an opinion concerning the appropriate standard of conduct. The jury then renders a verdict. Some prohibited acts are such obvious violations of the standard of care that experts may not have to be called. Among these prohibited acts are: having sexual relations with a client, and marrying a client.

The next section warns of fourteen situations to avoid. In each situation, the therapist is likely to be sued and must settle out of court or face losing at trial. In some situations, a plaintiff/client will elect not to pursue a case to conclusion and will either drop the charges or refer the matter to the licensing board for further action. The consequences for the therapist can be severe and might affect his or her entire professional career and family life. When *any* of these occurrences arises, beware! In our consumer-oriented society, even the appearance of impropriety can give rise to a lawsuit.

Activities to Be Avoided

1. Entering into a dual relationship of any type with a client: A relationship, as defined here, might include serving on a committee together; going to each other's homes for school, church, or political functions; attending cultural events; or any other activity wherein the client–therapist boundary might be made fuzzy. When in doubt, avoid the circumstance. Become a master of aversion.

In small communities, some contact with clients is hard to avoid, and there have been few cases when a simple "Howdy" in a supermarket has led to litigation. However, an effusive public hug, or having coffee or lunch together can cause, in the mind of the client, an impression that the therapeutic connection is now one of friendship. And that creates a dual relationship.

Historically, dual relationship situations start off very innocently. Soon, they are hard to control or terminate. Better to stop the possibility before it begins.

2. Blurring the boundaries between therapist and client: Therapists hear many of a client's intimate thoughts. Socially, a therapist can share intimacies with friends, colleagues, and business associates, but not clients. The roles of the therapist and client are clear and well defined. There is a boundary between the two, and the boundary is obvious and apparent at the moment therapy begins. As time and therapy proceed,

Informality, if misconstrued by the client, can have serious consequences.

the tendency is to become more casual and informal. Be careful. Informality, if misconstrued by the client, can have serious consequences.

3. Doing business with a client: There might be a time when it seems appropriate to sell or buy something—a used car, for example. Can you sell to or buy from a client? Doing business of any type is frowned on. Possibilities include buying or selling merchandise; using the client as a broker; having the child of a client mow the lawn or baby-sit; hiring the client as a secretary, typist, bookkeeper, public relations person, business manager, accountant, auto mechanic, plumber, lawyer, physician, and so on. Business opportunities may arise in the therapeutic relationship on occasion. Such activities are off limits to therapists.

Dr. Helen Mitchell visited with Bob and Susan in marital therapy. After about one year, the couple terminated therapy and obtained a divorce. Susan received custody of their child. Following termination, Bob, who was in the television production business and had been impressed with Dr. Mitchell, approached her about producing a one-hour tape describing her particular type of therapy. He would put up the financial investment, and she would invest her expertise. She was flattered, and the project began. It failed. Bob would have been happier if the tapes had sold and there had been a profit to be divided, but he was willing to accept the business loss.

Susan, two years later, was a law student at a state university and wished to receive more child support. When investigating her former husband, she was appalled to discover that, one year after therapy ended, he had gone into business with her therapist and had formed a corporation that she assumed (incorrectly) had made money. She was even more furious when, as a result of another court action, she discovered that there would be no increase in child support because her former husband made less money than before and had suffered a substantial business loss. Susan was poorer by almost $200 in court costs and $1,500 in attorneys' fees. Where could she vent her anger? She complained to the licensing board.

Dr. Mitchell spent some $3,000 for lawyers' fees to represent her, but she won the case before the licensing board and retained her license. She received only an educational letter as an admonishment.

What had started as a simple business venture became an ethical nightmare with malpractice implications. In addition, Dr. Mitchell has to explain the whole event every year, when she renews her malpractice insurance, and again when she requested inclusion on a managed care list of preferred providers.

4. Establishing a friendship with a client, or accepting the client's invitations to family or social events: Clients often want to show friendship or express appreciation to their therapist by inviting him or her to weddings, graduations, confirmations, bar mitzvahs, engagement parties, anniversaries, or other family events. The therapist, prior to the beginning of therapy, should set the boundaries and indicate to a prospective client that the connection between client and therapist precludes social contacts. If such a discussion takes place during intake, the client will not be insulted when there is a refusal.

5. Marrying a former client: After therapy ends, many clients and therapists date, court, get engaged, and ultimately marry. *This outcome is to be avoided.* In one state, the quarterly newsletter published by the licensing board contained the names of three therapists who were former residents of that state, all of whom had lost their licenses after marrying their former clients. And who filed the complaints? Either the former spouse of the client or the former spouse of the therapist. Marrying does not legitimate an inappropriate client–therapist relationship.

6. Accepting substantial gifts: A small gift of a few dollars' value, presented for the end-of-year holidays, *may* be acceptable. A huge or expensive gift is clearly not acceptable; it could easily cause the therapist to lose clinical objectivity. Children in play therapy are often anxious to please and will give drawings, decorated boxes, and small objects to the therapist. The authors are unaware of any cases wherein a child's gift led to legal action of any type, so such a token is presumed acceptable. But be aware. Small gifts of antiques and heirlooms have a tendency to increase in value. If a conflict arises between the client and the therapist, a question of exploitation may develop.

7. Trading or exchanging for services: Therapists must work for cash and be paid for their services in accordance with their customary, and perhaps published, schedule. Again, the problem is one of potential exploitation.

Dr. Franklin was an amateur musician who practiced therapy as a profession and piano as a hobby. His client, Julie, owned a beautiful, old, out-of-tune piano that she never played. She was moving and wanted to get rid of it because it took up too much space. She offered it to Dr. Franklin in exchange for twenty-five therapy sessions, estimating that the piano and the professional fee would be of about equal value.

The therapist, prior to the beginning of therapy, should set the boundaries and indicate to a prospective client that the connection between client and therapist precludes social contacts.

Dr. Franklin accepted the offer and had the piano tuned, resurfaced, and refurbished at his expense. At the end of twenty-five sessions, Julie continued to require individual therapy but had no money. She, with her lawyer, stated that Dr. Franklin had initiated the "trade" and had exploited her. She had the piano appraised. In its refurbished condition, it was worth much more than twenty-five sessions.

Was this exploitation? Not really. Was the trade a prohibited act? Yes. Trading items of value for services is to be avoided.

8. Making a misdiagnosis or exceeding one's level of competence: Therapists are not expected to be correct all the time. They are expected to use usual therapeutic standards in making each diagnosis, and to be able to back up the diagnosis with legitimate documentation. When a diagnosis is questionable, therapists should refer or consult rather than make a decision that might, in hindsight, be inappropriate. The best manner to reconcile differences is to consult with a colleague (or several colleagues), and to document the result of the consultation and how the consultants responded to the case. If a case is too difficult to handle or exceeds the competence of a treating therapist, making a referral to another competent professional is better than failing to recognize the limits of one's own level of competence.

When a diagnosis is questionable, therapists should refer or consult rather than make a decision that might, in hindsight, be inappropriate.

9. Accepting illegal or unethical remunerations: Such payments are violations of both the law and the ethical canons. A therapist cannot be paid a fee for referring clients to another therapist. Decisions to refer are founded on the best interest of the client, without any thought of remuneration for the referral. "Kickbacks" are inappropriate. It is possible to sell a practice, and the files in a practice, but only after permission is first obtained from the clients involved. Cross referrals are acceptable if they are in the best interest of the client. Clients can be referred when a therapist retires.

A therapist cannot be paid a fee for referring clients to another therapist.

10. Failing to make arrangements that accommodate the death of a client or a therapist: Death does not end responsibility. The therapist must make provisions, in his or her estate plan, for the disposition of client files in the event of the therapist's death. The intake form should state that, in the event of the death of the therapist, (1) another therapist of similar competence can take possession of a file and continue therapy if the client wishes, or (2) the client has a right to request a copy of his or her file to take to another therapist. The executor, although technically the successor to the deceased therapist, should not be privy to the contents of clients' files, especially if the successor is not a trained professional specializing in mental health.

The estate of the therapist owns the file, but the client or the client's executor is entitled to a copy at reasonable cost. However, in the event of the death of a client, the surviving therapist would be wise to petition a court for a ruling concerning the release of a client file to an executor or administrator, stressing the possibility that the client might not have wanted the file to lose its confidentiality. A court order will indicate whether the file is to be copied or delivered.

Upon the death of a therapist, the estate of the therapist owns the file but the client or the client's executor is entitled to a copy.

When a therapist's death is unexpected, the task for a colleague who volunteers or has been designated to resolve paperwork, insurance forms, closure of the practice, and so on, can be a nightmare. With some foresight and advance protection against chaos following an untimely death, the task can be less difficult. The death of the therapist or the client is always a possibility, and it should be acknowledged in the intake form and the therapist's estate plan.

11. Having sex with a client: Sex with a client is prohibited. Sex with a former client may violate the canons of ethics, depending on the time interval between the date of the last client contact and the date a social relationship begins. In general, **sex with a former client is a bad idea,** as is hugging, touching, sexy conversations, or dialogue concerning sexual topics that are not appropriate for a particular client's treatment plan. Remember: "Once a client, always a client."

12. Having sex with a client's relative: Therapists will be led into temptation in many situations. For example, children will be brought to therapy by single, eligible parents who find the therapist attractive. A therapist who knows a lot about a client's spouse might meet that spouse in a social circumstance after therapy has terminated—and after a divorce has been granted to the couple. Pastoral counselors often deal with families who have attractive relatives. School counselors often have consultations with children who are delivered to the counseling session by aunts, uncles, or cousins who are single and eligible. The list could go on and on. Relationships with any relatives of a client are to be avoided. In some case verdicts, therapists have been disciplined or sued for some social contact. To avoid being a test case, avoid having sex with individuals related to the client.

13. Revealing a client's identity in published works: When writing books, journal articles, mass media presentations, or lectures, use examples that present no potential breaches of confidentiality. If a real case is the basis of an example, change the sex, name, location, age, religion, and any other identifying data, of any persons described in the printed text. In a book such as this one, all the names and parts of all circumstances are fictitious, but if a client's situation can be easily identified and damage befalls the client, the client has a right to be upset. Confidentiality includes being identified. It is more than just a name.

When an article or any other source is published, no one connected with the real person should be able to identify the circumstances and connect the person and the event described.

When an article or any other source is published, no one connected with the real person should be able to identify the circumstances and connect the person and the event described. If the person described can identify himself or herself and chooses to tell everyone, the therapist is not at fault.

14. Revealing any private record: Carefully maintain the security of records. Each current file, whether in a manila folder or on a computer disk, must be maintained secure within a total security system. File drawers must be locked. Files stored in cardboard containers must be in a secure space, under lock and key. Computer access codes should require

Legal Lightbulb

- There are traditional areas in which therapists have been sued for malpractice. This chapter has listed some of the principal circumstances in which a vulnerable therapist has been held liable.

- Even if a therapist wins a case, the fallout is awesome because of the effects on subsequent malpractice policies, accountability to the licensing board, hospital privileges, and explanations to friends and professional colleagues or to managed care company panels.

- Litigation is public and open. Anyone can read the verdict and all the documents filed in a malpractice case.

- Malpractice premiums often rise when a case is filed. Sometimes, future professional liability policies are denied by the insurer.

- If damages exceed the policy limits, the therapist is personally responsible for the overage.

unique knowledge. Wherever there is a file, there is a confidentiality issue. The client is entitled to the security that every entry in a client file deserves. It is up to the professional to establish a protective system.

There is no way to practice a profession and be free from all possible risk. Some circumstances have proved to be riskier than others. Readers should seriously consider the list of prohibited activities and avoid them at all cost. A risk-free practice is not possible; however, with some caution and conservative responses, most risks can be minimized, and some can be eliminated.

27

Acts of Omission

Dr. Goshen, a successful therapist in private practice, had treated patients for nearly thirty years and was well respected and admired. Dr. Goshen had treated a relatively new client, Patrick, for five sessions. One day, when Patrick appeared for an appointment, he smelled of alcohol and had slurred speech. Dr. Goshen tried to continue with the session anyway. They talked for a while, but Dr. Goshen finally acknowledged that the session was fruitless. He asked Patrick to make another appointment. Patrick left, got into his car, and hit another car just as he left the parking lot. He seriously injured himself and the passenger in the other vehicle. Is Dr. Goshen liable? Should Dr. Goshen have made a referral to AA, or called in another therapist to consult immediately, while Patrick was in the office? Should he have detained Patrick until a ride home could be arranged? Should he have ordered black coffee or engaged a hotel room where Patrick could sober up? What would have been good practice?

The previous chapter defined malpractice and the elements that have to be alleged and proved in a malpractice action. The chapter also pointed out activities that, if carried out by a mental health professional, would or could be considered malpractice. Those were acts of *commission*, for which a therapist might be vulnerable or liable. However, malpractice also includes acts of *omission*; if a therapist *fails to take action*, he or she may also be liable. How might a therapist be obligated to offer a certain treatment plan, and then, by failing to act, be liable or vulnerable? What acts of omission can lead to a malpractice suit?

Activities to Be Pursued

1. Entering into a client–therapist contract, upon intake or during the initial interview, that protects the therapist: Throughout this book are numerous items that should be included in a comprehensive intake, consent, and waiver of rights form. The form should *include, but not be limited to*, provisions for fees and no-show charges; purposes, goals, and techniques of treatment; supervision (if any); exceptions to confidentiality; what to do with the file when the therapist or client dies; permission to refer when needed; names, addresses, and phone numbers of people to contact in the event the client presents a danger to self or others; written permission to call these individuals if the therapist believes it would be clinically helpful to do so; and perhaps a mediation or arbitration clause. (See Chapter 2 for examples.) Review your own intake and consent form. Does it protect you adequately while coordinating with the latest legal and ethical requirements?

Keep in mind that therapeutic modalities change. After a person has been in individual therapy for a while, a family systems approach may be indicated. Obtain a new consent, stating that members of the family will now be included in the therapeutic process, and that the technique and perhaps the goal of the therapy may be changing. Whenever the treatment plan changes from the terms originally consented to, a new form should be signed, or at least the record must reflect that a change was suggested, a discussion took place, and the client consented to the change.

Whenever the treatment plan changes from the terms originally consented to, a new form should be signed.

2. Making a referral, or at least seeking a consultation, when a problem exceeds the therapist's qualifications and experience: Few therapists can handle all problems of all clients. Situations arise wherein the learning, training, education, or experience of the therapist is not adequate to help the client cope with presenting problems. It is then appropriate to **refer** or **consult** with another therapist regarding the diagnosis, treatment plan, or psychological mix. Can this therapist treat this client? Is the treatment comfortable for both the client and the therapist?

The only time the question of referral is truly put to the test is when a complaint is filed with a licensing board, or a suit is threatened. Then the question arises: Should the therapist have made a referral or consulted with another therapist who has more expertise in the field? It is a question each therapist must ask himself or herself. When the therapist is not qualified or does not have enough experience to treat a problem, it is better to make a referral or bring in a consultant than to keep the client and hope for the best. Terminate treatment and refer or consult with someone more qualified, whenever there is any feeling of discomfort. Each therapist must establish his or her own guidelines.

When the therapist is not qualified or does not have enough experience to treat a problem, it is better to make a referral or bring in a consultant than to keep the client and hope for the best.

3. Using psychological tests when needed: Many therapists use the available psychological tests on a routine basis; others use them sparingly or not at all. When they are helpful, tests or all the tools of the trade should be utilized. When the client refuses or cannot afford the test, or when managed care will not permit testing, this fact should be noted in the file. Informed consent would dictate that available and appropriate tests be disclosed and discussed. Whether they are used or not, the reason for the choice made should be noted in the file. Testing is a clinical choice. A thorough record would include a note concerning a test's usefulness and the rationale for the decision.

4. Answering the answering service: Many therapists have printed in literature, on promotional folders, or on cards that they have a twenty-four-hour answering service. This implies that a client who calls will be called back within a reasonable time—usually, that business day or the next morning. It does not mean, literally, that there is an answering service. A client in crisis who calls the therapist is entitled to a return call within a reasonable time, even on weekends or when the therapist is on vacation and a relief therapist is on duty. Apply the usual yardstick. If you were a client in crisis, or had a problem so personal that it could be discussed only with the therapist, when would you like to receive the return contact? The sooner the better.

A frantic client who cannot reach the therapist could easily feel abandoned. And this is grounds for a malpractice action.

5. Checking every facility and individual to whom you give a referral, and making sure the resource you select can properly handle the client: Therapists refer to other therapists, hospitals, agencies, crisis centers, adoption agencies, AA, ALANON, Tough Love, and other community groups too numerous to mention. Some are general service providers with excellent supervision and credentials; others are highly specialized self-help groups. Each has excellence in a field, but a selection must be reviewed carefully before a referral is made. Calls, visits, and interviews with an agency would meet the minimum requirements, although a heavy investigation would be helpful when serious problems must be resolved.

Do not make any referrals without first checking references.

If you refer to an individual, make sure he or she has malpractice insurance. Next, call the malpractice carrier named, to check on the claims made, and call the licensing board to see whether any (or how many) complaints have been filed. Make no referral without checking references. A cause of action called "negligent referral" can be brought when a referral is made without properly checking credentials. Negligent referral can be easily avoided by establishing a method to systematically investigate before passing along the name of any other professional person, group, or agency.

Steve had been a therapist for about five years. Preferring not to handle clients who were a serious danger to themselves or others, he had the Crisis Hot Line number printed on his card. His answering machine also carried the message: "If there is an emergency, call the Crisis Hot Line, 972-123-4567."

In five years, only two clients had called the hot line. They were well satisfied with the results. Last week, another client called. The hot line had a recording: "We are temporarily out of service. We should again be on line on _____ 30, 20____ . Sorry."

The client was devastated. Steve was unavailable, and the client knew no one else to call.

Giving out out of date information is worse than giving out no information at all.

6. Taking homicide and suicide threats seriously: Proper intake and consent forms should give the therapist the right to call certain designated persons when a client clinically indicates to the therapist that the client might present an immediate threat to self and/or others. Those designated should be persons who, in the therapist's clinical judgment, might be in a position to prevent a homicide or suicide. In some jurisdictions, the police or a medical facility can be informed; in others, family members or the potential victim can be notified.

Family members, relatives, or other third parties involved with the patient will usually look for someone to blame and will seek financial compensation if a patient in therapy commits suicide, or kills or hurts another person. In almost every case of homicide or suicide, the friends or relatives will consult a lawyer. The case might not be filed against the therapist, or it may be screened out by the lawyer if he or she does not feel there is a fair possibility of substantial recovery. But litigation will be discussed, and a therapist must always be on guard.

If the therapist hears a client has killed, injured, or hurt someone or has committed suicide, the therapist should review the file immediately, call the malpractice carrier, and call a lawyer. The therapist can then, armed with legal advice, offer sympathy to the family without admitting liability. This is the time for damage control. Seek counsel. If nothing else, losing

A therapist could easily be challenged as being negligent if a technique were available but unknown to the therapist.

a client in this manner is traumatic for the therapist, and a procedure to grieve should be established.

7. Establishing a continuing education curriculum for self and staff: Therapists are charged with knowledge of the latest treatment possibilities and options, and must update their knowledge base periodically to ensure that the modalities being used have current validity. A therapist could easily be challenged as being negligent if a technique were available but unknown to the therapist. Some states have continuing education courses that offer the minimum requirements for preserving a license.

In addition, staff must be trained.

Ted told a local college placement bureau that he needed a student to replace his secretary during her summer vacation. The replacement was a pleasant, bright, and competent young man whose functions over the summer were to answer the phone and to book appointments. After several days, Ted happened to walk by the front desk and heard the hiree talking to his mother about a new client, who happened to be a neighbor. Ted insisted he immediately terminate the conversation, and began to reprimand him for breaching the confidentiality so necessary in a counselor's office. The young man replied: "I used to work in an ice cream shop and we gossiped about customers all the time. You mean a therapist's office is different? No one told me."

The negligence of the employee is the negligence of the employer, when acting in the course and scope of employment.

Staff must be trained concerning: the confidentiality of client information and files; the way to answer inquiries concerning clients and potential clients; what to say or not say to a process server; how to secure all paper and computer records; what can and cannot be said to colleagues and friends; how to camouflage clients and clients' files; and all other items that a new employee must know before becoming qualified to work in a therapist's office. Keep in mind that the negligence of the employee is the negligence of the employer, when acting in the course and scope of employment. Train employees; assign a person to be responsible for their training. Have a manual and insist that it be read by all new employees, and initialed. Failing to train a new or temporary employee because of stresses, pressures, or time constraints is no excuse.

8. Keeping parental rights in mind when treating a child: In general, either parent can give consent to the therapeutic treatment of a child, if the parents are married to each other. When parents are divorced, the rights, powers, and duties that confer parental rights are divided between the two parents. Often, the custodial parent has the normal rights of a parent, and the noncustodial or visiting parent has only the right to seek emergency treatment. In nonemergencies where assessment and treatment are needed, the consent of the custodial parent must be obtained. (This is why all divorce decrees and modifications of divorce decrees have to be read and reviewed.) In some states, there is a presumption that all parents are "joint" custodians of all children and have equal rights to consent to treatment. Texas and some other states call parents, following divorce, "sole or joint managing conservators" when the court divides the duties of parents. Other states use different terminology. Each jurisdiction has its own vocabulary. Before accepting a child as a client, a therapist must understand the local rules and terminology.

Children are often presented to therapists by divorced parents or guardians. If the parent has been divorced, **ask for and read the divorce decree and all modifications. If the parties were divorced in another jurisdiction and different legal jargon is used there, ask a lawyer in the state that granted the divorce to interpret the decree for you.** Only the custodial parent (usually, the parent designated in the decree), a legally appointed guardian, or a foster parent has the right to give informed consent to the therapeutic treatment of a minor child. Ask for and obtain a certified translation if the parties were divorced in a foreign country.

If the parent has been divorced, **ask for and read the divorce decree and all modifications.**

9. Contacting the police when necessary, especially if authorized by statute, and keeping this option open in consent forms: There is no better organization to have involved in homicide, suicide, or threat of harm than the local police. They respond quickly, can generally take a difficult situation in hand, and can, when they take charge, remove the therapist from liability. Check the state statute and determine when it is or is not appropriate to call a law enforcement agency.

10. Taking a lawyer to lunch: In the history of the legal profession, no lawyer is known to have ever refused a free lunch. The idea of taking a lawyer to lunch is advanced to suggest that lawyers and therapists are colleagues and should, on a regular basis, discuss common problems in an informal manner. Each therapist should have a lawyer who can be enlisted to bounce around ideas, make cross referrals, and check out small problems before they escalate into major violations. With a few inquiries, a lawyer knowledgeable in mental health law can be located. This networking can bring enormous benefits to members of both professions. As the relationship develops, the information exchanged can be very helpful.

Legal Lightbulb

- Acts of omission are as serious as acts of commission.

- When a therapist is on the witness stand as a defendant in a malpractice action, any review of any file will reveal omissions in treatment plans that might have been appropriate.

- Include in the treatment plan as many options as are reasonable, and tell why they were utilized or eliminated from consideration.

- Acts of omission and commission have shades of gray. The dark grays are to be avoided. When subtler issues arise, call the malpractice insurance carrier, a colleague, or a lawyer.

- Good news: Statistically, very few suits are filed.

A malpractice suit is a legitimate concern in a litigious society, but should not be viewed as an ogre on the horizon. Instead, the possibility of malpractice is a constant wakeup call. To avoid personal charges, the first step is to understand where you are vulnerable. This two-chapter unit on the topic has pointed out many areas where therapists have been held liable. With this information, malpractice suits can be more easily avoided or eliminated from your central concerns.

28

What to Do If You Get Sued

Dr. Hansen received, from an attorney, a letter containing allegations that suggested a possible abandonment of her client. Enclosed was a properly signed consent form asking Dr. Hansen to release all her client's records to the lawyer. What should she do?

~

At 8:00 A.M. one day, just as the first client was scheduled to come in, a stranger walked into Dr. Frank's office and handed him a legal process that turned out to be a notice of a malpractice suit. The allegations were awesome and, in Dr. Frank's opinion, ridiculous. But the suit had been filed, and he was named as defendant. He had to respond on or before the first Monday after twenty days from the date the process was served.

~

What should both therapists do?

There is no possibility of practicing therapy in a totally risk-free atmosphere. The reader can follow the thoughts in this book and minimize risks, but, in every profession, there are built-in risks that affect the practitioner. When the risk becomes a reality, a therapist can be sued.

Avoiding Litigation

Suits can often be curtailed if they are handled long before they reach a courthouse. Some of these suggestions may help:

- Listen to every complaint, no matter how trivial or small. If a short conference can ameliorate the situation, offer a free conference; if not, offer a free session. Clients seek the attention of the professional and wish to be heard. If appropriate, offer a complete session and discuss all the areas of discomfort. Most complaints can be eliminated in this manner.

- Include a mediation and/or arbitration clause in the intake contract. Differences can often be worked out with the help of an understanding and objective third person. Options that avoid confrontation and conflict can be considered and may lead to a result that satisfies all parties.

- When a hint of a suit appears, call the malpractice insurance carrier at once. Insurance companies are fonts of information about dealing with unhappy clients. They can suggest alternative methods for dealing with clients, and will often role-play the conversation. Malpractice insurance carriers are happier avoiding suits than winning in court. They are usually delighted to develop a scenario that avoids litigation.

- Sometimes, a carefully worded apology (without admitting liability), is all a client wants. Write one, but have your insurance carrier and lawyer review it before you send it out.

- Some suits simply cannot be avoided.

What to Do When Served with a Lawsuit

1. Call your malpractice insurance carrier at once: If, for some reason, there is no malpractice insurance, engage a lawyer immediately.

2. Assemble the entire client file, index it, and prepare a summary and chronology: Examine all corrections and make sure they can be explained. If some clarification is needed, make notes. *Do not* make any erasures or introduce any opaquing or changes into the original file.

3. Make three copies of the original file: Be prepared to mail one copy to the malpractice insurance carrier, which will undoubtedly want a copy of the file. Take another copy to a colleague to review. (Consent for collegial review should be contained in your intake and consent form.)

4. Read your malpractice insurance policy very carefully: Remember the maxim: "The big print giveth, the small print taketh away." Review the policy with your personal lawyer. Remember, the policy as written sets out the obligations of the insurance carrier. **Make sure you conform to every requirement of the malpractice policy. If you do not cooperate 100 percent, some of the rights under the policy may be forfeited.**

5. Do nothing without the advice and consent of the malpractice carrier: When you receive advice or direction from the insurance company's lawyer or claims manager, make a note of the instructions and follow them to the letter. Open a notebook and record *every contact* with insurance company personnel. Keep a log of every item or event that affects the suit. Don't discuss the litigation with anyone except the insurance company and your lawyer—and, perhaps, a trusted colleague. Offer meaningful input; other than that, put yourself in the hands of the insurance carrier's specialists. They will handle and process the claim; they have done it before. Insist that your representative in the insurance company keep you informed of all activities in the file, including settlement negotiations.

6. Participate with the lawyer in your defense against the charges: This is the time for personal involvement. Don't be afraid to ask questions and make suggestions. Lawyers aren't always knowledgeable when therapeutic problems are at issue. You may find yourself educating your lawyer, and that's fine. Consider retaining your own personal lawyer to consult with as the malpractice case progresses. Conflicts can arise between you and the insurance carrier, and the attorney retained by the insurance carrier will be caught in the middle. The insurance carrier may wish to settle a suit for $15,000, to avoid the higher cost of litigation. You, however, will want your name cleared. In some states, information regarding malpractice judgments and settlements must be sent to the therapist's licensing board. A practical settlement could cause serious licensing problems for the therapist, not to mention the loss of reputation and of future business and income.

7. Be prepared to answer a licensing board complaint: If your insurance carrier will not provide you with a licensing board defense through the same attorney, you should retain counsel. Make sure that you and your board-defense attorney coordinate with the malpractice case attorney. Admissions before the board and findings by the board can be introduced into evidence and can have a profound impact on a malpractice case. A board finding of unethical conduct can often lead to a quick settlement by your malpractice carrier and is dynamite in settlement negotiations.

Your Personal Well-Being

This may be the time to engage a personal therapist who will shepherd you through the litigation ahead. Insurance companies are not in a hurry to part with their money, and courts are so notoriously crowded that bringing a case to trail often takes years. Litigation has traditional delays and constant dilatory actions. Its stress is well known. There should be someone available to comfort you during these months of stress.

Most policies have limits, and beyond those limits, the insured (therapist) is personally or individually liable. In most cases, the limits are not a problem; but in high-dollar cases, they must be considered. If you must deal with a homicide or a suicide, it would be wise to consult an attorney to protect your assets and estate. Some maneuvering might be appropriate. Asset preservation requires careful planning and should not be undertaken without the help of an accountant and an attorney.

Why Few Suits Are Filed against Therapists

- Most therapists care about and respond to their clients.

- Proving a causal relationship or "proximate cause" between the actions of a therapist and damage to a client is difficult.

- Damages themselves, in dollar amounts, are hard to quantify. In many cases, damages are minimal and lawyers refuse to become involved.

- Once a suit is filed, the entire mental health record of the client becomes a matter of public record and is subject to examination by inquisitive strangers and the media.

- Therapy is still considered somewhat of an art form, and proving acts of negligence, commission, or omission is difficult. No two therapists would treat the same client the same way, and a judge or jury is aware of clinical differences. For these reasons, thorough documentation is critical.

- For a client who sues a therapist, future therapy is difficult to obtain. All therapists are litigation-shy.

- Mediation and arbitration have become popular alternatives to lawsuits and often lead to settlements that preclude litigation. A settlement may include a secrecy clause or an admission of no liability.

- A client who files a suit may have to wait years before the case comes to trial. Moving on with life while the problem is still open may be difficult. Plaintiffs may not see closure for years.

Once a suit is filed, the entire mental health record of the client becomes a matter of public record and is subject to examination by inquisitive strangers and the media.

Legal Lightbulb

- Malpractice insurance is essential for any therapist.

- Malpractice insurance policies must be read and understood. Questions should be asked if anything is unclear.

- Agency, university, or practice group insurance policies do not always cover all providers.

- Malpractice insurance policies, without endorsement, will not usually cover suits against managed care, wherein the therapist is a reluctant defendant.

- When a malpractice insurance policy covers a therapist, the carrier has the right to control the case. Let the carrier represent you unless there is an excellent reason *not* to give the case to the carrier's experienced legal staff. If conflicts arise, retain your own attorney to advise you.

- If you have no coverage (i.e., no insurance to indemnify you as a provider), contact a lawyer at once to provide a defense. Having adequate coverage deserves careful attention. A judgment against a therapist can ruin his or her credit for a period of years.

- Coordination between your malpractice defense and the licensing board's defense is critical. Each will impact the outcome of the other.

- Cooperate fully with the attorneys representing you, and be sure to tell them **EVERYTHING.** Your lawyers will not welcome courtroom surprises and cannot adequately defend you if they are not prepared.

This chapter has dealt with responding to a suit filed against a therapist for *malpractice*, which is a civil action for money damages. Ethical complaints filed with the various licensing boards are handled differently. Each board has its own rules and procedures. In some policies, the therapist who engages a lawyer for representation before the licensing board is entitled to reimbursement for up to $5,000. This reimbursement policy is not uniform, however.

Ethical complaints filed with the various licensing boards are handled differently.

Whether the problem is *civil*, as in malpractice; *administrative*, as in a complaint to the licensing board; or *criminal*, as in a charge against a therapist for assault, battery, sexual acts (in some states), or false imprisonment, a lawyer must be consulted.

SECTION EIGHT

MANAGED CARE

29

Confidentiality Issues

Jim, a 42-year-old department head for a medium size manufacturing company, sought assistance for a cocaine problem and utilized his company's health care benefits. Jim worked for a company that was self-insured for the medical and mental health claims of its employees, but retained an outside company to administer the plan and claims. Information regarding claims, limited to the name of the employee and the amount of benefits paid to providers of health care, was forwarded to Jim's employer's Human Resources Department, which was responsible for monitoring the claim fund.

Evelyn, the secretary in the Human Resources office, processed the information that payments had been made, on Jim's behalf, to a well-known local drug treatment facility. Jim had been admitted there for ten-day inpatient treatment. At lunch with Jim's boss's secretary, Evelyn shared what she had seen: that funds had been paid to the drug rehab facility on Jim's behalf. When Jim's boss's secretary returned to work, she passed the information on to Jim's boss.

When Jim returned to work, he found that he had been reassigned to an undesirable nonsupervisory position.

Unauthorized Disclosures

The flow of information regarding mental health care claims is fraught with the danger of unauthorized disclosures. The more eyes that view confidential information, the greater the risk of a breach of confidentiality. A therapist is required by managed care provider agreements to communicate confidential information regarding clients to managed care companies and payers of the clients' health care benefits. At a minimum, a therapist will have to provide the identification of the client, a diagnosis, a

The more eyes that view confidential information, the greater the risk of a breach of confidentiality.

treatment plan, the techniques used, the goals set, and an estimate of the required length of treatment.

Many payers require much more initial information; they may even request a detailed description of the client's reported problems. Others require access to all client information, including the therapist's progress notes. The type and quality of information vary from payer to payer. A recent federal district court decision [*Grijalva v. Shalala*, 1997 Westlaw 155392 (D. Ariz., March 3, 1997)] set out the components of a Medicare managed care appeals system and made clear that both the agency (or other party) reviewing the claim and the claimant were entitled to all information in the claimant's file. These guidelines for appeal systems will be carefully reviewed and evaluated by private payers. In connection with an appeal of a managed care decision, all information in a client's file, including the therapist's progress and case notes, could be subject to disclosure and review by the managed care company.

The Client's Consent

To guard against claims of breach of confidentiality when information is furnished to managed care companies or payers, a mental health practitioner should secure from the client, at the time of the first session, a consent to have the therapist provide to the managed care company, or other payer of the client's health care benefits, any and all information requested. A therapist should discuss and advise each client that, in these circumstances, information will have to be shared with the payer, and in the event of an appeal for denial of payment for services, all information in the client's file may have to be disclosed.

The client has the option of not seeking benefits under his or her health care plan and, instead, paying for services directly and personally.

The client has the option of not seeking benefits under his or her health care plan and, instead, paying for services directly and personally. The majority of clients, however, will opt to seek payment through their health care plan and should then be required to sign a consent for release of *all* information required by the payer or plan.

If Jim, the cocaine-addicted employee mentioned earlier, had known that information about his problem was going to be shared with other employees, he might have considered taking vacation time and paying out-of-pocket for his ten-day stay at the rehab clinic. The Human

Resources office only received information that $5,000 was paid to Hospital X on his behalf, but the hospital was well known in the community for treating drug dependency. It wasn't hard for the secretary or Jim's boss to correctly guess Jim's problem. Jim's chemical dependency counselor, who undertook Jim's treatment upon admission, is not responsible for the breach of confidentiality by the secretary. But he is charged with the responsibility to advise Jim regarding confidentiality and its exceptions, and to inform Jim that the health care plan requires the counselor to provide information to the plan's administrator—Jim's company.

The Therapist's Concerns

Before signing a provider agreement, a therapist should inquire about the kind of information a managed care company will require. Who will be reviewing the forwarded information? What training and experience will the reviewer have? What safeguards or procedures are in place to ensure that only necessary disclosure or review of confidential information will be done (i.e., who "needs to know" what)? If procedures are lax, training is poor, or inexperienced people will be receiving the information, it would be wise for the therapist to refuse to serve on the provider panel for that company.

After a provider agreement is signed, the therapist should assume, and should so advise a client, that all information may have to be disclosed to the managed care company. The therapist should then obtain the client's consent to disclosure of *all* information requested by the managed care company. If the client refuses to sign such a consent, the therapist should refuse to provide therapy unless the client agrees to pay directly and the provider agreement does not prohibit the therapist from taking direct pay for services from a client. Many provider agreements prohibit a therapist from billing a client directly for anything other than the client's co-pay. Under these circumstances, the therapist will have to decline to provide services and recommend the client seek referral to another therapist on the list of approved providers.

Many provider agreements prohibit a therapist from billing a client directly for anything other than the client's co-pay.

What if the client will consent to only partial disclosure of his or her file? A therapist who undertakes therapy with only a partial consent runs the risk of a claim being denied with no way to document an appeal in order

Sample Form

CONSENT TO DISCLOSURE OF CONFIDENTIAL
INFORMATION TO MANAGED CARE COMPANY

As a provider under contract with the managed care company providing your mental health care benefits, I am required to disclose information regarding your care to this company. Once the information is submitted, I have no control over it and cannot guarantee it will be appropriately safeguarded by the company, nor can I control how the information will be used. I may be required to share with the company all information in my files, including my personal case and progress notes. Please indicate, by signing below, your consent for me to provide the company with **all** information regarding your mental health care, including my personal case and progress notes, upon request.

I hereby consent to the undersigned therapist and members of his or her staff to disclose any and all information regarding my mental health care treatment requested by the managed care company that provides my mental health care benefits, upon request by that company.

_____   _____
Client   Date

_____
Social Security Number

_____   _____
Therapist/Provider   Date

to be paid. If the provider agreement prohibits direct billing of a client, then the therapist is not going to be paid. A therapist should pass on or reject any client who refuses to consent to disclosure of *all* information required by the managed care company.

The consent form shown on page 212 can be used as a separate document or included in a more comprehensive intake and consent form.

Legal Lightbulb

- Although payers initially require only general information regarding diagnosis and treatment, they may require substantially more information later on, especially during appeal of a decision denying benefits or payment.

- Prior to signing a managed care provider agreement, find out what information you will be required to provide. Ask about the training and experience of the people who will be reviewing the information. Make sure you also know their procedures for safeguarding client information.

- Prior to beginning therapy, a therapist has a duty to discuss *confidentiality* and its *exceptions and limitations,* including the information to be shared with a payer or managed care company.

- Let the client make the informed choice to consent or not to consent to disclose information to payers and managed care companies. Obtain the consent in writing, prior to the time when treatment commences.

- If a client refuses to consent or will consent to only a partial disclosure of information, a therapist should consider *not* providing services to that client.

- Always carefully review your provider contracts to learn whether direct billing of, and payment by, the client is an option.

- Document what is professionally appropriate. Keep in mind that the documentation might have to be shared with the managed care company.

30

Duty to Appeal

Suzanne, seeking counseling for stress and depression, called her managed care company for referral to a counselor. She was referred to Karen, a licensed counselor, and three visits were authorized. After three visits, Karen and Suzanne both called the managed care company to obtain authorization for additional sessions. The managed care company "gatekeeper" declined to authorize any additional sessions, and Karen discontinued therapy with Suzanne.

Two weeks later, Suzanne committed suicide. Her outraged family consulted a lawyer regarding a lawsuit against Karen and the managed care company. Karen consulted with her lawyer and was stunned to learn that she had cause for concern because she had made no attempt to pressure the managed care company to authorize additional sessions. Her single phone call may not be considered enough effort.

Therapists' Role as Patients' Advocates

Mental health professionals have a responsibility to their client that supercedes any limitations of an insurance contract or managed health care plan.

Mental health care professionals have an obligation to be patients' advocates when managed care decisions impact the quality or quantity of care provided for their clients. Their professional responsibility to their clients supersedes any limitations of an insurance contract or managed care health plan. The therapist is obligated to provide the client with treatment that is consistent with the standard of care the client would normally receive from the therapist. The ethical duties and responsibilities imposed by a licensing and statutory authority do not cease when the managed care company says "No."

Managed care companies are increasingly being held accountable when they make inappropriate decisions in order to save money—and so are providers who quietly go along with the managed care companies' decisions. Health care professional organizations are adopting

Sample Form

ETHICAL STANDARDS IN MANAGED CARE

1. Patient Advocacy Is Fundamental

The duty of patient advocacy is a fundamental element of the physician–patient relationship that should not be altered by the system of health care delivery in which physicians practice. Physicians must continue to place the interests of their patients first. *[American Medical Association Committee on Ethical and Judicial Affairs (AMA CEJA), Opinion 8.13(1), Managed Care; AMA Policy 285.982(1), Ethical Issues in Managed Care.]*

2. Advocacy for Patient Benefit

Regardless of any allocation guidelines or gatekeeper directives, physicians must advocate for care they believe will materially benefit their patients. *[Adapted from AMA CEJA, Opinion 8.13(1), Managed Care; AMA Policy 285.982(2)(b), Ethical Issues in Managed Care.]*

5. Appeals from Denials of Care

Adequate appellate mechanisms for both patients and physicians should be in place to address disputes regarding medically necessary care. In some circumstances, physicians have an obligation to initiate appeals on behalf of their patients. Cases may arise in which a health plan has an allocation guideline that is generally fair but in particular circumstances results in denial of care that, in the physician's judgment, would materially benefit the patient. **In such cases, the physician's duty as patient advocate requires that the physician challenge the denial and argue for the provision of treatment in the specific case.** Cases may also arise when a health plan has an allocation guideline that is generally unfair in its operation. In such cases, the physician's duty as patient advocate requires not only a challenge to any denials of treatment from the guideline but also advocacy at the health plan's policy-making level to seek an elimination or modification of the guideline. *[Adapted from AMA CEJA, Opinion 8.13(2)(d), Managed Care; AMA Policy 285.982(2)(d), Ethical Issues in Managed Care.]*

A physician should assist patients who wish to seek additional, appropriate care outside the plan when the physician believes the care is in the patient's best interests. *[Adapted from AMA CEJA, Opinion 8.13(2)(d), Managed Care; AMA Policy 285.982(2)(d), Ethical Issues in Managed Care.]*

principles requiring patient advocacy of their members on behalf of patients. For example, the ethical standards shown on page 215 were adopted by the Massachusetts Medical Society on November 8, 1996. They originated from or were adaptations of opinions of the American Medical Association.

Scope of Managed Care Companies' Contracts

It is important to remember that managed care contracts deal primarily with payment issues and not with a therapist's professional and ethical responsibilities to the client. With the emphasis that courts, consumers, professional organizations, and state licensing authorities are placing on patient advocacy and consumer rights, it is critical for mental health professionals to be prepared to document and ardently process the appeal of an inappropriate managed care decision.

The first step to take in preparing to meet this responsibility should be a thorough review and understanding of the provider's contract with the managed care company and the client's contract for benefits with the managed care company.

Ask for and review all written information disseminated by the managed care company with respect to benefits, procedures, claims, and appeals.

Ask for and review all written information disseminated by the managed care company with respect to benefits, procedures, claims, and appeals. Seek clarification in writing if you are unsure about or unfamiliar with anything in the materials you review. Learn the identities of the people you will be dealing with in the event of an appeal, and particularly note the documentation that may be required to support an appeal. Appeal processes vary with each company. If you are on several panels, it will be necessary to acquaint yourself with the policies and procedures of each company. Inroads are being made toward making companies more effective and providing honest systems of review and appeal, but the profession is a long way from mandated uniformity on the state or federal level.

After you have a good grasp of the managed care company's benefits, policies, and appeal procedures, you are ready to assume the referral of a client from that company. At the first session with the client, you should discuss the limitations imposed on you and the client by the managed care company, and the steps each of you will need to take if benefits, services, or payments of fees are denied. Anticipate denial, and decide in advance how it will be dealt with.

The Appeal Process

After therapy has commenced, keep detailed and accurate records that can be presented in the event of an appeal. Consider what information may be persuasive to a reviewer and decision maker during an appeal, and document all needed data in the client's file.

When a denial is announced and the appeal process begins, be sure to document, in detail, all phone calls, written requests, and information communicated to the managed care company. Carefully log the time, date, and identity of each person at the managed care company whom you contact by phone. You want to be able to look at jurors, eye to eye, and advise them that you did everything you possibly could do to secure the services or care you believed the client required. In effect, you are asking not to be blamed for damages the managed care company may have inflicted.

Carefully log the time, date, and identity of each person at the managed care company whom you contact by phone.

Provide the managed care company with support and documentation for your position, including, but not limited to, therapy and progress notes, test results, relevant research, learned treatises, and confirming opinions of colleagues. Be sure to have the client's informed consent before sharing any information from the client's file.

Fight for your client's rights outside the managed care appeal system if necessary. Write to your state's insurance commissioner, or to local or state mental health organizations. Let your local officials and state representatives and senators know the difficulties you and your client are encountering with a particular company. If your client is insured through employment, and the client consents, contact the benefits manager for the employer and explain the problems you and the employee are experiencing with the managed care company. Urge your client to contact these same potential sources of assistance. The client should also call and pressure the managed care company directly for a favorable decision. Clients who participate in a process are less likely to blame others (the therapist) if the process fails.

Fight for your client's rights outside the managed care appeal system if necessary.

Lastly, be persistent and insistent. Squeaky wheels get attention; sometimes, it is helpful to have the person reviewing the appeal know just how concerned you are about the outcome. With your firm resolve and the client's active involvement, the chances of a favorable decision are improved.

The Appeal Letter

An appeal letter will vary from managed care contract to managed care contract. However, after the agreement is reached, certain procedures should be established to ensure that the appellate process is pursued in accordance with the guidelines set out in the signed contract between the actual provider and the managed care company—in other words, all written information disseminated by the managed care company or the employer with respect to benefits, policies, procedures, claims, and appeals.

Seek clarification in writing if you are unsure about or unfamiliar with any terms or concepts in the published materials. If possible, consult with another provider who has been involved in the appellate process, and learn from your colleague's experience.

Discuss the provisions in the managed care contract prior to or at the time treatment commences. Should a claim be denied for any reason, the client should not be shocked or surprised by the action of the "gatekeeper" representing the managed care company. (The client must understand that the days have passed when the client and the therapist/provider were the sole determiners of the length of time services were to be rendered, or of the total nature and extent of managed care benefits.)

The following steps, taken in the sequence given, will prove helpful:

1. Outline the necessary actions as a time line:

    a. Make the telephone call seeking additional authorization.

    b. Forward the necessary documentation and file to the company for review.

    c. Write a letter supporting the documentation and requesting additional sessions.

    d. Request a written evaluation and explanation of the refusal to pay for further treatment.

    e. Write a letter seeking third-party review or peer review and reevaluation.

    f. Take any additional steps required in the contract.

    g. Request the specific reasons for denial of continued services.

2. Insert the time line for each transaction. Mark on a calendar the date on which each step is to be taken so that a claim is not denied

for technical reasons. Avoid a reply stating, for example: "You did not notify us of your dissatisfaction within 10 days as provided in the contract, and therefore you have forfeited your right to appeal."

3. Review the file and contract, to ensure that all data required for an appeal have been furnished to the managed care company.

4. Document every contact with the managed care company's authorizing agent (the gatekeeper), and follow up each contact with a written memorandum.

5. Keep the client informed of your efforts to seek additional services. Let the client know you are a "patients' advocate."

6. Seek mediation or arbitration if provided in the contract, or advise the client to seek legal advice if necessary. Your advocacy is toward the appeal process, not toward representing the client in litigation.

7. Establish a checklist that coordinates with the appellate process and monitors:

   a. Necessary documentation.

   b. Specific times appeal actions are to be taken.

   c. Processing of all the needed technical steps.

8. Keep a list of community resources to offer to the client in the event the appeal is denied. Regardless of the reason for the denial, be able to offer substitute options if your therapeutic services to the client have to be terminated. You can continue to provide services, *if permitted by the contract,* at a reduced fee or free, but if you cannot, or choose not to, continue treatment, community resources on a free or sliding fee scale basis should be offered to the client to avoid, as much as possible, claims or feelings of abandonment.

9. Make sure your file contains letters that support the client's condition and your professional opinion. Should the claim still be denied, accept the decision gracefully and inform the client that you have been his or her advocate in good faith and in accordance with the managed care guidelines and the contracts in force.

Legal Lightbulb

- Therapists have a duty to advocate for clients with managed care companies.

- A therapist's professional and ethical responsibility to a client will exceed and supersede any managed care contract. The managed care contract may limit a therapist's options, however, to provide additional services for free or for a fee upon denial of additional benefits.

- A thorough knowledge of the client's benefit contract with the managed care company is essential for client advocacy.

- Learn all you can about the appeal process and the people who will decide the appeal, before you meet with the client for the first time. Who are the players and what are their jobs and powers?

- Plan, from the first session, what to do if a denial occurs. Have an established in-office procedure.

- Detailed documentation of therapy and of efforts in the appeal process is critical for successful appeal to the managed care company as well as for defense at trial.

- Document your appeal (if the client consents) with therapy and progress notes, testing results, research or learned treatises, a colleague's confirming opinion, and so on.

- Failure to be an advocate and to vigorously pursue an appeal may be grounds for a malpractice action.

- If necessary, go outside the managed care system by contacting state insurance commissioners, politicians, and, with the client's consent, the employer.

- Communicate your resolve and seriousness about the care you believe your client needs, and urge the client to do likewise.

SECTION NINE

TEAMWORK

31

Legal Aspects of Delegating

In every organization and in every profession, there comes a time when it is necessary to delegate professional services to staff, technicians, other professionals, or specialists, not just mental health professions because of a conflict of interest, a lack of interest, or an excessive burden of responsibilities. When delegation is required, there are some questions to ask of oneself and others.

We rely here on an article titled and subtitled: "Patient [read *client*] Care Management Skills: Delegation and Supervision—Professional and legal aspects of delegating to staff members: Key questions to ask" [Source: *Healthweek* 2:26 (December 18, 1995)]. The article focuses on medical personnel, but the same guidelines can easily be applied to mental health professionals. Here is the substance of the questions:

- Is the delegatee stable enough for care delegation?
- Are the responsibilities stated in a current job description or scope-of-practice listing, and authorized by policy or procedure?
- Is the delegatee competent to perform the necessary tasks?
- Have all the necessary tasks been communicated clearly and reviewed?
- What degree of direction and supervision will the delegatee receive?
- Who will judge whether the delegatee is performing tasks correctly?
- Who will judge whether the client(s) is (are) benefiting from the care?
- What criteria will be used to declare a task completed correctly and safely?
- What criteria will be used to show positive response to the care?
- Has the delegator been given feedback by the delegatee?

Considerations When Delegating

- Has there been sufficient training within the practice to guarantee that the staff person is up to the responsibility and understands the internal procedures? Busy therapists are often reluctant to take time from income-producing practices to do the necessary training.

- Don't make assumptions about the knowledge of employees. A new employee may not know that therapeutic sessions are confidential and gossip will not be tolerated.

- Every professional entity should issue a training manual and appoint a professional to be responsible for the education of new staff.

- Employers are liable for the acts of employees when such acts occur in the course and scope of their employment. An employer would be held responsible if confidentiality were breached through office gossip.

- When a referral is made internally or externally, is there a proper protocol for checking out the person, agency, facility, or entity to whom the referral is made? A cause of action called "negligent referral" can be initiated when the delegation or referral is negligent, careless, or without proper foundation, or when the delegatee is not equipped, for any reason, to handle the client.

The Basics for Delegating Successfully

- Give adequate training.

- Verify malpractice insurance coverage.

- If licensed, call the licensing board to see whether any complaints are pending.

- Make sure the person performing the task has had adequate learning, training, experience, and education.

- Document internal training and keep a file on classes, continuing education, correspondence courses, and other indications that efforts were made to ensure the protection of the client.

Final Thoughts on Delegating Responsibility

A school counselor may refer or delegate to a specialist. A licensed marriage and family therapist (LMFT) may refer to an alcohol counselor if needed, or send children to a play therapist. A licensed professional counselor (LPC) may refer to a psychologist for extensive testing and a psychological workup. A psychologist may delegate a social worker to do a home study. Mental health professionals of all disciplines refer to each other or cross-refer when a client will benefit from additional expertise. Although delegation is to another professional, the responsibility of the delegator or referrer does not end. The questions concerning the appropriateness of the delegation must be asked, answered, and, if needed, explored fully.

Once active treatment begins, it can only be terminated by an appropriate procedure in accordance with professional standards. Delegation does not terminate professional responsibility. In most cases, continued involvement is needed until a formal termination is agreed on, entered into the clinical record, and properly documented.

A proper delegation of treatment may suit both the client and the provider, but the delegation must be handled properly—and often, gingerly.

32

Supervisor/Supervisee Responsibilities

Dale G. completed his master's degree in counseling and was under the supervision of Jack Hanson, PhD, LPC. Dale had to complete the requisite 2,000 hours of clinical, supervised practice before he could receive his license and practice independently.

Unknown to Dr. Hanson, Dale had, at a nearby lake, a house with a hot tub. Also unknown to Dr. Hanson was the fact that, on weekends, Dale invited "choice" clients to soak in the tub and receive a modified version of group therapy. Finally, a client complained to the licensing board, alleging sexual acts with Dale, a dual relationship, and numerous boundary violations. Dr. Hanson's first inkling of the problem occurred when he received a letter from the licensing board.

~

Cindy practiced and was being supervised in Susan's office. The two women were professional as well as social friends, and often went to lunch together. During lunch, they discussed problem clients in Cindy's practice. Susan would offer advice concerning treatment. Each week, after lunch, Cindy would record in her clinical notes: "Supervision this date" for each client discussed at lunch. Is this sufficient?

~

Dr. Rose Johnson rented a substantial office and sublet space to numerous other practitioners and interns whom she supervised. The intake and consent form signed by each client contained a clause stating that, although the client was initially referred to Dr. Johnson, she may utilize the services of the other providers and interns in her office if they are competent to handle the client. She conferred with each supervisee on a weekly basis—and more often, if deemed necessary. Dr. Johnson received a call at night from an unhappy client *who complained that an intern had just propositioned her. No touching, just inappropriate innuendo.*

A supervisor/supervisee relationship is similar to that of an employer/employee. The supervisor is responsible for the acts the supervisee performs in the course and scope of the supervision relationship.

At one time, supervision was less formal and the rights, obligations, and duties of the supervisor were less clearly defined.

Now, however, supervision has to be taken seriously and face-to-face supervision is required. At a minimum, each client has to be discussed periodically, and notations in the clinical record must indicate: the fact that the supervision took place; the nature of the supervision; the effect of the consult between the supervisor and supervisee; and any clinical changes in the diagnosis, evaluation, assessment, or treatment plan as a result of the supervision conference. For full protection, both the supervisor and supervisee should make **independent notations in separate files concerning the consult.**

General Guidelines

Over the years, each mental health discipline has published guidelines concerning supervision. Many of these have universal application and are stated as follows:

- When a state has published guidelines for supervision—for example, the credentials of supervisors, the hours needed, the methods to be used, or the records to be maintained—these rules have to be scrupulously honored.

- Certain requirements are stated for the supervisor. Check what those requirements are before beginning a supervised relationship.

- The supervising therapist must be trained in the area of supervision provided to the supervisee.

- Supervision of individuals within certain degrees of affinity or consanguinity is prohibited. Don't supervise a relative.

- In most jurisdictions, a percentage of clinical internship supervision must be "hands on" with clients.

- Some guidelines provide that the therapist can supervise only a certain number (perhaps two to nine) of supervisees at one time.

The supervising therapist must be trained in the area of supervision provided to the supervisee.

Some guidelines provide that the therapist can supervise only a certain number (perhaps two to nine) of supervisees at one time.

- Supervisees must notify clients of the supervision and supply the name and credentials of the supervisor.

- Supervisors may delegate to supervisees only such responsibilities as they can reasonably be expected to perform competently—given their education, training, or experience—either independently or within the level of supervision being provided.

- Supervisors must provide proper training and supervision to supervisees and take reasonable steps to see that such persons perform services responsibly, competently, and ethically.

- Supervisors must establish an appropriate process for providing feedback to supervisees.

- Supervisors are expected to evaluate supervisees on the basis of their actual performance when given relevant and established requirements.

- Supervisees shall keep and maintain documentation showing that their supervisor meets technical requirements and has the credentials to be a supervisor.

- A supervisor shall maintain and sign a record(s) to document: the date of each supervision conference; the minimum duration of _____ hour(s) per week of face-to-face supervision in individual or group settings; and the supervisee's total number of hours of supervised experience accumulated to (and including) the date of the supervision conference.

- A supervisee may not establish an independent practice while under supervision.

- In some states, a temporary license must be obtained before official supervision can begin.

- The supervisor may not be employed by the supervisee.

- The supervisee may usually, if agreeable to both, be employed on a salary basis or be a consultant or volunteer. All supervisory settings must be structured with clearly defined job descriptions and lines of responsibility.

- The full professional responsibility for the therapeutic activities of the supervisee shall rest with the supervisee's official supervisor.

- The supervisor shall ensure that the supervisee is aware of and adheres to the appropriate codes of ethics.

The supervisor may not be employed by the supervisee.

The supervisor shall ensure that the supervisee is aware of and adheres to the appropriate codes of ethics.

- A dual relationship between the supervisor and the supervisee may impair the supervisor's objective, professional judgment and should be avoided.

- A procedure shall be established for contacting the supervisor, or an alternate person, to assist in a crisis situation.

- All supervised experience must be on a formal basis, by contract or other specific arrangement, prior to the period of supervision. Supervision arrangements must include all specific conditions agreed to by the supervisor and the supervisee.

- If a supervisee enters into contracts with both a supervisor and an organization with which the supervisor is employed or affiliated, the contract between the organization and the supervisee will clearly indicate:

  —Where professional therapeutic treatment intervention will be performed.

  —No payment for services will be made directly by a client to the supervisee.

  —Clients' records are not the property of the supervisee.

  —The full responsibility for the therapeutic activities of a supervisee shall rest with the official supervisor.

  —Financial arrangements with the supervisee cannot extend beyond the period of supervision.

  —All supervised experience shall be in accordance with the canons of ethics of the profession.

- At any time during the supervised experience, and for any reason, if a supervisor determines that the supervisee may not have the skills or competence to practice independently, the supervisor shall develop and implement a written plan for remediation.

- States that require supervision for specialty recognition usually require that a plan be submitted for approval. Implementation and documentation of the plan are the responsibilities of a qualified supervisor.

- A supervisee who commits malpractice may be liable, together with his or her supervisor.

- In most cases, when a client files a complaint with the licensing board, the supervisor and the supervisee are both called to account for: their

A supervisee who commits malpractice may be liable, together with his or her supervisor.

activities; their acts of negligence, omission, or commission; or their failure to comply with the ethical standards of the profession.

- Don't assume the supervisee knows anything about professional ethics. In many graduate schools, the courses are theoretical and give little information concerning daily application. The supervisee must be diligently informed of ethical canons. Prepare a handout of the ethics requirements of the discipline, see that it is read, and have the supervisee initial the canons after reading the material. Have each supervisee read and initial (on each page) the code of ethics published by the designated licensing board.

The supervision publications of each state's licensing board must be consulted.

The various licensing boards—for therapists, licensed professional counselors, psychiatrists, social workers, marriage and family therapists, licensed chemical or drug abuse counselors, crisis intervention therapists, psychologists, and others—have issued guidelines for supervision. Published rules encompass the qualifications and responsibilities of supervisors and the responsibilities and requirements for supervisees. Each state is different, and each specific discipline promulgates its own guidelines. There is no universal set of rules on supervision. Common understandings are set out above, but, to be truly accurate, the supervision publications of each state's licensing board must be consulted.

To further complicate matters, some state and national organizations have published guidelines, the violation of which can lead to expulsion from the organization. In addition, some agencies, organizations, universities, insurance companies, and managed care panels have their own guidelines. This chapter sets out some of the rules. Active and curious therapists must review and coordinate all sources if they seek to practice in peace, free from worry and concern.

Supervision must be documented.

Most disciplines provide that graduates, interns, postdoctoral candidates, and future therapists undergo a period of supervision before they are prepared for independent practice. Following this "active" client contact and an evaluation of the input offered by the supervisor, the supervisor approves the supervision and the supervisee is authorized to practice independently. The liability of the supervisor is profound. During the period of supervision, the supervisor takes on a responsibility of immense proportions, and no legal document can exonerate the supervisor from the related obligations.

Legal Lightbulb

- The supervisor may be held responsible before the licensing board if the supervisee has violated ethical guidelines. The supervisor should, with due diligence, determine whether the supervisee is acting properly. This takes some "hands on" investigation.

- Supervision consultations must be documented and should include a review of the therapy to date, and any changes in the diagnosis, assessment, evaluation, treatment plan, or prognosis brought about by the consult.

- Supervision is more than casual exchanges of information over lunch, the phone, or cocktails. Ask the right questions. Document both the question and the answer.

- Supervision, to be objective, must be at arm's length. No family, friends, business associates, or other questionable relationships should be involved. When in doubt, don't supervise!

- Supervisors with huge clienteles cannot treat their clients wholesale and receive a kickback from supervisees. The substance, not the form, of the relationship will be reviewed if questioned by either a client or the licensing board.

- Supervision may occasionally be done over the phone, but mostly it should be face to face, with the file on the table.

- Supervision guidelines provide minimum standards. They are admissible in court to indicate what the supervisor or supervisee "should have done."

- Supervision must be disclosed to the client, together with the name and credentials of the supervisor.

- Supervision must be documented.

- The supervisor is responsible, legally, for the supervisee.

- The supervisee is responsible, also, for his or her own actions.

Appendix A

Bylaws for an IPA

MPH BEHAVIORAL HEALTH SERVICES, INC.
(A Texas Corporation)*

BYLAWS
ARTICLE ONE: NAME AND OFFICES

1.01   Name: The name of the Corporation is MPH Behavioral Health Services, Inc., hereinafter referred to as the "Corporation."

1.02   Registered Office and Agent: The Corporation shall establish, designate, and maintain a registered office and agent in the State of Texas. The registered office of the Corporation shall be at 350 Highway 183, Suite 206, Bedford, Texas 76022. The name of the registered agent at such address is Helen S. Shackowsky.

1.03   Change of Registered Office or Agent: The Corporation may change its registered office or change its registered agent, or both, by following the procedure set forth in Article 2.10 of the Texas Business Corporation Act. Any such change shall constitute an amendment to these Bylaws.

1.04   Other Offices: The Corporation may have offices at such places both within and without the State of Texas as the Board of Directors may from time to time determine or the business of the Corporation may require.

ARTICLE TWO: SHAREHOLDERS

2.01   Place of Meetings: All meetings of the Shareholders for the election of Directors and for any other purpose may be held at such time and place, within or without the State of Texas, as stated in the notice of the meeting or in a duly executed waiver of notice thereof.

2.02   Annual Meeting: An annual meeting of the Shareholders for the election of Directors and for the transaction of such other business as may properly come before the meeting shall be held each year on the first Monday in February, beginning in 20__, or such other date as may be selected by the Board of Directors from time to time. At the meeting, the Shareholders shall elect Directors and transact such other business as may properly be brought before the meeting.

---

* *Authors' Note:* Each state has its own incorporation statute, and the statutes vary slightly. Every lawyer has computer-generated forms available. The only special wrinkle is that certain professional disciplines have some corporate requirements that must be considered, and these requirements vary slightly from state to state.
   Section 8.09 discusses the inclusiveness intended by use of masculine nouns and pronouns.

2.03   Special Meetings: Special meetings of the Shareholders, for any purpose or purposes, unless otherwise prescribed by statute or by the Articles of Incorporation, or by these Bylaws, may be called by the President, the Secretary, the Board of Directors, or the holders of not less than one-tenth of all the shares entitled to vote at the meeting. Business transacted at a special meeting shall be confined to the subjects stated in the notice of the meeting.

2.04   Notice: Written or printed notice stating the place, day, and hour of the meeting and, in case of a special meeting, the purpose or purposes for which the meeting is called, shall be delivered not less than ten nor more than sixty days before the date of the meeting, either personally or by mail, by or at the direction of the person calling the meeting, to each Shareholder of record entitled to vote at the meeting. If mailed, such notice shall be deemed to be delivered when deposited in the United States mail addressed to the Shareholder at his address as it appears on the stock transfer books of the Corporation, with postage thereon prepaid.

2.05   Voting List: At least ten days before each meeting of Shareholders, a complete list of the Shareholders entitled to vote at such meeting, arranged in alphabetical order and setting forth the address of each and the number of voting shares held by each, shall be prepared by the officer or agent having charge of the stock transfer books. Such list, for a period of ten days prior to such meeting, shall be kept on file at the registered office of the Corporation and shall be subject to inspection by any Shareholder at any time during usual business hours. Such list shall also be produced and kept open at the time and place of the meeting during the whole time thereof, and shall be subject to inspection by any Shareholder during the whole time of the meeting.

2.06   Quorum: The holders of a majority of the shares issued and outstanding and entitled to vote thereat, present in person or represented by proxy, shall be requisite and shall constitute a quorum at all meetings of the Shareholders for the transaction of business except as otherwise provided by statute, by the Articles of Incorporation, or by these Bylaws. If a quorum is not present or represented at a meeting of the Shareholders, the Shareholders entitled to vote thereat, present in person or represented by proxy, shall have power to adjourn the meeting from time to time, without notice other than announcement at the meeting, until a quorum is present or represented. At such adjourned meeting at which a quorum is present or represented, any business may be transacted which might have been transacted at the meeting as originally notified.

2.07   Majority Vote; Withdrawal of Quorum: When a quorum is present at any meeting, the vote of the holders of a majority of the shares having voting power, present in person or represented by proxy, shall decide any question brought before such meeting, unless the question is one upon which, by express provision of the statutes or of the Articles of Incorporation or of these Bylaws, a different vote is required, in which case such express provision shall govern and control the decision of such question. The Shareholders present at a duly organized meeting may continue to transact business until adjournment, notwithstanding the withdrawal of enough Shareholders to leave less than a quorum.

2.08 Method of Voting: Each outstanding share, regardless of class, shall be entitled to one vote on each matter subject to a vote at a meeting of Shareholders, except to the extent that the voting rights of the shares of any class or classes are limited or denied by the Articles of Incorporation. The Board of Directors may, in the future, at their discretion, direct that voting be cumulative, according to any plan adopted by the Board. At any meeting of the Shareholders, every Shareholder having the right to vote may vote either in person or by proxy executed in writing by the Shareholder or by his duly authorized attorney-in-fact. No proxy shall be valid after eleven months from the date of its execution, unless otherwise provided in the proxy. Each proxy shall be revocable unless expressly provided therein to be irrevocable or unless otherwise made irrevocable by law. Each proxy shall be filed with the Secretary of the Corporation prior to, or at the time of, the meeting. Voting for Directors shall be in accordance with Section 3.06 of these Bylaws. Any vote may be taken viva voce or by show of hands unless someone entitled to vote objects, in which case written ballots shall be used. Cumulative voting is not prohibited.

2.09 Record Date—Closing Transfer Books: The Board of Directors may fix in advance a record date for the purpose of determining Shareholders entitled to notice of, or to vote at, a meeting of Shareholders, such record date to be not less than ten nor more than sixty days prior to such meeting; or the Board of Directors may close the stock transfer books for such purpose for a period of not less than ten nor more than sixty days prior to such meeting. In the absence of any action by the Board of Directors, the date upon which the notice of the meeting is mailed shall be the record date.

2.10 Action without Meeting: Any action required to be taken at any annual or special meeting of Shareholders, or any action which may be taken at any annual or special meeting of Shareholders, may be taken without a meeting, without prior notice, and without a vote, if a consent or consents in writing, setting forth the action so taken, is signed by the holder or holders of shares having not less than the minimum number of votes that would be necessary to take such action at a meeting at which the holders of all shares entitled to vote on the action were present and voted. Such consent or consents shall have the same force and effect as the requisite vote of the Shareholders at a meeting. The signed consent or consents, or a copy or copies thereof, shall be placed in the minute book of the Corporation. Such consents may be signed in multiple counterparts, each of which shall constitute an original for all purposes, and all of which together shall constitute the requisite written consent or consents of the Shareholders, if applicable. A telegram, telex, cablegram, or similar transaction by a Shareholder, or a photographic, photostatic, facsimile or similar reproduction of a writing signed by a Shareholder, shall be regarded as signed by the Shareholder for purposes of this Section 2.10.

2.11 Order of Business at Meetings: The order of business at annual meetings, and so far as practicable at other meetings of Shareholders, shall be as follows unless changed by the Board of Directors:

(a) Call to order.

(b) Proof of due notice of meeting.

(c) Determination of quorum and examination of proxies.

(d) Announcement of availability of voting list (see Bylaw 2.05).

(e) Announcement of distribution of annual reports (see Bylaw 8.03).

(f) Reading and disposing of minutes of last meeting of shareholders.

(g) Reports of officers and committees.

(h) Appointment of voting inspectors.

(i) Unfinished business.

(j) New business.

(k) Nomination of directors.

(l) Opening of polls for voting.

(m) Recess.

(n) Reconvening; closing of polls.

(o) Report of voting inspectors.

(p) Other business.

(q) Adjournment.

2.12 Credentialing Committee: Each and every individual who, from time to time, is a Shareholder in the Corporation, shall automatically be a member of a committee of all of the Shareholders of the Corporation to be called the Credentialing Committee of the Corporation. The Credentialing Committee shall be chaired by the President of the Corporation and shall be governed by the Articles of Incorporation and Bylaws of the Corporation and *Robert's Rules of Order, Newly Revised.* The duty of the Credentialing Committee shall be to meet from time to time, as convened by the President or at the written request of any three or more Shareholders, to determine for the Corporation which service providers the Corporation will contract for the providing of services. It is expressly understood and agreed that participation of the Shareholders on the Credentialing Committee shall not be deemed to be participation by the Shareholders in the operational management of the Corporation.

ARTICLE THREE: DIRECTORS

3.01 Management: The business and affairs of the Corporation shall be managed by the Board of Directors, which may exercise all such powers of the Corporation and do all such lawful acts and things as are not, by statute or by the Articles of Incorporation or by these Bylaws, directed or required to be exercised or done by the Shareholders.

3.02   Number: Qualification; Election—Term: The Board of Directors shall consist of not less than one member nor more than nine members; provided however, the Board of Directors in effect as of the date of effectiveness of these Bylaws consists of seven members. A Director need not be a Shareholder or resident of any particular state or country. The Directors shall be elected at the annual meeting of the Shareholders, except as provided in Bylaws 3.03 and 3.05. Each Director elected shall hold office until his successor is elected and qualified. Each person elected as a Director shall be deemed to have qualified unless he states his refusal to serve shortly after being notified of his election.

3.03   Change in Number: The number of Directors may be increased or decreased from time to time by amendment to these Bylaws, but no decrease shall have the effect of shortening the term of any incumbent Director. Any directorship to be filled by reason of an increase in the number of Directors shall be filled by the Board of Directors for a term of office continuing only until the next election of one or more Directors by the Shareholders; provided that the Board of Directors may not fill more than two such directorships during the period between any two successive annual meetings of Shareholders.

3.04   Removal: Any Director may be removed either for or without cause at any special or annual meeting of Shareholders by the affirmative vote of a majority, in number of shares, of the Shareholders present in person or by proxy at such meeting and entitled to vote for the election of such Director if notice of intention to act upon such matter is given in the notice calling such meeting.

3.05   Vacancies: Any unfilled directorship position, or any vacancy occurring in the Board of Directors (by death, resignation, removal, or otherwise), shall be filled by an affirmative vote of a majority of the remaining Directors though less than a quorum of the Board of Directors. A Director elected to fill a vacancy shall be elected for the unexpired term of his predecessor in office, except that a vacancy occurring due to an increase in the number of Directors shall be filled in accordance with Section 3.03 of these Bylaws.

3.06   Election of Directors: Directors shall be elected by majority vote.

3.07   Place of Meeting: Meetings of the Board of Directors, regular or special, may be held either within or without the State of Texas.

3.08   First Meeting: The first meeting of each newly elected Board of Directors shall be held without further notice immediately following the annual meeting of Shareholders, and at the same place, unless the Directors change such time or place by unanimous vote.

3.09   Regular Meetings: Regular meetings of the Board of Directors may be held without notice at such time and place as determined by the Board of Directors.

3.10 Special Meetings: Special meetings of the Board of Directors may be called by the President or by any Director on three days' notice to each Director, given either personally or by mail or by telegram. Except as otherwise expressly provided by statute, or by the Articles of Incorporation, or by these Bylaws, neither the business to be transacted at, nor the purpose of, any special meeting of the Board of Directors need be specified in a notice or waiver of notice.

3.11 Quorum—Majority Vote: At all meetings of the Board of Directors, a majority of the number of Directors then elected and qualified shall constitute a quorum for the transaction of business. The act of a majority of the Directors present at any meeting at which a quorum is present shall be the act of the Board of Directors, except as otherwise specifically provided by statute or by the Articles of Incorporation or by these Bylaws. If a quorum is not present at a meeting of the Board of Directors, the Directors present thereat may adjourn the meeting from time to time, without notice other than announcement at the meeting, until a quorum is present. Each Director who is present at a meeting will be deemed to have assented to any action taken at such meeting unless his dissent to the action is entered in the minutes of the meeting, or unless he files his written dissent thereto with the Secretary of the meeting or forwards such dissent by registered mail to the secretary of the Corporation immediately after such meeting.

3.12 Compensation: By resolution of the Board of Directors, the Directors may be paid their expenses, if any, of attendance at each meeting of the Board of Directors and may be paid a fixed sum for attendance of each meeting of the Board of Directors, or a stated salary as Director. No such payment shall preclude any Director from serving the Corporation in any other capacity and receiving compensation therefor. Members of any executive, special, or standing committees established by the Board of Directors, may, by resolution of the Board of Directors, be allowed like compensation and expenses for attending committee meetings.

3.13 Procedure: The Board of Directors shall keep regular minutes of its proceedings. The minutes shall be placed in the minute book of the Corporation.

3.14 Interested Directors, Officers, and Shareholders:

(a) If Paragraph (b) is satisfied, no contract or other transaction between the Corporation and any of its Directors, Officers, or Shareholders (or any corporation or firm in which any of them are directly or indirectly interested) shall be invalid solely because of such relationship or because of the presence of such Director, Officer, or Shareholder at the meeting authorizing such contract or transaction, or his participation in such meeting or authorization.

(b) Paragraph (a) shall apply only if:

(1) The material facts of the relationship or interest of each such Director, Officer, or Shareholder are known or disclosed:

(A) To the Board of Directors and it nevertheless authorizes or ratifies the contract or transaction by a majority of the Directors present, each such interested Director to be counted in determining whether a quorum is present but not in calculating the majority necessary to carry the vote; or

(B) To the Shareholders and they nevertheless authorize or ratify the contract or transaction by a majority of the shares present, each such interested person to be counted for a quorum and voting purposes; or

(2) The contract or transaction is fair to the Corporation as of the time it is authorized or ratified by the Board of Directors, a committee of the Board, or the Shareholders.

(c) This provision shall not be construed to invalidate a contract or transaction which would be valid in the absence of this provision.

3.15 Certain Officers: The President shall be elected from among the members of the Board of Directors.

3.16 Action without Meeting: Any action required or permitted to be taken at a meeting of the Board of Directors may be taken without a meeting if a consent in writing, setting forth the action so taken, is signed by all members of the Board of Directors. Such consent shall have the same force and effect as unanimous vote of the Board of Directors at a meeting. The signed consent, or a signed copy thereof, shall be placed in the minute book of the Corporation. Such consents may be signed in multiple counterparts, each of which shall constitute an original for all purposes, and all of which together shall constitute the unanimous written consent of the Directors.

ARTICLE FOUR: EXECUTIVE COMMITTEE

4.01 Designation: The Board of Directors may, by resolution adopted by a majority of the whole Board, designate an Executive Committee from among its members.

4.02 Number—Qualification; Term: The Executive Committee shall consist of one or more Directors. The Executive Committee shall serve at the pleasure of the Board of Directors.

4.03 Authority: The Executive Committee shall have and may exercise the authority of the Board of Directors in the management of the business and affairs of the Corporation except where action of the full Board of Directors is required by statute or by the Articles of Incorporation, and shall have power to authorize the seal of the Corporation to be affixed to all papers which may require it; except that the Executive Committee shall not have authority to: amend the Articles of Incorporation; approve a plan of merger or consolidation; recommend to the Shareholders the sale, lease, or exchange of all or substantially all of the property and assets of the Corporation other than in the usual and regular course of its business; recommend to the Shareholders the voluntary dissolution of the Corporation; amend, alter, or repeal the Bylaws of the Corporation or adopt new Bylaws for the Corporation; fill any vacancy in the Board of Directors or any other corporate committee; fix the compensation of any member of any corporate committee; alter or repeal any resolution of the Board of Directors; declare a dividend; or authorize the issuance of shares of the corporation. Each Director shall be deemed to have assented to any action of the Executive

Committee unless, within seven days after receiving actual or constructive notice of such action, he delivers his written dissent thereto to the secretary of the Corporation.

4.04   Change in Number: The number of Executive Committee members may be increased or decreased (but not below one) from time to time by resolution adopted by a majority of the Board of Directors.

4.05   Removal: Any member of the Executive Committee may be removed by the Board of Directors by the affirmative vote of a majority of the Board of Directors whenever in its judgment the best interests of the Corporation will be served thereby.

4.06   Vacancies: A vacancy occurring in the Executive Committee (by death, resignation, removal, or otherwise) shall be filled by the Board of Directors in the manner provided for original designation in Section 4.01.

4.07   Meetings: Time, place, and notice, if any, of Executive Committee meetings shall be as determined by the Executive Committee.

4.08   Quorum; Majority Vote: At meetings of the Executive Committee, a majority of the members shall constitute a quorum for the transaction of business. The act of a majority of the members present at any meeting at which a quorum is present shall be the act of the Executive Committee, except as otherwise specifically provided by statute or by the Articles of Incorporation or by these Bylaws. If a quorum is not present at a meeting of the Executive Committee, the members present thereat may adjourn the meeting from time to time, without notice other than announcement at the meeting, until a quorum is present.

4.09   Compensation: By resolution of the Board of Directors, the members of the Executive Committee may be paid their expenses, if any, of attendance at each meeting of the Executive Committee and may be paid a fixed sum for attendance at each meeting of the Executive Committee or a stated salary as a member thereof. No such payment shall preclude any member from serving the Corporation in any other capacity and receiving compensation therefor.

4.10   Procedure: The Executive Committee shall keep regular minutes of its proceedings and report the same to the Board of Directors when required. The minutes of the proceedings of the Executive Committee shall be placed in the minute book of the Corporation.

4.11   Action without Meeting: Any action required or permitted to be taken at a meeting of the Executive Committee may be taken without a meeting if a consent in writing, setting forth the action so taken, is signed by all the members of the Executive Committee. Such consent shall have the same force and effect as a unanimous vote at a meeting. The signed consent, or a signed copy thereof, shall be placed in the minute book. Such consents may be signed in multiple counterparts, each of which shall constitute an original for all purposes, and all of which together shall constitute the unanimous written consent of the Directors.

4.12 Responsibility: The designation of an Executive Committee and the delegation of authority to it shall not operate to relieve the Board of Directors, or any member thereof, of any responsibility imposed by law.

ARTICLE FIVE: NOTICE

5.01 Method: Whenever by statute or the Articles of Incorporation or these Bylaws notice is required to be given to any Director or Shareholder and no provision is made as to how such notice shall be given, it shall not be construed to mean personal notice, but any such notice may be given:

(a) In writing, by mail, postage prepaid, addressed to such Director or Shareholder at such address as appears on the books of the Corporation; or

(b) By any other method permitted by law.

Any notice required or permitted to be given by mail shall be deemed to be given at the time it is deposited, postage prepaid, in the United States mail.

5.02 Waiver: Whenever, by statute or the Articles of Incorporation or these Bylaws, notice is required to be given to a Shareholder or Director, a waiver thereof in writing signed by the person or persons entitled to such notice, whether before or after the time stated in such notice, shall be equivalent to the giving of such notice. Attendance of a Director at a meeting shall constitute a waiver of notice of such meeting except where a Director attends for the express purpose of objecting to the transaction of any business on the grounds that the meeting is not lawfully called or convened.

5.03 Telephone Meetings: Shareholders, Directors, or members of any committee may hold any meeting of such Shareholders, Directors, or committee by means of conference telephone or similar communications equipment which permits all persons participating in the meeting to hear each other. Actions taken at such meeting shall have the same force and effect as a vote at a meeting in person. The secretary shall prepare a memorandum of the actions taken at conference telephone meetings.

ARTICLE SIX: OFFICERS AND AGENTS

6.01 Number—Qualification; Election: Term:

(a) The Corporation shall have:

(1) A Chairman of the Board (should the Board of Directors so choose to select), a President, a Vice President, a Secretary, and a Treasurer, and

(2) Such other Officers (including one or more Vice Presidents, and assistant Officers and agents) as the Board of Directors authorizes from time to time.

(b) No Officer or agent need be a Shareholder, a Director, or a resident of Texas, except as provided in Sections 3.15 and 4.02 of these Bylaws.

(c) Officers named in Section 6.01(a) (1) above shall be elected by the Board of Directors on the expiration of an Officer's term or whenever a vacancy exists. Officers and agents named in Section 6.01 (a) (2) may be elected by the Board of Directors at any meeting.

(d) Unless otherwise specified by the Board at the time of election or appointment, or in an employment contract approved by the Board, each Officer's and agent's term shall end at the first meeting of Directors after the next annual meeting of Shareholders. He shall serve until the end of his term or, if earlier, his death, resignation, or removal.

(e) Any two or more offices may be held by the same person.

6.02   Removal and Resignation: Any Officer or agent elected or appointed by the Board of Directors may be removed with or without cause by a majority of the Directors at any regular or special meeting of the Board of Directors. Any Officer may resign at any time by giving written notice to the Board of Directors or to the President or Secretary. Any such resignation shall take effect upon receipt of such notice if no date is specified in the notice, or, if a later date is specified in the notice, upon such later date; and unless otherwise specified in the notice, the acceptance of such resignation shall not be necessary to make it effective. The removal of any Officer or agent shall be without prejudice to the contract rights, if any, of the person so removed. Election or appointment of an Officer or agent shall not of itself create contract rights.

6.03   Vacancies: Any vacancy occurring in any office of the Corporation (by death, resignation, removal, or otherwise) may be filled by the Board of Directors.

6.04   Authority: Officers shall have full authority to perform all duties in the management of the Corporation as are provided in these Bylaws or as may be determined by resolution of the Board of Directors from time to time not inconsistent with these Bylaws.

6.05   Compensation: The compensation of Officers and agents shall be fixed from time to time by the Board of Directors.

6.06   Chairman of the Board: The Chairman of the Board, if any, shall preside at all meetings of the Board of Directors and shall exercise and perform such other powers and duties as may be assigned to him by the Board of Directors or prescribed by these Bylaws.

6.07   Executive Powers: The Chairman of the Board, if any, and the President of the Corporation respectively, shall, in the order of their seniority, unless otherwise determined by the Board of Directors or otherwise are positions held by the same person, have general and active management of the business and affairs of the Corporation and shall see that all orders and resolutions of the Board are carried into effect. They shall perform such other duties and have such other authority and powers as the Board of Directors may from time to time prescribe.

Within this authority and in the course of their respective duties, the Chairman of the Board, if any, and the President of the Corporation, respectively, shall have the general authority to:

(a) *Conduct Meetings.* Preside at all meetings of the Shareholders and at all meetings of the Board of Directors, and shall be ex officio members of all the standing committees, including the Executive Committee, if any.

(b) *Sign Share Certificates.* Sign all certificates of stock of the corporation, in conjunction with the Secretary or Assistant Secretary, unless otherwise ordered by the Board of Directors.

(c) *Execute Instruments.* When authorized by the Board of Directors or if required by law, execute, in the name of the Corporation, deeds, conveyances, notices, leases, checks, drafts, bills of exchange, warrants, promissory notes, bonds, debentures, contracts, and other papers and instruments in writing, and unless the Board of Directors orders otherwise by resolution, make such contracts as the ordinary conduct of the Corporation's business requires.

(d) *Hire and Discharge Employees.* Subject to the approval of the Board of Directors, appoint and remove, employ and discharge, and prescribe the duties and fix the compensation of all agents, employees, and clerks of the Corporation other than the duly appointed Officers, and, subject to the direction of the Board of Directors, control all of the Officers, agents, and employees of the Corporation.

6.08 Vice Presidents: The Vice Presidents, if any, in the order of their seniority, unless otherwise determined by the Board of Directors, shall, in the absence or disability of the President, perform the duties and have the authority and exercise the powers of the President. They shall perform such other duties and have such other authority and powers as the Board of Directors may from time to time prescribe or as the senior Officers of the Corporation may from time to time delegate.

6.09 Secretary: The Secretary shall attend all meetings of the Board of Directors and all meetings of the Shareholders and record all votes and minutes of all proceedings in a book to be kept for that purpose, and shall perform like duties for the Executive Committee when required. He shall give, or cause to be given, notice of all meetings of the Shareholders and special meetings of the Board of Directors. He shall keep in safe custody the seal of the Corporation and, when authorized by the Board of Directors or the Executive Committee, affix the same to any instrument requiring it, and when so affixed, it shall be attested by his signature or by the signature of the Treasurer or an Assistant Secretary. He shall be under the supervision of the senior Officers of the Corporation. He shall perform such other duties and have such other authority and powers as the Board of Directors may from time to time prescribe or as the senior Officers of the Corporation may from time to time delegate.

6.10 Assistant Secretaries: The Assistant Secretaries, if any, in the order of their seniority, unless otherwise determined by the Board of Directors, shall, in the absence or disability of the Secretary, perform the duties and have the authority and exercise the powers of the Secretary.

They shall perform such other duties and have such other powers as the Board of Directors may from time to time prescribe or as the senior Officers of the Corporation may from time to time delegate.

6.11 Treasurer: The Treasurer shall have the custody of the corporate funds and securities and shall keep full and accurate accounts of all income, expenses, receipts, and disbursements of the Corporation and shall deposit all moneys and other valuable effects in the name and to the credit of the Corporation in such depositories as may be designated by the Board of Directors. He shall disburse the funds of the Corporation as may be ordered by the Board of Directors, taking proper vouchers for such disbursements, and shall render to the senior Officers of the Corporation and Directors, at the regular meeting of the Board, or whenever they may request it, accounts of all his transactions as Treasurer and of the financial condition of the Corporation. If required by the Board of Directors, he shall give the Corporation a bond in such form, in such sum, and with such surety or sureties as satisfactory to the Board, for the faithful performance of the duties of his office and for the restoration to the Corporation, in case of his death, resignation, retirement or removal from office, of all books, paper, vouchers, money, and other property of whatever kind in his possession or under his control belonging to the Corporation. He shall perform such other duties and have such other authority and powers as the Board of Directors may from time to time prescribe or as the senior Officers of the Corporation may from time to time delegate.

6.12 Assistant Treasurers: The Assistant Treasurers, if any, in the order of their seniority, unless otherwise determined by the Board of Directors, shall, in the absence or disability of the Treasurer, perform the duties and exercise the powers of the Treasurer. They shall perform such other duties and have such other powers as the Board of Directors may from time to time prescribe or as the senior Officers of the Corporation may from time to time delegate.

ARTICLE SEVEN: CERTIFICATE AND TRANSFER REGULATIONS

7.01 Certificates: Certificates in such form as may be determined by the Board of Directors shall be delivered, representing all shares to which Shareholders are entitled. Certificates shall be consecutively numbered and shall be entered in the books of the Corporation as they are issued. Each certificate shall state on the face thereof that the Corporation is organized under the laws of the State of Texas, the holder's name, the number and class of shares, the par value of such shares or a statement that such shares are without par value, and such other matters as may be required by law. They shall be signed by the President or a Vice President and either the Secretary or Assistant Secretary or such other Officer or Officers as the Board of Directors designates, and may be sealed with the seal of the Corporation or a facsimile thereof. If any certificate is countersigned by a transfer agent, or an assistant transfer agent, or registered by a registrar (either of which is other than the Corporation or an employee of the Corporation), the signature of any such Officer may be a facsimile thereof.

7.02   Issuance of Certificates: Shares (both treasury and authorized but unissued) may be issued for such consideration (not less than par value) and to such persons as the Board of Directors determines from time to time. Shares may not be issued until the full amount of the consideration, fixed as provided by law, has been paid. In addition, Shares shall not be issued or transferred until such additional conditions and documentation as the Corporation (or its transfer agent, as the case may be) shall reasonably require, including without limitation, the delivery with the surrender of such stock certificate or certificates of proper evidence of succession, assignment, or other authority to obtain transfer thereof, as the circumstances may require, and such legal opinions with reference to the requested transfer as shall be required by the Corporation (or its transfer agent) pursuant to the provisions of these Bylaws and applicable law, shall have been satisfied.

7.03   Legends on Certificates:

(a) *Shares in Classes or Series.* If the Corporation is authorized to issue shares of more than one class, the certificates shall set forth, either on the face or back of the certificate, a full or summary statement of all of the designations, preferences, limitations, and relative rights of the shares of such class and, if the Corporation is authorized to issue any preferred or special class in series, the variations in the relative rights and preferences of the shares of each such series so far as the same have been fixed and determined, and the authority of the Board of Directors to fix and determine the relative rights and preferences of subsequent series. In lieu of providing such a statement in full on the certificate, a statement on the face or back of the certificate may provide that the Corporation will furnish such information to any Shareholder without charge upon written request to the Corporation at its principal place of business or registered office and that copies of the information are on file in the office of the Secretary of State.

(b) *Restriction on Transfer.* Any restrictions imposed by the Corporation on the sale or other disposition of its shares and on the transfer thereof may be copied at length or in summary form on the face, or so copied on the back and referred to on the face, of each certificate representing shares to which the restriction applies. The certificate may, however, state on the face or back that such a restriction exists pursuant to a specified document and that the Corporation will furnish a copy of the document to the holder of the certificate without charge upon written request to the Corporation at its principal place of business, or refer to such restriction in any other manner permitted by law.

(c) *Preemptive Rights.* Any preemptive rights of a Shareholder to acquire unissued or treasury shares of the Corporation which are or may at any time be limited or denied by the Articles of Incorporation may be set forth at length on the face or back of the certificate representing shares subject thereto. In lieu of providing such a statement in full on the certificate, a statement on the face or back of the certificate may provide that the Corporation will furnish such information to any Shareholder without charge upon written request to the Corporation at its principal place of business, and that a copy of such information is on file in the office of the Secretary of State, or refer to such denial of preemptive rights in any other manner permitted by law.

(d) *Unregistered Securities.* Any security of the Corporation, including, among others, any certificate evidencing shares of the Common Stock or warrants to purchase Common Stock of the Corporation, which is issued to any person without registration under the Securities Act of 1933, as amended, or the securities laws of any state, shall not be transferrable until the Corporation has been furnished with a legal opinion of counsel with reference thereto, satisfactory in form and content to the Corporation and its counsel, if required by the Corporation, to the effect that such sale, transfer, or pledge does not involve a violation of the Securities Act of 1933, as amended, or the securities laws of any state having jurisdiction. The certificate representing the security shall bear substantially the following legend:

"THE SECURITIES REPRESENTED BY THIS CERTIFICATE HAVE NOT BEEN REGISTERED UNDER THE SECURITIES ACT OF 1933, AS AMENDED, OR UNDER THE SECURITIES LAWS OF ANY STATE AND MAY NOT BE OFFERED, SOLD, OR TRANSFERRED UNLESS SUCH OFFER, SALE, OR TRANSFER WILL NOT BE IN VIOLATION OF THE SECURITIES ACT OF 1933, AS AMENDED, OR ANY APPLICABLE BLUE SKY LAWS. ANY OFFER, SALE, OR TRANSFER OF THESE SECURITIES MAY NOT BE MADE WITHOUT THE PRIOR WRITTEN APPROVAL OF THE CORPORATION."

7.04   Payment of Shares:

(a) *Kind.* The consideration for the issuance of shares shall consist of money paid, labor done (including services actually performed for the Corporation), or property (tangible or intangible) actually received. Neither promissory notes nor the promise of future services shall constitute payment for shares.

(b) *Valuation.* In the absence of fraud in the transaction, the judgment of the Board of Directors as to the value of consideration received shall be conclusive.

(c) *Effect.* When consideration, fixed as provided by law, has been paid, the shares shall be deemed to have been issued and shall be considered fully paid and nonassessable.

(d) *Allocation of Consideration.* The consideration received for shares shall be allocated by the Board of Directors, in accordance with law, between Stated Capital and Capital Surplus accounts.

7.05   Subscriptions: Unless otherwise provided in the subscription agreement, subscriptions for shares shall be paid in full at such time or in such installments and at such times as determined by the Board of Directors. Any call made by the Board of Directors for payment on subscriptions shall be uniform as to all shares of the same series. In case of default in the payment on any installment or call when payment is due, the Corporation may proceed to collect the amount due in the same manner as any debt due to the Corporation.

7.06   Lien: For any indebtedness of a Shareholder to the Corporation, the Corporation shall have a first and prior lien on all shares of its stock owned by him and on all dividends or other distributions declared thereon.

7.07   Lost, Stolen, or Destroyed Certificates: The Corporation shall issue a new certificate in place of any certificate for shares previously issued if the registered owner of the certificate:

(a) *Claim.* Submits proof in affidavit form that it has been lost, destroyed, or wrongfully taken; and

(b) *Timely Request.* Requests the issuance of a new certificate before the Corporation has notice that the certificate has been acquired by a purchaser for value in good faith and without notice of an adverse claim; and

(c) *Bond.* Gives a bond in such form, and with such surety or sureties, with fixed or open penalty, if the Corporation so requires, to indemnify the Corporation (and its transfer agent and registrar, if any) against any claim that may be made on account of the alleged loss, destruction, or theft of the certificate; and

(d) *Other Requirements.* Satisfies any other reasonable requirements imposed by the Corporation.

When a certificate has been lost, apparently destroyed, or wrongfully taken, and the holder of record fails to notify the Corporation within a reasonable time after he has notice of it, and the Corporation registers a transfer of the shares represented by the certificate before receiving such notification, the holder of record shall be precluded from making any claim against the Corporation for the transfer or for a new certificate.

7.08   Registration of Transfer: The Corporation shall register the transfer of a certificate for shares presented to it for transfer if:

(a) *Endorsement.* The certificate is properly endorsed by the registered owner or by his duly authorized attorney; and

(b) *Guaranty and Effectiveness of Signature.* If required by the Corporation, the signature of such person has been guaranteed by a national banking association or member of the New York Stock Exchange, and reasonable assurance is given that such endorsements are effective; and

(c) *Adverse Claims.* The Corporation has no notice of an adverse claim or has discharged any duty to inquire into such a claim; and

(d) *Collection of Taxes.* Any applicable law relating to the collection of taxes has been complied with.

7.09   Registered Owner: Prior to due presentment for registration of transfer of a certificate for shares, the Corporation may treat the registered owner or holder of a written proxy from such registered owner as the person exclusively entitled to vote, to receive notices, and otherwise exercise all the rights and powers of a Shareholder.

7.10 Preemptive Rights: No Shareholder or other person shall have any preemptive rights of any kind to acquire additional, unissued, or treasury shares of the Corporation, or securities of the Corporation convertible into, or carrying rights to subscribe to or acquire, shares of any class or series of the Corporation's capital stock, unless, and to the extent that, such rights may be expressly granted by appropriate action.

ARTICLE EIGHT: GENERAL PROVISIONS

8.01 Dividends and Reserves:

(a) *Declaration and Payment.* Subject to statute and the Articles of Incorporation, dividends may be declared by the Board of Directors at any regular or special meeting and may be paid in cash, in property, or in shares of the Corporation. The declaration and payment shall be at the discretion of the Board of Directors.

(b) *Record Date.* The Board of Directors may fix in advance a record date for the purpose of determining Shareholders entitled to receive payment of any dividend, such record date to be not more than sixty days prior to the payment date of such dividend, or the Board of Directors may close the stock transfer books for such purpose for a period of not more than sixty days prior to the payment date of such dividend. In the absence of any action by the Board of Directors, the date upon which the Board of Directors adopts the resolution declaring such dividend shall be the record date.

(c) *Reserves.* By resolution, the Board of Directors may create such reserve or reserves out of the Earned surplus of the Corporation as the Directors from time to time, in their discretion, think proper to provide for contingencies, or to equalize dividends, or to repair or maintain any property of the Corporation, or for any other purpose they think beneficial to the Corporation. The Directors may modify or abolish any such reserve in the manner in which it was created.

8.02 Books and Records: The Corporation shall keep correct and complete books and records of account and shall keep minutes of the proceedings of its Shareholders and Board of Directors, and shall keep at its registered office or principal place of business, or at the office of its transfer agent or registrar, a record of its Shareholders, giving the names and addresses of all Shareholders and the number and class of the shares held by each.

8.03 Annual Reports: The Board of Directors shall cause such reports to be mailed to Shareholders as the Board of Directors deems to be necessary or desirable from time to time.

8.04 Checks and Notes: All checks or demands for money and notes of the Corporation shall be signed by such Officer or Officers or such other person or persons as the Board of Directors designates from time to time.

8.05 Fiscal Year: The fiscal year of the Corporation shall be the calendar year.

8.06 Seal: The Corporation Seal (of which there may be one or more examples) may contain the name of the Corporation and the name of the state of incorporation. The Seal may be used by impressing it or reproducing a facsimile of it, or otherwise. Absence of the Corporation Seal shall not affect the validity or enforceability or any document or instrument.

8.07 Indemnification:

(a) The Corporation shall have the right to indemnify, to purchase indemnity insurance for, and to pay and advance expenses to, Directors, Officers and other persons who are eligible for, or entitled to, such indemnification, payments, or advances, in accordance with and subject to the provisions of Article 2.02–1 of the Texas Business Corporation Act and any amendments thereto, to the extent such indemnification, payments, or advances are either expressly required by such provisions or are expressly authorized by the Board of Directors within the scope of such provisions. The right of the Corporation to indemnify such persons shall include, but not be limited to, the authority of the Corporation to enter into written agreements for indemnification with such persons.

(b) Subject to the provisions of Article 2.02–1 of the Texas Business Corporation Act and any amendments thereto, a Director of the Corporation shall not be liable to the Corporation or its shareholders for monetary damages for an act or omission in the Director's capacity as a Director, except that this provision does not eliminate or limit the liability of a Director to the extent the Director is found liable for:

(1) A breach of the Director's duty of loyalty to the Corporation or its shareholders;

(2) An act or omission not in good faith that constitutes a breach of duty of the Director to the Corporation or an act or omission that involves intentional misconduct or a knowing violation of the law;

(3) A transaction from which the Director received an improper benefit, whether or not the benefit resulted from an action taken within the scope of the Director's office; or

(4) An act or omission for which the liability of a Director is expressly provided by an applicable statute.

8.08 Amendment of Bylaws: These Bylaws may be altered, amended, or repealed at any meeting of the Board of Directors at which a quorum is present, by the affirmative vote of a majority of the Directors present thereat, provided notice of the proposed alteration, amendment, or repeal is contained in the notice of such meeting.

8.09 Construction: Whenever the context so requires, the masculine shall include the feminine and neuter, and the singular shall include the plural, and conversely. If any portion of these Bylaws is ever finally determined to be invalid or inoperative, then, so far as is reasonable and possible:

(a) The remainder of these Bylaws shall be valid and operative; and

(b) Effect shall be given to the intent manifested by the portion held invalid or inoperative.

8.10 **Table of Contents; Headings:** The table of contents and headings are for organization, convenience, and clarity. In interpreting these Bylaws, they shall be subordinated in importance to the other written material.

MPH Behavioral
Health Services, Inc.,
A Texas Corporation

By: _____
Helen S. Shackowsky, President

Appendix B

PARTNERSHIP AGREEMENT

This agreement is made on February 1, 20__ between James Hathaway of 3638 Ridgecove, Rockwall, Rockwall County, Texas 75032, Sylvia Wainright of 1467 Royal Lane, Apt. 645, Dallas, Dallas County, Texas 75210, and Benjamin Stickle of 14679 Allenway, Plano, Collin County, Texas 75462, who are referred to in this agreement as "partners."

The partners form a partnership under the Texas Revised Partnership Act as a registered limited liability partnership per § 3.08 of the Texas Revised Partnership Act pursuant to the following terms and conditions which are stated in this partnership agreement.

RECITALS

1. The partners are mental health professionals licensed to practice as professional counselors in Texas.

2. The partners have each been sole practitioners in their respective mental health specialties.

3. The partners desire to enter into a partnership for the practice of counseling. (Practice of: Psychology, Social Work, Marriage and Family Therapy, Addictions Therapy, Play Therapy, etc.)

In consideration of the mutual covenants contained in this agreement, the parties agree as follows:

I. PURPOSE AND NAME

A partnership is created and shall be known as 3P Wellness Center, LLP, and shall be for the practice of counseling as regulated by the laws of the State of Texas, and the Code of Ethics of the American and Texas Counseling Associations.

II. DURATION

The partnership commences on February 1, 20 __ and continues in effect until terminated by operation of law or by the agreement of the partners as provided in Article XX.

III. CONTRIBUTIONS

The partnership shall be capitalized at $45,000.00, consisting of the contribution of their existing three counseling practices, with values stipulated at $10,000.00 each and a cash contribution of $5,000.00 each, receipt of which is hereby acknowledged.

IV. OFFICE EQUIPMENT

All office equipment that presently is on the premises to be occupied by the partnership belongs to Benjamin Stickle but shall remain on the premises for use by the partnership.

The equipment shall remain the personal property of Benjamin Stickle and the partnership shall pay him $250.00 per month rental for the use of the equipment.

V. SHARES IN PARTNERSHIP

The partners are entitled to share in the partnership profits and losses, as follows:

James Hathaway   33 ⅓ percent

Sylvia Wainright   33 ⅓ percent

Benjamin Stickle   33 ⅓ percent

VI. FEES

All fees received by any partner, whether for counseling services rendered, grants, consultation fees, or any other service, shall be the property of the partnership and shall be treated as ordinary partnership income. Personal property received as a gift by a partner may be retained by that partner as his or her separate property.

VII. DUTIES OF PARTNERS

Each partner shall contribute his or her full time and all of his or her skills to the partnership business. Each partner is responsible for the consultation, evaluation, and treatment of those clients desiring care in that partner's mental health specialty area as follows:

James Hathaway specializing in addiction/chemical dependency therapy

Sylvia Wainright specializing in children/play therapy

Benjamin Stickle specializing in adolescents/family therapy

Each partner may be called on to consult with any other partner regarding the consultation, evaluation, and treatment for any client of the other partner, for any purpose whatever.

VIII. LIMITATIONS ON DUTIES

The partners shall not engage in the practice of counseling in any manner or form except for the benefit of the partnership unless the prior written consent of the remaining partners is obtained. This prohibition shall apply equally to services performed without a fee.

A partner shall not obligate the partnership by acting as guarantor or surety on a note, discharging any debts owed to the partnership for less than full consideration, loaning partnership money to third parties, or contracting any indebtedness for the partnership in excess of $150.00 ($ ____ . ____) without the prior written approval of the remaining partners.

IX. PRIVATE DEBTS

Each partner shall hold the partnership harmless on any private debt that he or she has incurred, and should the partnership be held liable for any personal indebtedness of a partner, that partner's share of the annual profits shall be debited a corresponding amount.

X. EXPENSES

The partnership shall pay all expenses incurred by the partnership and those of each partner incurred in the course of partnership business, except as follows:

Each partner shall obtain, maintain, and use an automobile of his or her personal selection for performing the duties required in the partnership business. The costs and expenses for obtaining, operating, and maintaining the automobiles shall be the personal obligations of each partner, and the partner shall hold the partnership harmless for such expenses.

XI. PROFITS AND LOSSES

A monthly profit and loss statement shall be prepared for the partnership by a certified public accountant selected by the partners, reporting the monthly partnership net profits or losses for distribution. These figures shall be controlling on all parties, and the reported net profit or loss shall be distributed proportionately to partners based on their percentage interest in the partnership on the 30th day of each month. All errors in the statements must be noted and corrected within 2 months after release of the statement figures, or they shall be binding.

XII. DRAWS

The partners are entitled to obtain advance disbursements of money from the partnership to meet anticipated business expenses. A draw shall be made on the basis of a voucher submitted by the partner, and each partner shall file a monthly expense account statement, reconciling all expenses with draws he or she has obtained during the reporting period. (Alternatively, periodic draws can be agreed on in advance in a specific sum.)

XIII. GOOD FAITH

The duties of each partner are of a fiduciary nature relating to the remaining partners in the partnership, and each partner owes a duty of complete disclosure of all business transactions and good faith in his or her dealings on behalf of and with the partnership and the remaining partners.

XIV. BANKING

The partnership shall maintain a business banking account at Bank One located at 4625 Main Street, Richardson, Texas. All the receipts of the partnership shall be deposited in this account, and all partnership and partners' authorized business expenses shall be disbursed from this account.

XV. BOOKS OF ACCOUNTS

A complete set of books of accounts, organized and maintained using approved accounting practices, shall be established by the partnership's accounting firm. The books shall be retained at the principal place of the partners' business and shall be open for inspection by any partner at all reasonable hours.

XVI. ACCOUNTING

The fiscal year of the partnership is from January 1 to December 31, each year, a date corresponding to the fiscal year used by the partners in their former individual practices. The accounting basis used shall be cash. The accounting firm shall prepare, in addition to the monthly profit and loss statements, the annual profit and loss statements, financial statements, annual audits, and valuations of partners' interests.

XVII. INSURANCE

The partnership shall procure and maintain a policy of liability insurance providing malpractice insurance for each of the partners for $2,000,000.00 for each occurrence and $5,000.000.00 total coverage per partner.

XVIII. NEGLIGENCE

Each partner is personally and individually liable for repayment to the partnership of any sum paid out by the partnership in excess of insurance coverage provided in Article XVII where the negligence or misconduct of the partner has been determined to be the cause of the insurance settlement or suit.

XIX. TERMINATION

The partnership is terminated either by operation of law or on written notice from any partner desiring to terminate the partnership to the remaining partners. A notice of termination must be given at least six months prior to the intended date of termination.

XX. LIQUIDATION

On the termination of the partnership, either by operation of law or election of a partner, the existing business of the partnership shall be completed with special consideration being given to appropriate referral and termination of all existing clients of the partnership. Client files shall be maintained by the partner providing services to a client. The office equipment shall be returned to Benjamin Stickle and all assets of the partnership shall be liquidated. After discharging all obligations of the partnership, all remaining proceeds shall be distributed to the partners on a basis proportionate to their interest in the partnership. In the event there are insufficient assets to discharge all obligations of the partnership, the partners shall be liable for the remaining obligations on a basis proportionate to their interest in the partnership.

Dated February 1, 20__

_____

James Hathaway

_____

Sylvia Wainright

_____

Benjamin Stickle

Appendix C

ARTICLES OF INCORPORATION: PROFESSIONAL CORPORATION

ARTICLES OF INCORPORATION OF CARL DAVIDSON, JR., PHD, PC

The undersigned, acting as incorporator of a professional corporation under the Texas Professional Corporation Act, adopts the following articles of incorporation:

ARTICLE 1. NAME AND TYPE OF CORPORATION

The corporation's name is Carl Davidson, Jr., PhD, PC. The corporation is a professional corporation, as that term is defined in law.

ARTICLE 2. DURATION

The duration of the corporation's existence is perpetual or until dissolved on a vote of the shareholders as later provided for in these articles.

ARTICLE 3. PURPOSE

The purposes for which this corporation is formed are:

1. To engage in the practice of psychology; to counsel with individuals, families, and groups; to do psychological testing; to employ knowledge of psychological techniques, human capabilities, and conscious and unconscious motivation to assist people to achieve more adequate, satisfying, and productive emotional adjustments and improved emotional and mental health; and to do research related to these endeavors.

2. To own property, enter into contracts, and carry on the business that is necessary or incidental to the accomplishment or furtherance of the professional service to be rendered by the corporation.

3. The professional services of the corporation shall be carried on only through officers, employees, and agents who are licensed in the State of Texas to render professional psychological services.

ARTICLE 4. PRINCIPAL OFFICE

The address of the corporation's current principal office is 600 Meadow Rd., Suite 104, Dallas, TX 75231.

ARTICLE 5. CORPORATE POWERS

The corporation has all of the rights and powers now or hereafter conferred on professional corporations by the laws of the State of Texas, including: to own property, enter into contracts and carry on the business that is necessary or incidental to the accomplishment or furtherance of the professional service to be rendered by the corporation.

ARTICLE 6. INCORPORATOR

The name and address of the incorporator is:

Name
Carl Davidson, Jr., PhD

Address
5826 Dondo Drive
Dallas, TX 75218

ARTICLE 7. DIRECTORS

The number of directors constituting the initial board of directors is one, and the name and address of the initial director is:

Name
Carl Davidson, Jr., PhD

Address
5826 Dondo Drive
Dallas, TX 75218

The initial director shall hold office until his successor(s) are elected and qualify as provided in the bylaws. Thereafter, the term of office of each director is one year, and each director shall remain in office until the election and qualification of a successor.

The number of directors set forth in these articles and constituting the initial board of directors is the authorized number of directors until that number is changed by a bylaw duly adopted by the shareholders.

The initial director and each subsequent director of the corporation are licensed or otherwise duly authorized to perform the professional service that the corporation may render.

ARTICLE 8. BYLAWS

The initial director shall submit the proposed bylaws to the shareholders at a meeting to be held for that purpose not more than thirty (30) days following the issuance of the Certificate of Incorporation. Following the adoption of bylaws by the affirmative vote of three-fourths of the shareholders, the internal affairs of the corporation are to be regulated and managed in accordance with such bylaws.

ARTICLE 9. SHAREHOLDERS

The name and address of the individual who is to be the shareholder of the corporation is:

Name   Address
Carl Davidson, Jr., PhD   5826 Dondo Drive
                              Dallas, TX 75218

The initial shareholder and each subsequent shareholder of the corporation are licensed or otherwise duly authorized to perform the professional service that the corporation shall render.

ARTICLE 10. SHARES AND REQUIRED CAPITAL

The total number of shares and the par value, if any, of each class of stock that the corporation is authorized to issue are as follows: 10,000 shares of $00.01 par value.

The amount of the stated capital with which the corporation shall begin business is $1,000.00

No shares may be sold, transferred, or owned by any person who is not licensed or otherwise duly authorized to perform the professional service that the corporation renders.

Each outstanding share of ownership in the corporation shall be entitled to one vote. Cumulative voting is not allowed. All questions shall be determined by a majority vote of shares present in person or by proxy, unless otherwise provided in these Articles or in the bylaws of the corporation. All voting matters shall be governed by the bylaws of the corporation.

The shareholders of this corporation shall have the preemptive right to subscribe to any issue of shares or securities of the corporation.

Any shareholder who becomes disqualified to perform the services to be rendered by the corporation or if a person succeeds to shares of the corporation and that person is not licensed or otherwise duly authorized to perform the professional service that the corporation shall render, he or she shall immediately transfer the shares to the corporation or other shareholders for the consideration stated in the shareholder's stock purchase agreement or in any other manner allowed by law if the shares cannot be transferred by the shareholder agreement.

ARTICLE 11. DISSOLUTION

The corporation may be dissolved at any time by the affirmative vote of the holders of three-fourths of the outstanding shares of the corporation at a meeting called for that purpose or by unanimous written consent of all the shareholders without a meeting.

In the event of such dissolution, the corporate property and assets shall, after payment of all debts of the corporation, be distributed to the shareholders, each shareholder to participate in such distribution in direct proportion to the number of shares held by such shareholder.

If there are two or more shareholders of record, then no one shareholder may cause the dissolution of the corporation by his or her own independent action.

ARTICLE 12. REGISTERED OFFICE AND REGISTERED AGENT

The name and address of the initial registered agent is:

Name	Address
Carl Davidson, Jr., PhD	5826 Dondo Drive
	Dallas, TX 75218

ARTICLE 13. LICENSED PROFESSIONALS

The director and shareholder is duly licensed or otherwise legally authorized to render in Texas the specific kind of professional service to be rendered by the corporation.

ARTICLE 14. INDEMNIFICATION

The corporation shall indemnify any director or officer, former director or officer of the corporation, or any person who may have served in the capacity of director or officer of another corporation in which it owns shares of stock or of which it is a creditor, against expenses actually and necessarily incurred by that person in connection with the defense of any action, suit, or proceeding in which he or she is made a party by reason of being or having been such director or officer. The corporation may purchase and maintain liability insurance for such persons. The corporation will not indemnify any such director or officer in relation to matters as to which he or she shall be adjudged liable for negligence or misconduct in the performance of his or her duty. Indemnification will not be deemed exclusive of any other rights to which such director or officer may be entitled under any bylaw, agreement, vote of shareholders, or otherwise.

In witness whereof, I, the undersigned incorporator of this corporation, have executed these articles of incorporation on March _____, 20__ .

_____
Carl Davidson, Jr., PhD

The State of Texas
County of Dallas

I, the undersigned Notary Public, do hereby certify that on the _____ day of March, 20__, personally appeared before me Carl Davidson, Jr., PhD, who being by me first duly sworn, declared that he is the person who signed the foregoing document, and that the statements therein contained are true and correct.

_____
Notary Public, State of Texas
My commission expires:_____

Appendix D

ARTICLES OF INCORPORATION: GENERAL CORPORATION

ARTICLES OF INCORPORATION OF MPH BEHAVIORAL HEALTH SERVICES, INC.

We, the undersigned natural persons of the age of 18 years or more, acting as incorporators of a corporation under the Texas Business Corporation Act, adopt the following Articles of Incorporation for the corporation:

ARTICLE I. NAME

The name of this corporation is MPH Behavioral Health Services, Inc.

ARTICLE II. DURATION

The period of its duration is perpetual.

ARTICLE III. PURPOSE OR PURPOSES

The purposes for which the corporation is organized are as follows:

(a) The transaction of any or all lawful business for which corporations may be incorporated under the Texas Business Corporation Act and which is authorized or approved by the board of directors of this corporation;

(b) To carry on any other trade or business which can, in the opinion of the board of directors of the company, be advantageously carried on in connection with or auxiliary to those described in clause (a) of this Article III, and to do all such things as are incidental or conducive to the attainment of these objects or any of them;

(c) To enter into any lawful arrangements for sharing profits and/or losses in any transaction or transactions, and to promote and organize other corporations;

(d) To have and to exercise all rights and powers that are now or may subsequently be granted to a corporation by law.

The above shall be construed as objects, purposes, and powers and their enumeration shall not limit or restrict in any manner the powers now or subsequently conferred on this corporation by the laws of Texas.

The objects, purposes, and powers specified in these articles of incorporation shall, except as otherwise expressed, be in no way limited or restricted by reference to or inference from the terms of any other clause or paragraph of these articles.

The objects, purposes, and powers specified in each of the clauses or paragraphs of these articles of incorporation shall be regarded as independent objects, purposes, or powers.

The corporation may in its bylaws confer powers, not in conflict with law, upon its directors in addition to the foregoing and in addition to the powers and authorities expressly conferred upon them by statute.

ARTICLE IV. CAPITALIZATION

The aggregate number of shares which the corporation shall have authority to issue is one hundred thousand (100,000) shares of $00.01 par value. The corporation is authorized to issue only one class of stock. All issued stock shall be held of record by not more than 35 persons. Stock shall be issued and transferred only to (1) natural persons, (2) estates, or (3) a trust as defined in the Internal Revenue Code provision defining a qualified "small business corporation."

ARTICLE V. ISSUANCE OF SHARES

The corporation will not commence business until it has received for the issuance of its shares consideration of the value of One Thousand Dollars ($1,000.00), consisting of money, labor done, or property actually received, which sum is not less than One Thousand Dollars ($1,000.00).

The shareholders of this corporation shall have the preemptive right to subscribe to any and all issues of shares or securities of this corporation but shall not have the right to cumulative voting.

ARTICLE VI. REGISTERED OFFICE

The street address of its initial registered office is 600 Preston Avenue, Suite 520, Dallas, Dallas County, Texas 75210, and the name and address of the initial registered agent is:

Name   Address
Shirley Jameson   600 Preston Avenue
                                    Suite 520
                                    Dallas, TX 75210

ARTICLE VII. DIRECTORS

(a) The number of directors constituting the initial board of directors is three (3), and the names and addresses of the persons who are to serve as directors until the first annual meeting of the shareholders or until their successors are elected and qualified are:

Name	Address
Shirley Jameson	600 Preston Avenue Suite 520 Dallas, Texas 75210
Adrian Burns	600 Preston Avenue Suite 520 Dallas, Texas 75210
Cynthia Reynolds	600 Preston Avenue Suite 520 Dallas, Texas 75210

(b) The number of directors of the corporation set forth in clause (a) of this article shall constitute the authorized number of directors until changed by an amendment or a bylaw adopted by the vote or written consent of the holders of a majority of the then outstanding shares of stock of the corporation.

ARTICLE VIII. INDEMNIFICATION

The corporation shall indemnify any director or officer, former director or officer of the corporation, or any person who may have served in the capacity of director or officer of another corporation in which it owns shares of stock or of which it is a creditor, against expenses actually and necessarily incurred by that person in connection with the defense of any action, suit, or proceeding in which he or she is made a party by reason of being or having been such director or officer. The corporation will not indemnify any such director or officer in relation to matters as to which he or she shall be adjudged liable for negligence or misconduct in the performance of his or her duty. Indemnification will not be deemed exclusive of any other rights to which such director or officer may be entitled under any bylaw, agreement, vote of shareholders, or otherwise.

ARTICLE IX. INCORPORATORS

The names and addresses of the incorporators are:

Name	Address
Shirley Jameson	600 Preston Avenue Suite 520 Dallas, Texas 75210
Adrian Burns	600 Preston Avenue Suite 520 Dallas, Texas 75210

Cynthia Reynolds

600 Preston Avenue
Suite 520
Dallas, Texas 75210

For the purpose of forming this corporation under the laws of Texas, we, the undersigned, constituting the incorporators of this corporation, have executed these Articles of Incorporation on this _____ day of January, 20__.

_____
Shirley Jameson
Incorporator

_____
Adrian Burns
Incorporator

_____
Cynthia Reynolds
Incorporator

The State of Texas
County of Dallas

I, the undersigned Notary Public, do hereby certify that on the _____ day of January, 20__, personally appeared before me SHIRLEY JAMESON, who being by me first duly sworn, declared that she is the person who signed the foregoing document, and that the statements therein contained are true and correct.

_____
Notary Public, State of Texas
My commission expires: _____

The State of Texas
County of Dallas

I, the undersigned Notary Public, do hereby certify that on the _____ day of January, 20__, personally appeared before me ADRIAN BURNS, who being by me first duly sworn, declared that he is the person who signed the foregoing document, and that the statements therein contained are true and correct.

_____
Notary Public, State of Texas
My commission expires: _____

The State of Texas
County of Dallas

I, the undersigned Notary Public, do hereby certify that on the _____ day of January, 20__, personally appeared before me CYNTHIA REYNOLDS, who being by me first duly sworn, declared that she is the person who signed the foregoing document, and that the statements therein contained are true and correct.

_____
Notary Public, State of Texas
My commission expires: _____

References and
Reading Materials

I. CURRENT INFORMATION

FMS (FALSE MEMORY) FOUNDATION
  3401 Market Street, Suite 130, Philadelphia, PA 19104-3318;
  215-387-1865

MENTAL HEALTH LAW REPORTER
  Bonnie Becker, editor, 951 Pershing Drive, Silver Spring, MD 20910-4464;
  301-587-6300

PRACTICE STRATEGIES
  A Business Guide for Behavioral Health Care Providers, 442½ East Main Street, Suite 2,
  Clayton, NC 27520; 919-553-0637

PSYCHOTHERAPY FINANCE
  Managing Your Practice and Your Money, P.O. Box 8979, Jupiter, FL 33468;
  800-869-8450

II. REFERENCE BOOKS

Lawless, Linda L.
  *Therapy, Inc.—A Hands-On Guide to Developing, Positioning, and Marketing Your Mental
  Health Practice in the 1990s* (John Wiley & Sons, Inc., 1997)

Psychotherapy Finance *Managed Care Handbook—The Practitioner's Guide to Behavioral
  Managed Care* (Ridgewood Financial Institute, Inc., 1995)

Roach, William H., Jr., and The Aspen Health Law Center
  Medical Records and the Law (Aspen Publishing, Inc., 1994)

Stout, Chris E., Editor-in-Chief
  The Complete Guide to Managed Behavioral Healthcare (John Wiley & Sons, Inc., 1996)

Wiger, Donald E.
  *The Clinical Documentation Sourcebook—A Comprehensive Collection of Mental Health
  Practice Forms, Handouts, and Records* (John Wiley & Sons, Inc., 1997)

III. ORGANIZATIONS WITH PERIODIC PUBLICATIONS ON LAW AND MENTAL HEALTH

American Association of Marriage and Family Therapists

American Association of Pastoral Counselors

American Bar Association (Especially mental health or hospital law sections)

American Counseling Association

American Medical Association

American Mental Health Counselors Association

American Psychiatric Association

American Psychological Association

National Association of Social Workers

Note: All state licensing boards publish lists of licensed practitioners who have been disciplined by the boards. Usually, the names of the individuals who have been disciplined are given, together with the rule allegedly violated.

IV. LIBRARY LIST FOR BACKGROUND

Banton, Ragnhild, *The Politics of Mental Health* (1985)

Beis, Edward B., *Mental Health and the Law* (1984)

Dutton, Mary Ann, *Empowering and Healing the Battered Woman* (1992)

Hunter, Edna J., Editor, *Professional Ethics and Law in the Health Sciences* (1990)

Kermani, Ebrahim J., *Handbook of Psychiatry and the Law* (1989)

Lidz, Charles W., *Informed Consent, A Study of Decision Making in Psychiatry* (1984)

Nadelson, Carol C., Editor, *Marriage and Divorce* (1984)

National Institute of Mental Health, *Handbook of Mental Health Consultation* (1986)

Pederson, Paul, *Handbook of Cross-Cultural Counseling and Therapy* (1985)

Rosner, Richard, MD, Editor, *Ethical Practice in Psychiatry and the Law* (1990)

Shuman, Daniel W., *Law and Mental Health Professionals* (1990)

Stout, Chris E., Editor, *The Complete Guide to Managed Behavioral Healthcare* (1996)

U.S. Department of Health and Human Services, *Legal Opinions on the Confidentiality of Alcohol and Drug Abuse Patient Records, 1975–1978* (1980)

Index